PROJECT MANAGEMENT
AN INTERNATIONAL PERSPECTIVE

PROJECT MANAGEMENT
an International Perspective

Ralph Keeling

First published 2000 by
MACMILLAN PRESS LTD
Houndmills, Basingstoke, Hampshire RG21 6XS
and London
Companies and representatives
throughout the world

ISBN 0–333–77764–6 hardcover
ISBN 0–333–77765–4 paperback

A catalogue record for this book is available from the British Library.

This book is printed on paper suitable for recycling and made from fully managed and sustained forest sources.

10 9 8 7 6 5 4 3 2 1
09 08 07 06 05 04 03 02 01 00

Designed and formatted by
The Ascenders Partnership, Basingstoke
Illustrations by *Ascenders*

Printed and bound in Great Britain by
Antony Rowe Ltd
Chippenham, Wiltshire

Published in the United States of America by
ST. MARTIN'S PRESS, INC.,
Scholarly and Reference Division,
175 Fifth Avenue, New York, N.Y. 10010

ISBN 0–312–23291–8

To Olivia for her patience, forbearance and help

ARRANGEMENT OF CHAPTERS

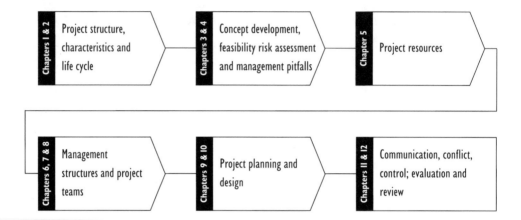

Chapters 1 & 2 — Project structure, characteristics and life cycle

Chapters 3 & 4 — Concept development, feasibility risk assessment and management pitfalls

Chapter 5 — Project resources

Chapters 6, 7 & 8 — Management structures and project teams

Chapters 9 & 10 — Project planning and design

Chapters 11 & 12 — Communication, conflict, control; evaluation and review

CONTENTS

Chapter 3

FEASIBILITY AND RISK ASSESSMENT

Chapter 4 **AVOIDING MANAGEMENT PITFALLS**

Chapter 5 **PROJECT RESOURCES**

Chapter 6   **PROJECT MANAGEMENT STRUCTURES**

Chapter 7   **BUILDING THE PROJECT TEAM**

Chapter 8 **PROJECT TEAM SELECTION**

Chapter 9 **PROJECT PLANNING AND DESIGN**

Chapter 12

REVIEW, REVISION AND EVALUATION

LIST OF FIGURES

ABBREVIATIONS AND TERMS

activity	A unit of work contributing to project completion
activity on node (A–N) diagrams	Diagrams or precedence networks in which details are recorded on the node itself
actual authority	Properly delegated authority to act; for example to contract on behalf of an owner or proprietor
ACWP	Actual cost of work performed – direct and indirect costs of a body of work
actual date of completion (or actual finishing date)	The actual date of completing a given activity
actual commence-ment date	The actual date on which an activity was started
arrow diagram	A flow chart or diagram to show a sequence of activities, represented by arrows and numbers
ADB	Asian Development Bank
assumptions	Factors that may affect the ability of the project to achieve its purposes or goals
AusAID	Australian Agency for International Development
baseline	A project schedule used as a standard against which progress is measured
BCWP	Budgeted cost of work performed
BCWS	Budgeted cost of work scheduled
benchmark	An established standard for comparison
BNFL	British Nuclear Fuels Limited
BOT	Build, operate and transfer. A procedure in which an organization or consortium is contracted to construct, commission and operate a facility before handing it over as a going concern
BOOT	Build, own, operate and transfer
CAA	Civil Aviation Authority
CAD	Computer-aided drafting
CAD/CAM	Computer-aided drafting and manufacture
calendar	A calendar of project events and resources to include holidays, training periods, reviews, and so on
calendar unit	The time used in a project schedule
cause and effect analysis	The process of identifying the causes and effects of performance problems or opportunities

cluster evaluation	An evaluation of the long-term results of a number of closely related projects
concept	The rationale behind a project proposal
concurrency	The practice of conducting a number of key project activities at the same time; for example, development of an essential process with manufacture or construction
concurrrent engineering (simultaneous engineering)	The practice of controlling the conduct of closely linked aspects of a project at the same time
crashing (compression)	Shortening a project schedule by allocating increased resources
critical activity	An activity with zero or negative float on the critical path
critical path	A sequence of linked activities in a network diagram that takes most time to complete. Therefore, delay in completing one or more steps in the sequence would delay project completion
control	Aligning actual and planned performance by monitoring results and taking corrective action
CPM	Critical path method. A network technique based on activity and project duration to determine sequence and float times
cost plus contract	A contract in which the supplier is reimbursed on a basis of actual cost and an additional sum to cover work done
contingency planning	Management planning for the purpose of coping with, or minimizing, the effect of project risks
CSIRO	Commonwealth Scientific and Industrial Research Organization
DCF	Discounted cash flow
deliverables	The desired outcomes or results of a project activity or a complete project
EET	Earliest event time
earned value	A method of analysis comparing planned and actual performance to assess progress in terms of cost and time
earliest finish	The earliest time at which an activity can finish
earliest start	The earliest time at which an activity can begin
EIS	Environmental impact statement
ERR	Economic rate of return
elapsed time	Time needed to complete an activity
exception report	A report of major variance between planned and actual progress
FAA	Federal Aviation Authority
fast tracking	Compressing the project schedule by conducting sequential events concurrently

feasibility study	A detailed study of the feasibility, risks and implications of a project proposal
finish date/time	The date or time on which the activity is to be completed
finish float	Time remaining after completion of an activity before the next activity must begin
finishing activity	The last activity in a project
free float	The available time between the end of an activity and the start of the next one assuming that preceding activities have been carried out at their earliest times and following ones can be commenced at their earliest start times
free float early	The leeway when both events take place as early as possible
free float late	The leeway when both events take place as late as possible
Gantt chart	A chart providing a logical picture of activities required to complete a job, showing sequence, duration, and time for start and completion. The chart may be drawn to allow both planned and actual times and linked to cash-flow predictions
goal	A desired result – less far-reaching than an objective but more general and specific than a deliverable
histogram	A form of vertical bar chart forming a graphic display of, for example, activity or consumption over time
ICAO	International Civil Aviation Organization
initiating	The process of commencing a task, activity or project
impact	In project work, generally used to refer either to the way in which the project will affect the lives of people or the effect of achievement of the project's long-term goals
independent float	The minimum leeway between two events when they are conducted as closely together as possible
interdependencies	Relations between organizational functions where one function or task is dependent on others
IR	Industrial relations
IRR	Internal rate of return
ISO	International Standards Organization
IT	Information technology
JIT	Just-in-time procedures
lag	Delay between the start and end of an activity, or completion of one activity and starting the next
latest start	The latest date or time by which an activity must start without lengthening the critical path or delaying project completion
latest finish	The latest date or time by which an activity can end without delaying the project
lead	An overlap between activities when a task starts before the completion of its predecessor
LET	Latest event time

life cycle	A standard concept of the life of a project (or a product) in which it passes through a series of phases
logical framework (logframe)	A conceptual and analytical tool for analysing project opportunities, options and possible outcomes
management of projects	The overall strategy of introduction or control of a programme, series or a group of projects
master plan	The main project plan or schedule, showing strategies, tactics, principal activities, events and milestones
master schedule	An overall schedule of all major events and activities
matrix organization	An organization structure in which projects rely on staff and/or functional departments for products or services
MAUT	Multi-attribute utility technique – a process for choosing between possible solutions
MOU	Memorandum of understanding
micro-scheduling	Scheduling activities of very short duration
milestone	A term used by some project planners to indicate a significant stage in project progress
multi-project analysis	An analysis of the interaction between projects sharing resources or a comparison between related projects
negative float	A term used in highlighting activities that must start before completion of their predecessors
network analysis	Identification of earliest and latest start and finishing times applicable to project activities
network diagram	A flow chart or diagram showing a sequence of activities and events
mission objectives	The total outcome for which the project is designed
NPV	Nett present value
NGO	Non-government organization
objectives	desired outcomes of a project (these can be immediate, related to an activity or phase, or long-term)
ongoing operations	The continuing activities of long-term operations
parallel activities	Activities that can be carried out at the same time
parties at interest	Individuals or groups with a special interest in a project, usually the client or principal, senior management, project manager, project team and/or specific public interest (stakeholders)
PDD	Project design document
performance indicators	Measures of project performance
PERT	Programme evaluation and review technique. The use of critical path methods to plan, monitor and evaluate the progress of a project or activity
phase	A stage or period in the project life cycle, usually a series of related activities

PID	Project implementation document
precedence notation	Information entered on activity or event nodes in a network
predecessor	An activity that must be completed before the start of its successor
preliminary proposal	An initial proposal setting out the project idea and seeking acceptance and support
programme	Sometimes not distinguished from 'project' but usually taken to mean a group of similar or related projects
project	'A temporary endeavour undertaken to create a unique product or service' – a discrete undertaking set up to achieve specific objectives in a limited time, usually with its own management, staff and resources
project charter	A document defining project purpose, assigning responsibility and providing authority for the use of resources to conduct a project activity
project life cycle	A sequence of phases showing stages of progress in the course of the life of a project (see life cycle)
project management	The use of means, concepts and techniques to run a project and achieve its objectives
project plan	A formalized scheme for the conduct and control of project activity leading to the achievement of its goals and objectives
project schedule	A schedule of project activities, events and, possibly, resources
project scope	The sum of products (deliverables) and services to be provided by the project
resource	Finance, materials, equipment, manpower, management and other things required for the conduct of a project
resource levelling	Reduction and minimization of peaks and troughs in resource needs to achieve economical use of resources and better workflow
RFQ	Request for quotation
RFT	Request for tender
risk	The chance that outcomes will not occur as planned
risk analysis	Analysis of the causes and probable effects of risk
risk identification	Identification and classification of anticipated project risks
scope	The sum of products (deliverables) and services to be provided by the project
sector analysis	A process for identifying possibilities for improving sector performance
stakeholder	Persons, groups or organizations in any way involved in or affected by the project (see parties at interest)
SIS	Sociological impact statement
start float	Excess time between the earliest and latest start times for an activity

starting activity	The initial activity of a sequence
suboptimize	Doing the best with a function or activity without cost to the project as a whole
subproject	A group of activities amounting to a small project within the scope of a larger project; for example, the development of a process or manufacture of materials needed for the main project
successor	An activity reliant for its start on the finish of a previous one
superficial activity	An activity with negative float that has fallen behind schedule
sustainability	A term used to denote the lasting or continuing impact of a project outcome
target finish	A date/time on which an activity or an entire project is scheduled for completion
task	One of the work elements of a project
technology	The technical implications or means of accomplishing difficult or complex tasks
trade-off	Taking less on one measure, for example, performance, in order to do better with another, such as schedule or cost
total float	The period of extra time in activities that may be conducted without prejudice to the final completion of a project
TQC	Total quality control
TQM	Total quality management
uncertainty	Having only partial information about a situation or outcome
UNDP	United Nations Development Programme
UNICEF	United Nations Children's Fund
UNO	United Nations Organization
USAID	United States Agency for International Development
VPI	Verifiable performance indicators
WB	World Bank
WBS	Work breakdown structure

PREFACE

New technology has resulted in dramatic advances in human achievement, new expectations, developments in leadership styles and means of achieving previously unattainable objectives. One consequence of change is a massive increase in recourse to the project method, and in the number and diversity of new projects and project concepts. People of every nationality and background are increasingly drawn to project work as instigators, sponsors, advisers, managers or members of project teams.

The need for another book on project management became apparent when I had to train a group of professionals destined for major overseas projects and discovered that, with a few notable exceptions, such as P.W.G Morris's monumental work *The Management of Projects* and publications of the project management institutes, many texts were of limited practical value to the sponsor, generalist project manager or student because they were overtaken by time or described the discipline from narrow, parochial or specialized viewpoints.

When a project is well structured and running smoothly, its challenges can be stimulating and enjoyable. But an ill-conceived, ill-defined or badly managed project can become a nightmare for all concerned, lead to financial disaster and prejudice many a promising career. It is a sad fact that far too many ambitious and worthy projects are abandoned, or fail to achieve objectives, because of startling inadequacies in feasibility, planning or implementation.

For the inexperienced, the offer of a project role sometimes entails pressure to accept ill-considered risks, ill-founded, preconceived assumptions, or unsuitable routines that inhibit effective management and freedom of action and prejudice ultimate success. When this occurs, a through understanding of established project techniques and adherence to sound principles is the only way to retrieve the project and bring about a satisfactory outcome.

The purpose of this book is to outline the basic principles of establishing, managing or participating in a successful project.

I have attempted to illustrate lessons of experience that result in better practice and lead to a 'quality control' approach in each project phase, commencing with the initial concept through feasibility, planning management and control to the final evaluation.

After discussing project characteristics, I have attempted to deal with subjects in the sequence in which they usually occur, beginning with the concept, feasibility, risk and consideration of resources. These issues often come up in discussion before the selection of key staff who will become involved in detailed planning, project design and management to culminate in handover, the final report and follow-up evaluation. As the project develops, topics inevitably overlap to form a mix of interrelated activity.

In selecting case studies, I have tried to present a wide diversity of subject, situation, scale and geographical location. All are based on actual events but, for reasons of confidentiality, sensitivity and legality, identities of individuals and organizations are not always divulged. While I attempt to illustrate selected points with each case, all have other implications from which readers may draw additional conclusions.

The book is intended for all those who commission, sponsor, manage or participate in project work. I hope it will be of value to students of management, principals, practising project managers, project contractors and the many professionals or specialists who are increasingly being drawn to project leadership through expertise in other disciplines.

Ralph Keeling

THE NATURE OF A PROJECT

1.1   WHAT CONSTITUTES A PROJECT?

Of the many and various definitions, that adopted by the Project Management Institute says it all in a few words: 'A temporary endeavor undertaken to create a unique product or service'. It implies a limited timespan, a target date for completion and an outcome different from that produced in the course of operational routine.

The method is far from new. Projects have been going on since the dawn of time but in recent years the method has proliferated, reaching new heights of sophistication and popularity. Most projects of ancient civilizations were related to power, worship or the construction of great monuments. Cost, of overriding importance today, was of scant significance to despotic rulers of old and time, now so highly valued and closely tied to project cost, was of secondary importance. On rare occasions a case in which time was synonymous with success would occur. In the fifth dynasty, a pyramid in Egypt, at Abusir, was not finished in time for the death of its sponsor and the great tomb was eventually completed to house the remains of another dignitary.

This fine disregard for time extended to building the great cathedrals. Construction extended over hundreds of years and successive generations of stonemasons were employed in their building. Then the overriding considerations were beauty, durability of structure, and quality of workmanship. As the years progressed, cost and time assumed increasing significance. A study of the great houses of Europe tells many a sad story of ambitious owners who, having failed in financial planning, were reduced to poverty by escalating project cost.

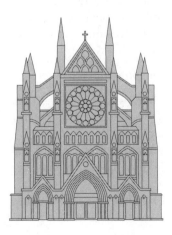

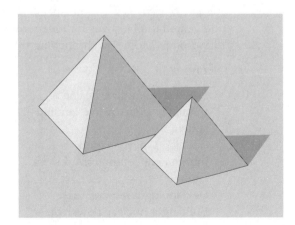

1

1.2 PROJECTS OF TODAY

Contemporary projects come in many forms and sizes. Some are of short duration, inexpensive enterprises lasting but a few days and needing minimal resources. Medium or long-term projects, on the other hand, may be ambitious undertakings over many years, incurring vast financial and material resources, high levels of technical and scientific skill, and complex management structures. All projects, however, have these characteristics in common:

- They are separate undertakings.
- They have a discrete purpose and objectives.
- They are of limited duration.

Most projects will also have:

- target dates for commencement and completion;
- their own resources (including finance and staff);
- their own management and management structure.

The work of a project remains separate from routine operations even though its result may be a direct contribution to the long-term plan. A project is planned, financed and managed as a separate activity and, being divorced from routine work, it is easier to plan, monitor and control the project and avoid the need to overload those responsible for day-to-day work. It is easier to engage or allocate staff, specialist expertise, finance and material resources, tend to cost and evaluate results without the complications of involvement in any long-term operation.

1.3 SCOPE AND OBJECTIVES

Another important distinction between projects and ongoing activities is in the nature of scope and mission objectives (Figure 1.1). Here, the emphasis is different; project scope is rigidly defined, limited by time and resources, and project objectives are more specific. Most ongoing operations, on the other hand, are geared to objectives for long-term return on investment and survival. Compare these project topics with ongoing operations:

Project	*Ongoing activity*
Establishing a new business	Running an established business
Installing a microwave landing system	Providing air traffic control facilities
Building a new seaport	Running an ocean terminal
Introducing computerized stock control	Routine inventory management
Developing a mineral lease	Profitable ore production
Building a nuclear power plant	Providing a constant power supply

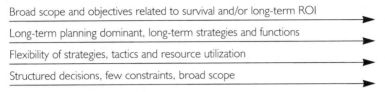

Ongoing, long-term routines

Broad scope and objectives related to survival and/or long-term ROI

Long-term planning dominant, long-term strategies and functions

Flexibility of strategies, tactics and resource utilization

Structured decisions, few constraints, broad scope

Project

Fixed duration

Limited scope
Precise objectives

Planning outcomes
predictable and precise

Control dominant

Figure 1.1 Comparison of ongoing and project characteristics

1.4 FEATURES AND BENEFITS OF THE PROJECT METHOD

Salient features of the project method include:

- *Simplicity of purpose.* The project has easily understood goals and objectives.
- *Clarity of purpose and scope.* The project can be clearly described in finite terms, its objectives, scope, limitations, resources, management, quality of results, and so on.
- *Independent control.* The project can be protected from market or other fluctuations affecting routine operations.
- *Ease of measurement.* Project progress can be measured against clear targets and performance standards.
- *Flexibility of employment.* The project management can employ or co-opt specialists and experts of high calibre for limited periods without prejudice to long-term staffing arrangements.
- *Conducive to team motivation and morale.* The novelty and special interest of project work is attractive to individuals and conducive to the formation of enthusiastic and self-motivated teams.
- *Sensitivity to management and leadership style.* Though sometimes capable of self-management, teams of self-motivated experts react critically to some styles of leadership.
- *Helpful to individual development.* Work with an effective project team is conducive to accelerated personal development and capability.

- *Conducive to secrecy and security.* Projects may be protected from hostile action or intelligence activity for defence, research, product development or the safety of market-sensitive or high-value products.
- *Portability.* As separate entities, projects may be carried out in remote locations, foreign countries, and so on.
- *Ease of allocation.* Management or the conduct of an entire project may be let out to contract, for example on a build, operate and transfer (BOT) agreement.

Under these circumstances, the range of projects in operation is boundless. It covers subjects as diverse as space exploration, satellite development, undersea recovery, motorway construction, building an international airport, the delivery of medical facilities or humanitarian aid to needy communities in the Third World or the development and transfer of sophisticated technology. With the availability of increasingly sophisticated management aids and control systems, the project method has become a powerful instrument of change and increasingly used in the development of routines and systems within organizations.

Successful experience in multi-project management and simultaneous engineering techniques is increasing and has led to their proliferation in a variety of innovative situations, for example Toyota (Cusumano and Nobeoka, 1998).

1.5 PROJECT DURATION

Labelling projects has much to do with the customs of industry sectors and those of project sponsors and owners. For convenience, many people classify projects in terms of duration and three broad classifications are common. These are illustrated in Figure 1.2.

Figure 1.2 Labelling by duration

Short term	Medium term	Long term
1 month to 1 year	To 2 years	2 years +

Years   0   1   2   3   4   5 10

1.6 CAPITAL, COMMERCIAL AND GOVERNMENT PROJECTS

Most major projects are long-term endeavours, but duration is not the sole criterion. Capital projects are usually large undertakings with a formal management structure calling for heavy capital investment (usually in excess of $10m).

Large commercial and government projects are often let out to one or more contractors who conduct research, develop and supply products or services to non-routine specifications. In cases where a contractor is responsible for both development and production, experience underlines the wisdom of imposing stringent penalty clauses and strict performance guarantees.

1.7 PROGRAMMES

Many organizations, such as international aid agencies, research institutions or the defence forces and space agencies, conduct lengthy programmes of related projects to achieve broad overall or far-reaching objectives in a particular field. Some of these are in the form of a project series; others may be self-standing modular projects designed to achieve a separate but contributory result which is often integrated with the work of other agencies with interests in the same theatre of operations or field of activity.

1.8 PROJECT SERIES

In a variety of sectors such as commerce, aeronautic, pharmaceutics and so on, organizations will conduct a series of projects, each as a separate step in the achievement of a particular mission objective. For example, if development of a new process is a prerequisite of production, uncertainty over the outcome of research or development may dictate the wisdom of completing all or some of the development before detailed planning or implementation of the production requirement. This enables progress to be assessed before moving to the next step in the sequence, limits the overall risk and provides valuable information as a basis of planning the important stages in the sequence.

1.9 MULTI-PROJECT ORGANIZATIONS

Consultants and contractors specializing in project work, such as construction or mechanical engineering contractors, are often organized as multiple project organizations with a pool of expertise and resources on hand to provide service to project owners and sponsors. The benefits of this kind of specialization are obvious in so far as ability to offer a variety of readily available specialist resources is concerned. Spreading the cost of resources across a number of projects might be expected to result in useful economies of scale although these advantages are not always passed on to the project owners.

1.10 MULTIPLE PROJECTS WITHIN ORGANIZATIONS

Organizations conducting ongoing operations are increasingly resorting to the use of projects to achieve organizational or technical change, for example to introduce new inventory control or quality systems. One such example is the Toyota initiative (Cusumano and Nobeoka, 1988).

1.11 TECHNOLOGY TRANSFER AND KNOWLEDGE MANAGEMENT PROJECTS

A rapid increase in the amount of knowledge, its complexity and value has resulted in project work related to the management of knowledge as opposed to information and data. Knowledge can be managed as an asset and projects may be designed to create knowledge repositories, and improve access (Davenport, DeLong and Beers, 1998).

1.12 PROJECT MANAGEMENT IN GLOBALIZING ECONOMIES

Extension and transfer of many operations to areas of plentiful and inexpensive labour has led to projects entailing a mix of investment, infrastructure, the establishment of new facilities, transportation, and training for inexperienced workforces.

Special problems have to be overcome in transitory or developing economies. Some countries (particularly in Asia) whose economies were buoyant have become unstable or sluggish and transitory economies have not developed as expected.

With the increasing trend towards globalization, organizations conditioned to government favouritism, protection or, in some cases, nepotism, may find themselves suddenly 'left out in the cold' and stripped of favoured status.

Progressive governments encourage improvement in the management of public and business organizations and, more specifically, in production and marketing. In Korea, for example, government protection for export-driven industries is becoming a thing of the past. Extensive training in project management 'based on the soil of the locality' rather than dependence on transfer of knowledge from the more advanced countries is recommended (Sung Woong Hong, 1997).

1.13 MANAGERIAL FOCUS

Running a project calls for ability in all management disciplines but the short-term nature of project work demands special application, discipline and technique. Concentration of effort calls for a rather special kind of manager and focus of management activity. As we have observed, the objectives and focus of most long-term and ongoing operations are geared to factors for survival, growth, long-term return on investment, service and so on – objectives necessitating flexible strategies and long-term perspectives. Project management, on the other hand, focuses on the essentially limited term of the project life cycle, day-to-day and step-by-step progress. Leadership and team development are vital ingredients of project management but in terms of day-to-day activity, planning and control are still dominant.

1.14 THE CHARACTERISTICS OF A PROJECT MANAGER

Projects have no luxury of time, so a manager cannot 'grow into the job'.

The manager is:

1. the hub around which all activity revolves;
2. the link between the internal and external stakeholders and organizations;
3. regulator of progress, speed, quality and cost;
4. leader and motivator of project personnel;
5. communicator and negotiator in all things affecting the project;
6. controller of finance and other resources.

Opinions on the characteristics of the ideal project manager vary but few are in doubt that they differ in some important respects from those engaged in managing many ongoing endeavours.

Turner (1997) offers the following list in Chapter 7 of *The Shorter MBA – A Practical Approach to the Key Business Skills*:

- strong, forceful but acceptable personality – diplomacy and advocacy should be strong traits;
- intelligence with independence of mind;
- proven ability in at least one branch of work essential to the project;
- an appreciation of areas of work outside his experience and the ability to see things as a whole;
- a vital interest and concern to see the project completed;
- an ability to direct and delegate technical work;
- business acumen – financial procedures, contract law, etc. – and entrepreneurial dynamism;
- energy and persistence.

(Reproduced by permission of HarperCollins, Publishers, London)

case study

The Southern Meat Works

The meat division of a major food conglomerate decided to design, build and operate a 'state of the art' abattoir in the southern counties.

The General Manager, Meats and Poultry, was an enlightened executive whose experience was backed by a degree in agriculture and an MBA. His concept for the Southern Meat Works was that it should become a model project and showpiece for the company. Quality and hygiene were to conform to the highest national and international standards and an essential feature of its export capacity was the inclusion of separate facilities for meat processing to meet the requirements of both Islamic and Jewish markets.

▶

The General Manager stipulated that the factory be managed by a top-rate, world-class executive and it was considered desirable that, as chief executive of this important subsidiary, the manager should assume a role in the design, construction and commissioning of the plant.

With the aid of the Group Personnel Manager, a recruitment specification was developed, salary and conditions specified and recruitment procedures initiated on a worldwide basis.

This led to the preparation of a short list of six prime candidates who were interviewed by a panel of senior executives of the parent company.

All candidates seemed well qualified and the panel anticipated some difficulty in choosing between such good applicants. However, the results of the interviews were disappointing.

The panel was unanimous in their assessment of the high quality of all candidates but unable to agree on a suitable choice to fill the needs of the job, and further attempts at recruitment proved equally unproductive.

As the matter became urgent, the opinion of a well-respected consultant, who had completed other assignments for the parent company, was sought in the hope that he could assist in filling the position.

Prior to re-interviewing short-listed candidates, the consultant examined the recruitment specifications and then delivered his advice with a measure of diplomacy.

This amounted to an opinion that the recruitment specification contained basically conflicting personal characteristics. For practical purposes it could not be filled. The problem was simply that two different managers were required, each of whom could be recruited from the short-listed candidates.

The best manager for the construction and equipping phase was a South African applicant with engineering qualifications, building and refrigeration experience, applied to the meat industry, combined with a forceful personality and somewhat autocratic attitude. The reason for his failure to meet initial selection criteria was the panel's misgivings over his managerial style which seemed to be in conflict with that of the company and the expectations of the workforce.

On the basis of his record in meat marketing, commercial management, leadership and industrial relations, an applicant with abattoir experience but limited design and engineering background was selected to manage production and ongoing operations.

The Southern Meat Works case illustrates the incompatibility that is occasionally experienced between the characteristics of managers well equipped for the needs of a project situation and those of an ideal manager for a long-term operation. Of course, the characteristics of the person selected in this case study for the design and construction phase might not meet the needs of some other projects but the fact remains that success in one aspect of management is no certain criterion of success in another.

1.15 VULNERABILITY TO FRAUD

Some projects are, because of their transitory nature and finite span of activity, vulnerable to acts of dishonesty. This problem is not confined to projects in countries or circumstances where corruption is deeply ingrained into the social culture. Nor is fraud confined to loss of funds. It can be found in a variety of circumstances leading to illicit gain, for example deliberate failure to complete on schedule to increase income or incur penalty payments, diluted quantity or quality of work or supplies, sabotage leading to penalty rates for additional work, demands for bribes to avoid industrial action, and so on.

An additional purpose of day-to-day monitoring and scrutiny of activity and quality is prevention of fraud. It is sometimes desirable to provide for independent scrutiny of tendering procedures, contractual arrangements and financial disbursements, and, in the planning process, consideration should be given to the introduction of controls to prevent, or ensure early disclosure of, dishonesty.

Control mechanisms should be designed and understood to safeguard both the project and the integrity of its participants who might otherwise come under unfounded and harmful suspicion.

Controls should be effective without inhibiting the manager's freedom of activity, but in the final analysis, the best safeguard is a manager's complete familiarity with day-to-day activity, progress and costs by monitoring and effective control.

1.16 PROJECT WORK AND EQUAL OPPORTUNITY

Project specialists are not limited by age, sex or nationality. Since the Queen of Sheba built a reservoir at Aden's Mt Shamshan to provide water for the spice routes, women have been successfully involved in project management. Men and women of all nationalities, some well past the customary age of retirement, have been recruited in the search for vision, talent and ability.

The nature of project enterprise has thus provided opportunity for a range of exceptional talent that might not achieve recognition in routine work.

1.17 THE PROJECT LIFE CYCLE

Every project undergoes a series of phases from its conception to the point of completion. Each phase has its own needs and characteristics. As the project passes through these phases, the cumulative amount of expended resources and time will increase and unexpired time and resources will diminish. This series of phases is known as the project life cycle.

An understanding of the life cycle is important to successful project management because significant events occur in logical progression and each phase must be properly planned and managed.

THE TRIBAL CARPET

In the lives of the Baluchi Nomads, a most prized family possession is a richly coloured, hand-woven carpet. The tribespeople live a wandering existence, often with little money and few possessions. The design and weaving of a carpet is an activity of great family significance in this arid and inhospitable landscape. It will probably be woven in a large pit close to a huddle of dwellings and, from time to time, moved considerable distances before the task is lovingly completed. The procedure goes like this:

Conceptual phase

Following a betrothal or some other significant family event, a discussion initiates the project. The head of the family leads the discussion and senior members state their ideas about the design, cost and source of finance before a final decision is made to proceed.

Planning phase

A professional designer is paid to prepare a selection of suitable plans for consideration and animated discussion takes place before a final choice of design and colour is reached. A new and intricate design may cost as much as 40,000 rials (about $500).

Implementation (execution) phase

Resource provisioning

When the design has been agreed and the price negotiated, the next step is to select materials – wool, hemp, cotton or some other material for the warp and weft, wool for the carpet pile and dye to produce the rich colours of the complicated design.

The designer will accompany the villagers to market to select the wool and cotton. Materials are bought undyed and when the bargaining process is concluded the parties go to the dyemaker where the exact shades are discussed. The first stage of manufacture consists of the dyeing process which takes a long time. Vegetable or aniline dyes are mixed and the required quantity of wool is coloured in each of the several shades to complete the

▶

design. Wool dyeing is an ancient art calling for considerable skill. It is important that the correct amount of wool is dyed in each colour, or the cost will rise and quality suffer, for it may not be possible to match the dye accurately enough to produce more of any particular shade and any excess in one colour will result in a shortage in another.

Manufacture

The carpet is made on a large timber frame (loom) across which the warp and weft are stretched during the hand-knotting process. Timber is not plentiful and circumstances dictate whether this essential equipment is made for the job, borrowed or traded from another family. Other tools will include a tika – a small, razor-like knife, a special comb, scissors and containers in which the wool will be dyed.

The work of carpet making is an ancient art practised by nomadic people for thousands of years. Training takes place from childhood and every tuft of wool is carefully inserted and knotted by hand. When the carpet is completed, it is washed in clear stream water and taken to a contractor for the pile to be shaved to an even finish.

Termination phase

The finished carpet is ironed and left in the lanes and alleys of the tribal village so that passing feet may enhance its beauty. It is then passed to the people for whom it was made.

This simplest of undertakings has the same life cycle and follows the basic sequences of a large and complex project.

Familiarity with the project life cycle enables those involved to understand the logical sequence of events, recognize bounds or 'milestones', and know where the project stands in the continuum of activities that progress from start to finish. It helps the manager to anticipate changes in character and pace, the build-up of pressure as costs accumulate and time and resources diminish, recognize when special reviews, revisions or priority reappraisals are due and understand the needs of each phase. It also provides points of reference from which team members can asses progress, and see what is still to happen during the project life-span. An executive joining a project after its inception can see exactly where he/she is 'getting on', and review prior activity. If a step in the logical progression is omitted or inadequately performed, or if information is insufficient, the matter can be rectified before further steps are taken.

This is an important safeguard because a project is a monolithic structure, each stage being built on the foundation of its predecessor. Major problems are inevitable if an earlier stage provides an unsound foundation for what is to follow.

1.18 THE LIFE CYCLE AND PROJECT QUALITY

The life cycle also becomes an instrument of quality. This applies to the conduct of the project itself, as quality expectations are established between each phase, and to its 'deliverables' or products, where the life cycle provides reference points for confirmation of product quality.

Many problems of project quality can be pre-empted by sound feasibility and risk assessment in the conceptual phase, and careful planning and accurate specification in the planning phase. Rectifying quality failures becomes progressively costly as the life cycle progresses.

Life-cycle and quality relationships are well described in *The Handbook of Project Based Management.* (Turner, 1993). With the passage of time and as completion dates grow near, uncertainty over project outcome diminishes, significant revisions become more difficult and the cost of accelerating activity escalates (Archibald, 1992).

1.19 PHASES (STAGES) OF THE PROJECT LIFE CYCLE

The phases are:

1. Conceptualization
2. Planning
3. Implementation (execution)
4. Termination

Figure 1.3
Volume and intensity of activity in the project life cycle plotted against time and finance

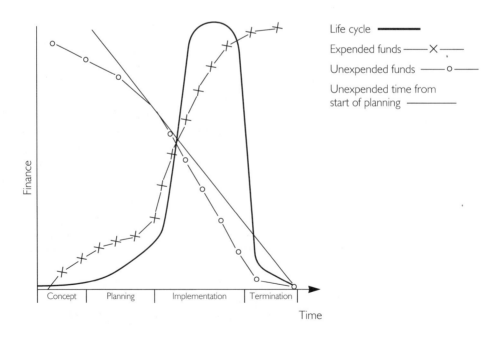

Conceptualization

This is the point of departure, starting with the seed of an idea, an awareness of need or a desire for some major development or improvement.

There may be no conscious intention to use the project method as a means of achieving the desired result and the desirability of mounting a project may become clear as ideas develop.

Preliminary goals are considered and ideas on costs, potential benefits, feasibility and scope receive initial consideration, possibly with ideas on problem areas, alternative approaches and ways of overcoming difficulty.

The project proposal

As the idea becomes established, it may be necessary to seek approval from principals or other parties who might, in some way, be affected by the project. In such cases, a project proposal will usually be prepared, setting out rationale, proposed methods, estimated costs, benefits and other details.

The feasibility study

When a decision for action is reached, practicalities, feasibility and risk are re-examined in greater detail, usually with the benefit of a structured feasibility study. This will offer recommendations as to how the project should proceed, the scale and form it should take, its scope, duration, objectives and so on.

Planning

Formal planning begins when a decision has been taken to proceed. By this stage, ideas on objectives and some aspects of the plan will have received initial consideration. They must now be reviewed, and project objectives clarified.

The project structure and management will be planned and, probably, a manager and senior specialist staff selected.

As the foundations on which the planning hierarchy will be based, objectives for the project mission and component activities must be clear and measurable. Activity, finance and resource plans will be developed and integrated with the communication pattern, standards for quality, security and administration.

Life-cycle progress reviews

Master plans will provide for periodic reviews of progress, reporting structures and the possibility of revision. Review programmes are usually based on:
- time – for example, every two or three months and to conform with set accounting periods;
- at strategic points:

  1. completion of the planning phase and, when the project is to be carried out by a consortium or contractor, prior to signing agreement;
  2. during the implementation phase (usually prior to peak activity);
  3. towards commencement of the termination phase.

Implementation (execution)

This is a period of concentrated activity when plans are put into operation. Each activity is monitored, controlled and coordinated to achieve project objectives. Work efficiency will be directly related to the quality of the plans already formulated, the effectiveness of administration, technology, leadership and control. Reviews of progress are conducted and plans updated or revised when necessary.

Termination

This phase includes preparation for completion, preparation for handover, handing over duties and follow-up activity such as disposal of machinery and equipment, closure of bank accounts or termination of drawing facilities, perform-ance assessment and reallocation of project personnel, courtesy calls and similar formalities, project assessment and evaluation, and preparation and presentation of the project terminal report. In some cases there may be a later evaluation to assess the sustained effects of the project after its results have been in practice for a reasonable period of time.

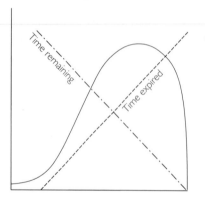

Figure 1.4 Project life cycle plotted against time

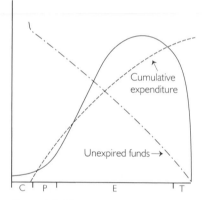

Figure 1.5 The project life cycle, cumulative expenditure and remaining finance

1.20 COMPARISON OF LIFE-CYCLE CHARACTERISTICS

Every project goes through the four life-cycle phases but different projects have somewhat different life-cycle curves. Figure 1.6 illustrates the different character-istics of two projects of similar project cost, one the research and development of an important ethical pharmaceutical, the other the construction of a casino in the USA. Although project costs may be comparable, the intensity of activity is quite different because of the nature of the work.

Figures 1.7, 1.8 and 1.9 show typical sequences of events in various types of project.

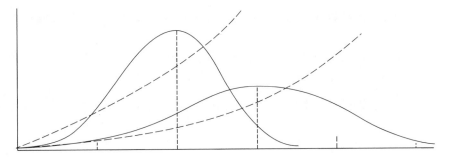

Figure 1.6
Comparison of
project life-cycle
characteristics –
pharmaceutical
development and
construction

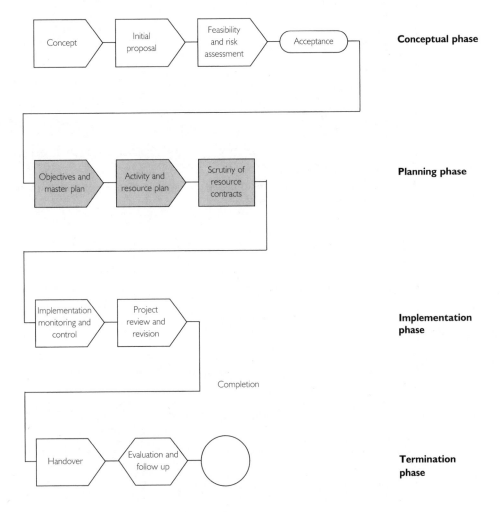

Figure 1.7
Typical
sequence of
events during
the project life
cycle

Conceptual phase

Planning phase

Implementation phase

Termination phase

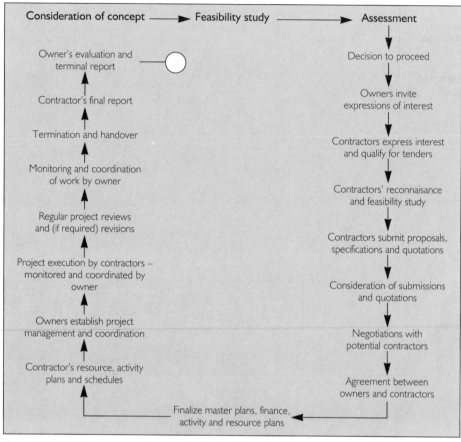

Figure 1.8 Typical sequence of events during the life cycle of an owner-managed project using contractors

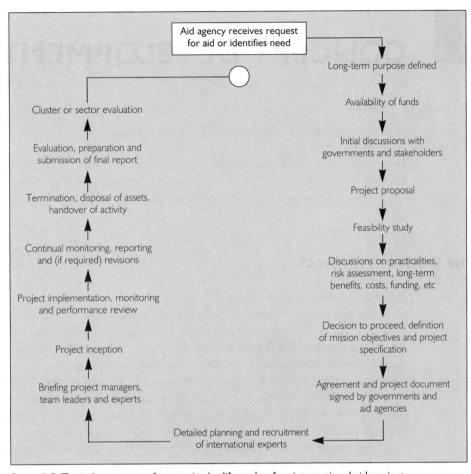

Figure 1.9 Typical sequence of events in the life cycle of an international aid project

REVIEW AND DISCUSSION QUESTIONS

1. Explain the main differences between a project and an ongoing activity and discuss examples.
2. List at least six features or benefits of the project method.
3. Discuss examples of projects having similar cost but different life cycles and levels of activity.
4. Give three examples of the use of the project method as used to implement change within an organization.
5. Compare the special qualities of a good project manager with those of a good manager of an ongoing operation.
6. Consider the activities that occurred in each phase of the life cycle of a project of your experience; consider whether the correct sequence was followed, which, if any, steps were omitted and the consequences of any omissions.

2 CONCEPT DEVELOPMENT

The best laid schemes o' mice and men gang aft aglae R. BURNS

This chapter deals with three fragile aspects of project work – concept acceptance, development and concept preservation, and offers examples of the many threats to the concept that occur at different stages of project life and a number of related issues.

2.1 THE BIRTH OF A PROJECT

A project is an engine of change. It is conceived when someone sees a need for progress, when there is likely to be a period of discussion, speculation, a 'tossing around' of pros, cons and ideas without much decisive action until the concept assumes an identifiable form. As the idea takes shape and desirability has been agreed, it is important to clarify the exact purpose of the project, that is, draft objectives, scope, outcome and cost, and to identify stakeholders (those who will be involved and others who might be advantaged or disadvantaged if it were to come to fruition). Proponents 'think through' their assumptions and expectations, reassess practicality, and discuss the tactics and methods by which the project might be brought to a satisfactory conclusion. It is helpful to 'sound out' the concept, test the reactions of others and exchange ideas with potential supporters and those who might offer advice or guidance. However, experience underlines the prudence of selectivity in choosing confidants, for many a good idea has been killed in infancy by hasty rejection or the covert opposition of someone with antipathy to change or a situation that might threaten a private agenda.

2.2 WEIGHING THE ALTERNATIVES

Project development is a continuous process of considering alternatives. This is particularly true during the conceptual stage. Test the concept by questioning:

1. Exactly what should be achieved?
2. Which outcomes are important (needs), which are desirable but less important (wants)?
3. What should not be included (impediments)?
4. How could the project 'vision' best be achieved?
5. How long will it take to achieve results and when would it be sensible to start?

6. How much will it cost and who would pay for it?
7. What opposition might be encountered, why, and from whom?

2.3 CONSIDERING METHODOLOGY

Alternative ways of achieving project objectives may come up for consideration. It is a good idea to explore each of these rather than dismiss any less attractive options. A clear and detailed picture of each alternative will lead to a reasoned decision on merits and a better final choice. Relative merits can be debated better if the favoured course is not readily accepted by potential stakeholders, so consideration of concept alternatives may later be helpful in overcoming opposition.

2.4 PITFALLS AND CONCEPT PRESERVATION

Many pitfalls can be attributed to a simple breakdown in communication and project concepts are vulnerable to misunderstanding and manipulation. Unless difficulties are overcome in the initial stages, differing perceptions and aspirations of potential stakeholders may develop into false expectations. As these become deeply rooted, a disastrous level of conflict may develop with those whose cooperation could have led to a successful project launch. The case study gives an example.

case study

TOO MANY COOKS – THE YOUTH TRAINING PROJECT

The youth training project was mooted by the director of an Industry Training Association. The idea was that by subsidizing a pre-employment period of properly structured job training, private firms would be encouraged to employ school leavers whom they would otherwise be reluctant to train in clerical, commercial or manufacturing skills. It was calculated that training subsidies would be offset by a reduction in unemployment payments. Payment of a subsidy to organizations would be subject to an approved training schedule, proper record keeping and reports of satisfactory training performance.

The Training Association's intention was that training would be simple, effective and systematic. It would be based on an analysis of job needs and conducted by qualified company personnel on the employers' premises.

The concept was considered by the Minister for Employment and Training without much thought as to how it might best be conducted nor under-

▶

standing of how the project should be structured. He called for submissions from representatives of the country's vast and deeply entrenched Technical Education Network, Apprenticeship Boards, Trades Unions and Local Education Authorities. Representatives of these bodies discussed the scheme's possibilities with their friends (usually in the absence of any real competence in the practicalities of commercial or industrial training), and formulated separate ideas of how the scheme would work and the benefits that might accrue to their respective organizations. Armed with these preconceived and partisan notions, each indicated qualified support for the proposal with an expectation of a paid appointment to the Steering Committee.

A Project Steering Committee was set up under the chairmanship of the Director of Technical Education, and the Minister, who represented a marginal electorate and was under pressure to reduce unemployment, embarked on a costly publicity campaign, in which he and the government were portrayed as originators of a new and revolutionary initiative to reduce youth unemployment.

From an early stage, it was clear that the commonsense concept envisaged by the Industry Training Advisor was neither understood by nor attractive to members of the committee. The Director of Education called for educational entry standards and detailed college curricula for all training courses; the Director, Technical Education, demanded that the training be conducted through the medium of technical college courses; trades union representatives called for lectures on the union movement to be conducted by their representatives as a mandatory requirement of all courses; and representatives of Departments of Education, Employment and Training wished to staff the scheme with administrators, training advisers and inspectors provided by their departments (it transpired that, at that time, none of these departments had people with credible experience of up-to-date commercial and/or industrial training in their employ).

Twelve months later, discussions continued. A formidable number of additional staff had been recruited to public departments and project expenditure exceeded $7m. Three programmes for a total of 41 trainees had been approved through the complex and convoluted system, and a further 20 people were to commence training. The 20 new trainees were destined for an already overstaffed public department. It was ironic that one of their first sessions of practical training consisted of shredding more than $3m worth of government pamphlets boasting the success of the youth training initiative.*

* The youth training project is a composite of projects conducted in two different countries.

What lessons can be learned from this tragedy of errors and how could it have been averted?

1. **Keep control of the concept.**
   The training adviser's concept was sound. He knew how to make it work and he had the credibility to secure the cooperation of employers on whose participation the scheme would depend. Those who became involved in the concept did not. Their support was given for the wrong reasons. *It is unwise to surrender the project concept without a proviso on how it should be implemented.*

2. **Beware of sponsors who seek personal salvation or gain.**
   The minister had his own agenda, probably unrelated to the real purpose of the original proposal.

3. **Beware of empire builders and false profits.**
   In this case, representatives of other sectors were concerned with preserving the status quo and antipathetic to the industrial training concept of which they had no first-hand experience. Few had anything of value to contribute to the project but used it as a tool for advantage in their own spheres of operation.

4. **Insist on unambiguous and attainable objectives.**
   Project scope and objectives were not clearly defined at an early stage.

5. **Beware the open cheque book.**
   Beware of projects that have no clear terms of reference, credible assessment of costs, benefits or fixed budget allocations.

6. **Confirm stakeholder support.**
   The original concept would have been attractive to employers but the prospect of bureaucratic control and academic involvement was not conducive to their acceptance or support.

7. **Don't count your chickens.**
   A project can benefit from the right sort of publicity at the right time. Publicity for this project was damaging, being released for the wrong reasons and based on anticipation of unrealistic results that were not forthcoming.

8. **Conduct a responsible feasibility study.**
   Most importantly, a well-structured feasibility study conducted by experts would have established sound guidelines and provided a workable foundation for the project.

THE AIRBORNE EARLY WARNING SYSTEM

Because of its cost, the UK AEW project is a well-publicized example of concept abandonment.

In the Cold War period of the early 1970s, the Royal Air Force needed a high altitude electronic surveillance system. The Army also wanted accurate, high altitude intelligence but had no airborne assets on which to mount it. To meet RAF needs, the Ministry of Defence advocated development of a British Airborne Early Warning System (AEW) and agreement was reached for its development and commissioning by 1982 at a cost of about £22m.

Management and control was vested in MoD (Air) teams to control each specialist aspect of development, and contracts for airframe and avionics were awarded to Marconi Avionics and Hawker Sidley Aviation. The aircraft had to be capable of remaining aloft for prolonged periods and the radar had to be versatile. Urgency of need led to a decision that airframe and electronics would be developed concurrently.

As the project progressed, management control problems became apparent and, by 1980, the project was behind schedule and costs were thought to have escalated to over £318m (Morris, 1994).

Meanwhile, by 1983, the Army had MoD support for a research programme called CASTOR – Corps Airborne Stand-off Radar. Development was based on a reliable and versatile Pilatus Britten–Norman Islander conversion and Ferranti Defence Systems multi-mode radar. This was extensively tested and, by 1985, had proved the success of the Moving Target Indicator concept, now the basis of modern target acquisition systems (Ashley, 1999).

Meanwhile, with the AEW project, problems with radar, software development and computer processing had been reported and, about 1984, one of the contractors agreed to absorb some cost and accepted a new, incentive-based contract. Even so, in 1986, with short-term success still in doubt and continually rising costs, the concept was abandoned and the project cancelled. Costs of over £800m were written off. (The Nimrod Project and its aftermath are well documented in P.W.G. Morris' book *The Management of Projects*, Thomas Telford, 1994.)

Analysis of the AEW project brought to light many lessons in project management, including:

- the advantages of using a single project manager;
- the risks involved in concurrent development of untried technologies.

Although technologically different, a comparison of the two radar projects confirms these points and the advantages of limited scope and reliance, where possible, on 'footholds' of established technology.

The concept of a UK AEW was temporarily abandoned at heavy cost but the Nimrod airframe with its endurance capability has delivered valiant service in intelligence gathering and surveillance operations throughout the world.

In 1999, after research and development programmes lasting from the mid-1980s, the MoD established a £750m project to meet the combined needs of air and ground forces.

2.5 PROBLEMS OF CONCURRENCY

As with the Sydney Opera House (in which case the concept won through to completion), amongst other things, the UK AEW project illustrates:

- the danger of project compression, and concurrency;
- the danger of fragmented management, and the difficulty of controlling cost and subcontractors engaged in complex development work.

2.6 CONCURRENT (SIMULTANEOUS) ENGINEERING CONCEPTS

Overcoming many problems encountered in the past, better practices for managing concurrency have been successfully developed for projects of limited scope, specific objectives and a sound basis of past experience. In *The Role of Concurrent Engineering in Weapons System Acquisition*, Winner (1998) mentions 'A systematic approach to integrated concurrent design of products and related processes including manufacturing and support' and the way in which the approach encourages developers to consider all elements of the product life cycle. The technique is also receiving attention in the construction industry (Love, Gunasekaran and Li, 1998).

To reduce time frames for such things as product development and to reduce the problems of project control, simultaneous engineering (SE) management techniques have been developed with considerable success in some manufacturing, and in specialized industries (Figure 2.1).

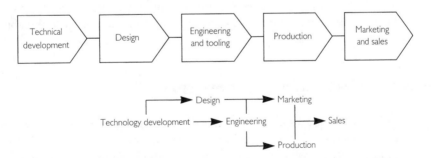

Figure 2.1 Sequential and simultaneous engineering (team) concepts in new product design and introduction

Evidence of success in simultaneous (concurrent) management is most often identified with projects of limited objectives, clear definitions of scope, unified leadership and very close cooperation between functions. All these features are more easily achieved in internal projects, and in Japan, dedicated multidisciplinary teams or 'task forces', working in close cooperation to solve, for example, design and development problems, have met with considerable success in reducing development times, and improving quality and production processes.

An industry leader in these processes is the Toyota Motor Corporation which has succeeded in containing lead times and combining a broad range of possible designs to achieve 'what may be the fastest and most efficient vehicle development cycles' (Sobek, Ward and Liker, 1999); for example, the Toyota forklift truck design cycle (Maylor, 1996).

2.7 INNOVATIVE AND DEVELOPMENTAL CONCEPTS IN MAJOR PROJECTS

Many worthy and ambitious concepts call for the development or adaptation of new technology. But, being difficult to assess, the costs and outcomes of new process development make risk assessment and planning very difficult. Risks are multiplied and difficulties more frequent when research or development in several areas is conducted concurrently, for example with construction or production. The project concept is obviously safer when implementation is based on well-tried methods. Nevertheless, despite having begun without definition of or experience in essential technique, many imaginative and ambitious projects based on a 'grand vision' survive. The Sydney Opera House (Chapter 9) was commissioned before the problems of its construction and exterior treatment had been solved. In the Channel Tunnel project linking England and France, funding was sought well before many essential specifications had been developed. Solving design problems was a costly business and problems of excavation posed difficulty for the consortia responsible for this work. Major problems had to be overcome in funding the immense cost of this venture.

But, despite cost escalation, controversy and public criticism, the Sydney Opera House and the Channel Tunnel are both examples of projects now commonly regarded as great and successful achievements. Planning inadequacies, management problems and astronomical costs are long forgotten because the concepts, in each case, were sound.

2.8 PROGRAMME AND MULTI-PROJECT CONCEPTS

Multi-project management links a set of projects strategically, by portfolio planning, technologically because of common components, or through overlapping project management, for example in the form of a programme.

Programme concepts involving a series of geographically, sector (Figure 2.2) or company-linked projects are common in the experience of large companies and international agencies. The heavy cost of some infrastructure concepts frequently results in an integrated programme reliant on several financing agencies whose programmes are linked by sector or common interest.

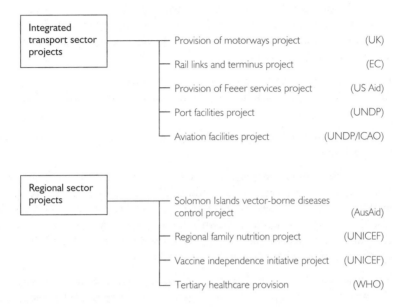

Figure 2.2 Examples of integrated sector programmes

On a smaller scale, commercial organizations and public utilities encounter situations in which a need for new product development, the introduction of total quality management, or organizational change, for example business re-engineering, point to the desirability of a series of small linked projects that can be conducted concurrently within the organization. In such cases, the projects might be assigned to a project manager or coordinator.

Business re-engineering (Andrews and Stalick, 1994), management reorganization, the introduction of new methods, practices for improvement, employee attitudes or similar concepts often involve a multiplicity of activities that result in small internal projects that can be run concurrently with good results.

2.9 DIFFICULT CONCEPTS

The transition from concept to project implementation is often fraught with difficulty and many excellent or deserving causes fail to survive the process of conception.

SAVING THE PATAGONIAN TOOTHFISH

The Patagonian toothfish was discovered near Macquarie Island in 1994. It is one of the largest species of fish known to occur in the Antarctic and lives at ocean depths of between 600 and 3200 metres. The fish is named for its large razor-sharp teeth and lives for up to 30 years, growing up to 2 m in length and 100 kg in weight.

Properties of the toothfish are unique. The flesh contains a high level of Omega 3 fatty acids which have become recognized for their health benefits in combating asthma.

In the markets, it sells for as much $11 per kg, making it an attractive target for illegal fishing.

Assessments of fishery status are carried out by different agencies, including the Commonwealth Scientific and Industrial Research Organisation (CSIRO). In 1997, as little is known about the species, CSIRO announced a joint $2.9m CSIRO, Australian Antarctic Division and fishing industry research programme to establish sustainable fishing levels and study the effect of the fishery on other parts of the complex sub-Antarctic ecosystem.

The Australian Fisheries Management Association consults with industry and non-government groups, and to manage the Macquarie Island Development Fishery (MIDF) on a sound ecological basis, MIDF has established two expertise-based groups to advise on a variety of issues.

The Commission for the Conservation of Antarctic Marine Living Resources (CCAMLR) has stated an intention to back proposals to 'make use of satellite-linked vessel monitoring systems mandatory, to increase reporting of illegal vessels, to improve CCAMLR's vessel register and to tighten licensing and port controls' (Hill and Vale, 1998) and a number of vessels have been arrested, impounded and subjected to heavy penalties for illegal fishing.

Toothfish populations are now under extreme pressure from high levels of illegal fishing which are also responsible for the death of endangered birds, including the albatross (Hill and Vale, 1998).

The diversity of commercial, national and international agencies, the nature of vested interests and practical difficulties in policing the vast Antarctic Oceans make effective coordination of effort difficult and despite the valuable activities of various agencies, policing action by the Royal Australian Navy, Coastguard, Greenpeace activity and considerable lobbying by fisheries interests, no coordinating individual or group seems able to unite potential sponsors with the resources to establish total project coordination.

Many worthy concepts fail to reach the proposal stage because of an inability to identify a single sponsor or a cohesive group with the power, determination or opportunity to fully coordinate all aspects of the concept.

The case of the Patagonian toothfish is an example of the many problems confronting a would-be project developer. Despite extensive expertise and funding opportunities, the practical difficulties of bringing together the many agencies, funding sources and fragmented interests involved present a formidable obstacle.

In cases of this kind, the best (sometimes the only) alternative is closer coordination, and the development of additional, linked sector projects, by the agencies and organizations concerned.

case study

A GLOBAL PROBLEM – THE DISPOSAL OF NUCLEAR WASTE

Despite a fall in enthusiasm for nuclear power since the 1986 meltdown of the Chernobyl reactor and failures that led to mounting concern over safety, world production of nuclear waste continues to increase and its disposal presents increasingly pressing and contentious world problems. In Russia alone, recharging and repairing civilian ships with atomic devices forms up to 1200 cubic metres of liquid waste annually, spent fuel rods are stored on a barge in Murmansk harbour and the cost of cleaning up nuclear sites in the north west is around $44 million, according to BNFL.

The United States, Great Britain and France are some of the other countries with major problems in disposing of radioactive materials resulting from activities that range from decommissioning weapons to the reprocessing of fuel rods, and the principle of the International Non-Proliferation Treaty that each country will be responsible for the disposal and storage of its own nuclear waste products must soon come under pressure.

Some nuclear materials have a long half-life, remaining radioactive for over 50 000 years, and disposal technology has been the subject of major research projects. The cost of waste disposal is immense, and facilities for it, being highly capital-intensive, offer opportunities for substantial revenue to any country willing and able to safely accept the potentially hazardous material.

Few areas of public concern evoke such emotional or vociferous comment, attracting both informed and a wealth of uninformed opinion. For this reason, projects involving any form of nuclear activity tend to remain on a confidential basis until feasibility and the possibility of acceptance can be assessed.

In 1999, the concept of a $16 billion nuclear waste dump in Western Australia, under consideration by Pangea, an international consortium, attracted press

▶

coverage following parliamentary exchanges and, despite assurances that no official meetings or communication had taken place, allegations of discussions between Pangea representatives and members of state and federal governments were the subject of considerable comment.

The plan was said to have received the backing of the US government. It was also claimed that such a repository would add a massive 1 per cent to Australia's GNP and create over 50 000 jobs.

Speculation on the plan's scale, earning potential and economic benefits included assertions that Australia had a responsibility to participate in the storage of waste originating from uranium exports and so on. Western Australia has many prospective uranium mines within its vast land area, and guarded or tentative claims of possible support by influential people were suggested (Rose and Grove, 1999).

A suitable disposal site would be an unfaulted rock bed in a remote, unpopulated region. In addition to the site in Western Australia, some parts of China, Russia or Canada might be suitable, but only Australia and Canada are politically stable and of course, both these countries are highly sensitive to nuclear issues.

This Pangea concept is said to favour a location in the Centralian Superbasin, a stable area of ancient sandstone that lies in a remote desert region near to Aboriginal reserves and close to the South Australian border.

Feasibility of the proposal is based on a combination of deep underground mining techniques and the use of synthetic rock technology, a process developed by the Australian National University (ANU) and patented in 1979. This uses intense heat and compression to lock the waste into a crystalline structure of synthetic minerals or rock. ANU is a joint patent holder with the Australian Nuclear Science and Technology Organization (ANSTO). Subsequent development led to patenting the process under the trade name of 'Synroc'.

A French process of mixing waste with molten glass provides a temporary disposal option lasting about 50 years, when the waste has to be reprocessed and reburied in deep, fan-cooled caverns. Synroc, it is claimed, will last indefinitely and requires no temporary storage.

Construction of a repository in which radioactive material might be safely stored in a system of deep underground caverns was considered feasible by engineers well versed in mining and similar operations, who pointed out its similarity to that of a modern gold mine (Amalfi, 1999).

In Arizona, Pangea Australia's president stressed the importance of 'moral and ethical values' in the quest for public and political acceptance, relegating the economic benefits to secondary significance in the argument.

To facilitate some of the immense problems of stakeholder communications, and public acquiescence, Pangea Resources were said (no doubt amongst other measures) to have recruited a media relations organization, former advisers to the Premier of Western Australia and Lands Minister (Priest, 1998) and an international expert on the transportation of nuclear materials.

Despite expressions of public concern, opposition of environmentalists and anti-nuclear lobbies and forthright political promises to veto nuclear waste proposals, the concept is based on a problem that is unlikely to disappear. Pangea Resources can hardly expect short-term agreement but with so much at stake and massive financial backing from major users of nuclear energy, they may well feel that time is on their side.

In September 1999, the company opened an office in Perth.

The synroc nuclear waste disposal process

Based on an original plan of the synroc process developed at the Australian National University in Canberra

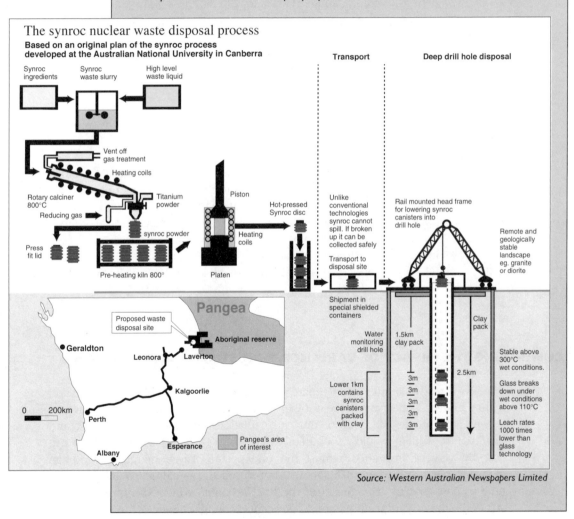

Source: Western Australian Newspapers Limited

The prelude to this nuclear waste proposal illustrates the fragility and speculative nature of project conception. This is accentuated when the process is complex, controversial or the proposal involves untried technologies related to issues of deep public doubt or concern. In a project of this nature the number of potential stakeholders is enormous and lengthy periods of research, explanation, risk analysis and reassurance and political negotiation are likely to ensue.

2.10 SEEKING ACCEPTANCE AND SUPPORT

The politics of acceptance and support cannot be systematized or covered by generalities. However, a reminder of simple ground-rules may not come amiss. These include:

- Invest time and money 'up front' identifying stakeholders and their concerns – even when plans are still tentative, this saves time and resources later (Laufer, 1997).
- Identify potential stakeholders early and, when possible, get them involved.
- Marshal support from the 'true believers' – enthuse peers and immediate superiors to provide encouragement and basic help.
- Show benefits in realistic but attractive terms.
- Don't play down difficulties or problems; assess the risks and show ways of overcoming them.
- Be realistic about costs and risks but stress benefits.
- 'Picket the heights' – get support from top people – in as many areas as possible.
- Anticipate opposition and be forewarned – think why proposals might attract opposition, and from whom, and prepare a rational defence.
- 'Play a straight bat' – don't gloss over problems; be factual and, of course, honest. A project cannot work on a basis of false information.
- Support proposals with logical framework structures showing major assumptions on which the project proposals are based and what results would be verifiable.

2.11 CUSHIONING THE IMPACT OF VARIANCE, ADJUSTMENT AND REVISION

We have already said that an adequately managed project should end on time and within budget but it would be foolhardy to commence a project without any leeway whatsoever. Because of the close relationship between time, cost and quality, it is prudent to allow for variance (say up to 10 per cent) in total time and cost by way of insurance against the unexpected. Large margins encourage extravagance and slipshod management but in practice, small gains and losses of time or cost tend to average out in the final accounts which, in normal circumstances, will not vary from within 10 per cent of budget target.

2.12 OWNER'S REVISIONS DURING PROJECT IMPLEMENTATION

A project owner will not normally change the concept, but calls for some form of revision after commencement are not uncommon. Full implications of any new proposal should be carefully assessed. Apart from essential planning changes that the revision would entail, it may have a major impact on the overall concept, timing and nature of the project outcome. It is important to consider the full effect of a revision on project implementation, including resource availability, allocation, staffing, cost and cash flow. Additional costs, which are usually borne by the owners, should be agreed before the revision is accepted.

REVIEW AND DISCUSSION QUESTIONS

1. Discuss projects of your knowledge in which the concept was abandoned or compromised and the likely causes of failure.
2. What tests should be applied to a new concept to establish clear understanding and test its suitability?
3. Bring to mind a project that failed because it was pursued for the wrong motives; consider how the concept might have been preserved and successfully implemented.
4. Discuss the dangers of project compression and concurrency in a strategic project involving both technological development and production.
5. Consider the concept of a project of which you have personal knowledge and assess the extent to which the original concept was maintained and the events and considerations that led to its outcome.
6. Consider how you might best set about gaining acceptance for an innovative or controversial project.
7. Think of a number of concepts that would be best satisfied by means of programmes or a project series and consider how they might be split into a number of projects.
8. Consider tactics that might be effective in establishing a project for the disposal of small quantities of radioactive material (for example, for medical or clinical use).
9. Consider and discuss the next case study.

case study

GOODBYE SUBIC BAY

Changing alliances, technology and revised defence estimates are amongst the reasons for the closure of defence bases. Over the past few years, the US Base Realignment and Closure Commission (BRAC) has planned the reduction or elimination of several hundred US military installations worldwide.

▶

Administrators are well practised in the logistics of base closures, dismantling equipment, transport storage, mothballing ships or aircraft and disposal of assets by sales and so on, but defence departments are not the only stakeholders in such projects.

The concept of base closure is associated with political or sociological issues and consequences of closing important installations can be traumatic to the local community.

Bases attract direct and indirect employment, that is, civilians employed in the base itself and those in trade (shopping, transport and recreation facilities for military personnel, and so on).

In an isolated region, a base closure is often linked to hardship and massive unemployment. After a long period of dependency on the base and adaptation to its needs, local communities should not be left without any measures to cushion the loss of income and facilities. Base closure usually involves vacating areas of land, buildings and services, many which might be redeveloped for other purposes. In tandem with the closure project, many state, local governments or private individuals may initiate projects for redevelopment of vacated military facilities. One such plan was at Subic Bay in the Philippines, another adopted by the Commonwealth of Massachusetts for the installation known as Fort Devens.

The Fort Devens plan was for:

- avoidance of adverse fiscal effects on the town;
- orderly redevelopment;
- accelerated job creation;
- environmental protection;
- strong local control of development.

(*Source:* McManus and Burke, 1997)

Exercise task

9.1   Consider essential concept differences between base closure and base reuse plans.

9.2   Discuss the concept of a redevelopment plan, what such a project might involve, when it should be implemented and how it should be linked with the closure project.

9.3   Consider possible problems related to redevelopment, for example infrastructure modification, incompatibility of power, sewerage, water or telephone installations, and so on.

3 FEASIBILITY AND RISK ASSESSMENT

The bearings of his observation lays in the application of it ...   C. DICKENS

3.1   INITIAL PROPOSALS AND FEASIBILITY STUDIES

After initial consideration of concept and potential, the next step is usually a preliminary proposal to gauge the reaction of stakeholders and elicit support. If reactions are favourable, a feasibility study and risk assessment will probably follow. One of the most important steps of successful project development, the feasibility study is all too often neglected or inadequately carried out.

3.2   THE INITIAL PROPOSAL

The purpose of the initial proposal is fourfold:

1. to introduce the concept;
2. to test the reactions of potential stakeholders;
3. to elicit support;
4. to establish a basis for feasibility assessment.

The initial proposal identifies the project and sets the ball rolling. It explains the background, need, purpose of the project and offers a broad outline of expected costs and benefits. Some detail will be conceptual, possibly a little 'broad-brush', but the proposal will include available hard data to support the project concept and it will probably recommend a feasibility study. In some cases, the recommendation will be extended to suggestions on feasibility study scope, objectives, terms of reference, probable cost and even who should carry it out. The main purpose of the proposal is to persuade, 'sell' the concept and attract support. So at this stage, it is unwise to pre-empt a decision or complicate initial impressions. The proposal should concentrate on central issues and avoid unnecessary detail of the mechanics of planning and implementation.

3.3   PROPOSALS TO PARTICIPATE

Project proposals of a slightly different kind are made by would-be contributors, individuals or firms who specialize in project work and seek to manage, conduct or contribute to a project by providing research, consultancy, manufacture or some other service. These proposals are likely to follow a feasibility study and occur in response to a project owner's invitation to tender.

In the case of large projects, the participation proposal may reflect intensive effort and costly preparation on the part of the would-be contractor who has made a detailed investigation into the feasibility, cost, risks and profit potential of the proposed contribution

3.4 THE FEASIBILITY STUDY

After the concept has been provisionally accepted, a feasibility study is usually required. This important step is often disregarded but to embark on any major project without an adequate feasibility study would be foolhardy in the extreme, as many individuals, organizations and governments have discovered to their cost!

The study will investigate practicalities, ways of achieving objectives, strategy options, methodology, and predict likely outcomes, risks and the consequences of each course of action.

In a written report, it will confirm (or otherwise) the need and concept, propose objectives, scope, strategies and benefits and offer a 'ball-park' estimate of costs. The report will probably advise on timing, staffing, terms of reference and logistics. It will report on the nature and extent of any threats to project success and the extent and consequences of risk.

In the case of long-term or complex projects, the study may be a substantial undertaking with detailed terms of reference. It is likely to need special funding and managerial resources, and entail in-depth research or investigation by consultants or other specialists. The feasibility study is likely to become the foundation on which project definition and rationale will be based so the quality of its conduct and information is likely be reflected in all subsequent project activity.

A well-conducted study will prove a good investment and offer a sound basis for decisions, clarification of objectives, logical planning, minimal risk and a successful, cost-effective project.

Finally and importantly, it is largely on the basis of the feasibility study that the financier will base the assessment of project risk, potential value and suitability for investment or financial backing.

3.5 INVESTIGATING FEASIBILITY

The feasibility study is a reconnaissance of the whole area of the project proposal. It should present a balanced picture incorporating all aspects of possible concern, that is:

1. **Existing data**
    - Many studies benefit from experience of similar operations and pre-recorded data derived from similar projects or operations.

2. **Scope, objectives and assumptions**
   - Apart from confirming (or otherwise) project need, scope and objectives, the study should test the assumptions expressed in the initial proposal.
3. **Strategy outline**
   - The study may result in an outline strategy for the project (what, when, where, how and by whom, and so on).
4. **Financial analysis** (external factors, where relevant)
   - The economy of the country or region (for example, stable, transitory, developing), trends, threats detailed, factual information and analysis.
5. **Financial analysis** (project basis)
   - Cost estimates should be realistic and the study may be required to investigate or suggest sources of equity. (Bear in mind the difficulty of raising capital for high-risk or politically sensitive projects, and ventures involving unproven technologies or projects in unstable regions.)
6. **Assessment of return on investment and effort**
   - Assess the expected return from project effort and investment (ROI) and/or other benefits, including sustainability in the case of training, organizational change, international aid, development or relief projects.
7. **Risk assessment**
   - Identification and classification of possible threats or risks to ultimate success.
   - An assessment of risk levels and consequences with an appreciation of methods of risk limitation or avoidance; assessment of financial risk.
8. **Sources of project support**
   - List supporters and advocates for the project (possible or confirmed) and agencies or special facilities that might be advantageous to acceptance or implementation.
9. **Technological assessment**
   - Technology – technological feasibility – tested, developmental or exploratory; level of technological risk – danger (if any) of cost overruns due to development costs; emergent technology – trends and outlook for relevant technologies.
   - Opportunities for the acquisition of expertise by contract, by merger, joint venture, and so on.
10. **Political analysis** (when appropriate)
    - Political assessment, and any implications on project issues (including choice of personnel, security, personal safety and so on); areas of possible support, conflict or opposition.
    - Level of political stability, economy, inflation, and so on.
    - Government involvement – national, state or regional government participation in the project, cost sharing – patronage; profit sharing – benefits, incentives, and so on.
    - Requirements for legislation, approvals, permissions and licences.
    - Nationalistic attitudes, dissident factions or groups, bias against overseas interests, multinational or international operations.
    - Opportunity for beneficial involvement with areas of influence.

11. **Environmental impact assessment** (EPA)
- Precise nature and extent of project impact on the environment (if any).
- Details of environmental management to be included in project structure to conform with desired, agreed or mandatory requirements (ISO 14000 series and so on).

12. **Sociological impact assessment** (if appropriate) **and stakeholder identification**
- Assessment of the project's impact on the social structure, and initial identification of affected individual or group stakeholders.

13. **Project management structure and administration**
- Outline of proposed management structure.
- Key personnel – special qualifications, outline job specifications, and so on.
- Administration, support for expatriate personnel, security, housing, welfare and safety.

14 **Project resources**
- Summary of important resource needs
- Identification of sources of supply
- Preferred type of contract
- Details of preliminary estimates

3.6 WHO WILL CONDUCT THE FEASIBILITY STUDY?

In small organizations, executives with limited project experience are apt to charge a 'bright' junior manager with responsibility for the feasibility study. This is a useful exercise in initiative and personal development, but it does not always result in project success. The outcome will depend on the nature of the project, the incumbent's training, ability and background, and the quality of the briefing.

The feasibility study is an investment in knowledge. It is of prime importance and, to be of value, it must be done by able and qualified people, and it may justify the employment of a specialist team. For a new unbiased view, special knowledge or experience, professional advisers or management consultants may be the best choice. In either case, terms of reference should be carefully drafted.

3.7 STUDY TEAMS FOR LOGIC-BASED PROPOSALS

The type of project and nature of activity will determine the composition of the team and the selection of its members. If assessment can rely on a body of existing knowledge, logic and experience, for example motorway, shopping centre construction or machinery design, the study team would almost certainly include an engineer with appropriate experience of the processes involved.

Reasoned arguments will be based on mature experience of similar projects, methods and well-understood technology, and technical problems will be readily foreseen; pre-recorded data applicable to many tasks and processes will be available; recommendations will be predictable and should result in an accurate forecast of costs, risks and results.

But the fact that some, apparently straightforward, propositions encounter opposition or active resistance on environmental, ecological, sociological or industrial grounds should not be overlooked.

3.8 TERMS OF REFERENCE FOR THE STUDY

Terms of reference are usually based on the background described in the project proposal as qualified by discussion, study objectives, direction, scope and focus. They will include the structure of the study team, staffing, the responsibilities of each team member, coordination of work, limits of authority and any other matters relating to the study, with constraints, for example limits on time and cost, and special restrictions – people who for some reason may not be consulted, secrecy or security needs, limitations on travel, and so on. In cases of doubt or concern over a particular aspect of the proposal such as technical feasibility, the capability of an overseas workforce or the sustainability of project improvements, the questions to be answered should be defined.

3.9 BRIEFING THE STUDY TEAM

The quality of the briefing will determine the study's effectiveness and the way that it is conducted. Formal briefing sessions should be backed by appropriate documentation. Written authorization to conduct the study may be necessary. The briefing should include:

1. Outline of project concept and initial assessment of need
2. Project background (including the initial proposal)
3. Scope, purpose and objectives of the study and when and where it is to take place (geographical area)
4. Composition of the team and areas of individual responsibility
5. Study budget, authority to engage or co-opt personnel
6. Sources of information (places, people, processes, sites, and so on); previous approaches for information; possible sources of opposition
7. Constraints or limits to the project – time, finance, political, climatic, market conditions, and so on
8. Requirement for technological, political, sociological or environmental impact assessment, and areas of special concern (confidentiality, secrecy, and so on)
9. Report format; to whom the report should be directed; number of copies required

3.10 CONDUCTING FEASIBILITY STUDIES

Because of the varied nature of project work, it is difficult to offer advice on the conduct of feasibility studies. However, a few useful ground-rules may not come amiss:

- Get as much information as possible before commencing the study.
- Make a study plan – who to see, what questions to ask, where to go, what to see and so on – and revise it regularly.
- Test preconceived ideas and prejudices. Listen to opinions but test their validity.
- Don't become wrongly influenced or caught up in someone's bandwagon.
- Differentiate between fact and opinion.
- Be aware of the nature and strength of deeply held opinions and feelings that might result in opposition or delay in completing the project.
- Obtain and record facts wherever possible.
- Be aware of possible risks; consider their consequences and how these difficulties might be overcome.
- Remember that you are an ambassador for the project and that your courtesy, acceptability and image may have a telling effect on future success.
- Don't be afraid to consider alternatives; give an honest and unbiased opinion.

3.11 WHAT SHOULD BE COVERED IN THE FEASIBILITY REPORT?

The coverage and layout of a feasibility study report is a matter of common sense and will be decided by the circumstances of the study. In practice, a list of typical report headings would include:

1. **Identifying information**
   Title
   Place and date of the study
   Composition of the study team
   Terms of reference and study objectives

2. **Executive summary**
   Brief description of study activities
   Summary of conclusions
   Summary of recommendations

3. **Body of the report**
   Contents
   List of annexes and exhibits
   Terms of reference
   Detail of investigations for each aspect of the study

4. **Conclusions**
   Conclusions relating to feasibility, consequences, benefits, likely costs, anticipa-

ted problems, hazards and possibility of failure in any area, assessment of success probabilities, possible alternatives

5. **Recommendations**
   Recommendations to proceed
   Proposed project duration
   How to proceed
   Draft project objectives for each area of the project
   Resources that will be required
   Project financing
   Management and staffing
   Framework for project control and review
   The purpose and objectives of key jobs

6. **Annexes and exhibits**
   Master charts of proposed project events
   Copies of relevant data
   Maps, charts, tables and so on
   Draft position descriptions for key personnel
   Financial estimates and cash flow prediction
   Threat and risk assessment

3.12 PROJECT RISKS

Before becoming involved in a project, owners, sponsors and prospective financiers will want:

- to be assured of project feasibility;
- to assess the possibility of threat to the desired outcome;
- to consider the consequences of potential project risk and be assured that it can be managed.

There is an element of risk in all projects. In some, the risks are minimal, while others are highly risk-prone. Risk management is a continuous process throughout the life of all projects, beginning with the feasibility stage when foreseeable risks are identified, classified and assessed.

A serious threat may cause the project to be modified or abandoned but, in most cases, planning will be able to provide risk avoidance mechanisms to reduce the probability of trauma and/or minimize the consequences.

Risk management takes place in four stages:

1. Risk identification
2. Risk assessment
3. Risk analysis
4. Risk elimination

3.13 RISK IDENTIFICATION

Risks may stem from:

- *the project itself – for example, decisions on method, specification, technology, finance, and so on.* These may be related to investment decisions (for example, in relation to a comparison of costs and benefits) or issues connected with project strategy and planning; that is, some strategies involve a greater element of risk than others.
- *unplanned occurrences,* some of which may be insurable, related to accident, fire, sabotage, and so on.
- *external causes* related to political situations, environment or economic downturn.

Consequences of a risk range between minimal and traumatic, affecting either:

- project outcome and achievement of objectives (the project will fail partly or completely), or
- duration, that is, serious time overrun and late completion, excessive cost and/ or failure to deliver specified results or quality during the project's life cycle.

Techniques of risk identification include history research or 'hindsight reviews' (evaluation of past experience of similar projects and processes).

Some sectors such as construction and infrastructure have a history of high risk, particularly in relation to cost overrun, quality and late completion, especially in certain geographical areas. In Hong Kong, a study of factors associated with project delay and cost escalation identified a range of basic problems from 'insufficient or incorrect design information' to 'poor co-ordination with sub contractors' (Shen, 1997).

Other techniques include 'check lists' and project simulations (in which risk factors emerge) and intensive 'brainstorming' sessions based on the ways in which adverse conditions might arise.

However, the most direct, probable and important risks are usually apprehended and investigated in the feasibility study, which may also identify indicators to alert managers to the onset of an impending problem. Risk patterns, including those of politically sensitive projects or risks involving concurrent development of untried technology, tend to conform to a curve of normal distribution in which most risks are of low impact and can be forestalled by good planning, or dealt with in the course of normal management activity. The vital few, probably less than 20 per cent in number (Figure 3.1), may be decisive and justify special measures.

3.14 RISK ASSESSMENT

Risk assessment takes account of:

- the nature of possible risk(s);
- the probability of risk (risk probability factors);

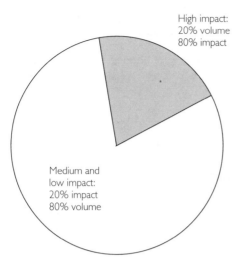

High impact:
20% volume
80% impact

Medium and
low impact:
20% impact
80% volume

Figure 3.1 Risk volume and impact

- the consequences of risk;
- means, costs and consequences of minimizing or underwriting risks.

Difficulty of risk assessment increases exponentially with time-span. For this reason, risks related to strategic and long-term projects are more difficult to assess and greater reliance has to be placed on probability factors and feasibility judgements. Conversely, as the time span or unexpired project time diminishes, risk probability is easier to assess and the impact more easily defined and quantified but even the more simple remedies may become progressively expensive to apply.

3.15 RISK ANALYSIS

Benefits of risk analysis include:

- greater reliance on logic and more systematic planning;
- inclusion of alternative tactics and methods to reduce the consequences of trauma during project implementation;
- quantification of risks and consequences to influence strategic decisions.

There are many programmes to assist with risk analysis in specialist circumstances such as construction or mechanical engineering activities (where historical data on costs, error and task timings are often available) and for in-company projects, for example computer modelling for product development or marketing decisions.

This level of information is seldom available to sponsors of innovative or strategic projects involving concepts with a wide range of variables and little historical precedent (such as the nuclear waste project described in Chapter 2). As with risk assessment, risk analysis in strategic projects has to rely heavily on personal judgement. Risk evaluation techniques include:

- activity network analysis (PERT, CPM, precedence networks, and so on);
- decision trees;
- expected value estimation;
- sensitivity analysis.

3.16 ACTIVITY NETWORKS AND ANALYSIS

The main use of activity networks in risk analysis is to isolate activities and events that might cause significant delay and to estimate the cost of 'crashing' or accelerating progress to bring the project back on schedule.

Most project schedules use Programme Evaluation and Review Technique (PERT), Critical Path Method (CPM) or a form of precedence network (Chapter 10). These methods map out the logical sequence of project activities, showing interdependencies (activities that are dependent on the completion of some other task before they can be started) and the expected duration of each activity. CPM traces the path that cannot be shortened (Figure 3.2). If the diagram covers the entire project, the length of this path will be the total project duration. Events on the critical path that take longer than expected or begin late will delay project completion. Time and cost being closely related, project delay is likely to result in extra cost. A long delay may result in penalties or heavy cost overrun.

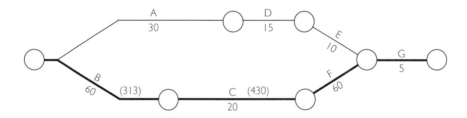

Figure 3.2 Segment of construction sequence with critical path – the risk-sensitive critical path is shown as a heavy line

'Crashing' (speeding up critical activities by increasing resources, such as labour and/or machinery) can be expensive (Figure 3.3). If the estimated duration of an activity is doubtful, or the work vulnerable to complication or delay, the cost of crashing may be very important (Figure 3.4).

To help assess their significance, risks may be categorized by probability and impact in a logical framework (Figure 3.5).

Activity	Depends on	Duration (days)	Daily labour cost (1 shift)	Daily machine cost	Daily labour cost (2 shifts)
A	–	30	$4 000	$2 000	$10 000
B	–	60	$6 000	$1 000	$15 000
C	B	20	$2 000	$1 000	$5 000
D	A	15	$4 000	$2 000	$10 000
E	D	10	$2 000	–	$5 000
F	C	60	$8 000	$3 000	$20 000
G	E & F	5	$5 000	$1 000	$10 000

Material usage is not changed by accelerated activity

Crash cost of 20 days from Activity B

Planned cost $

Labour 60 days @ $6 000   360 000

Machine cost 60 days @ $1 000 60 000

Total   420 000

Crash cost $

Labour 20 days @ $6 000   120 000

20 days @ $15 000   300 000

Machines 40 days @ $1 000   40 000

Total   460 000

Therefore cost of reducing activity B to 40 days would be $40 000

Figure 3.3 Sequence table and calculation of additional cost of reducing the duration of an activity

Activity	Normal time (days)	Crash time (days)	Total normal cost $	Total crash cost $	Max. time reduction (days)	Daily crash cost $
310	21	12	2100	4800	9	300
322	30	20	4000	6500	10	250
313	60	40	6000	9000	20	150
420	30	10	3000	4500	20	150
430	20	10	2000	3000	10	100
Totals			17 100	27 800		
Cost of crashing all activities				$10 700		

Figure 3.4 Summary of crash costs for a series of selected activities

Degree of impact on category	Risk probability		
	Improbable	Probable	Very probable
Minor effect on Category A & B	Priority 3	Priority 3	Priority 2
Serious effect on Category B	Priority 2	Priority 2	Priority 1
Severe effect on Categories A & B	Priority 2	Priority 1	Priority 1

Category A   Might compromise concept or project outcome
Category B   Might result in major delay or cost escalation

Figure 3.5 Risk classification table

3.17   USING DECISION TREES AND EXPECTED VALUES

Decision trees and expected value comparisons (described in Chapter 10) are another useful method of comparing risk factors. They map out alternative paths using known and estimated costs and values under a range of possible circumstances. They are often used in connection with expected values and become progressively effective as the accuracy of statistical information and forecasting improves.

Where monetary values are involved in the assessment, the expected value method is often used. The expected value is reached by multiplying the estimated product of an event by its probability.

The example shown in Figure 3.6 relates to the possibility of project delay due to difficulties in development. In this case, cost of delay is estimated to be $100 000 per month and it is considered that the project could be delayed for up to 10 months.

The services of a scientific adviser could be obtained for a fee of $50 000 and it is considered that the effect of his or her professional advice would probably reduce the duration of the delay.

The proposition is considered in the light of three possible delay periods, 10, 8 and 5 months respectively, (a) if the adviser is not engaged and (b) with the services of the scientific adviser, taking into account different probabilities for each delay period and the cost of the adviser (if appointed) to reach an 'expected value' figure.

3.18   SENSITIVITY ANALYSIS

The primary reason that sensitivity analysis is important to decision makers is that real-world problems exist in a dynamic environment (Anderson, Sweeney and Williams, 1991).

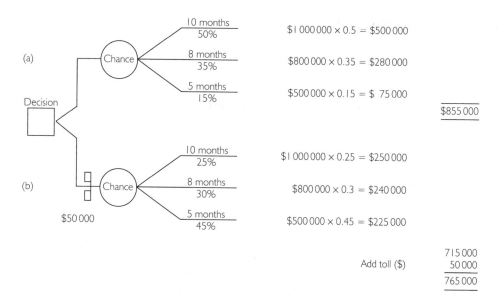

Figure 3.6 Simple delay reduction decision using expected values

In project work, sensitivity analysis concentrates on the effect of risk from changes that might occur during project implementation. Many will come to light in the feasibility study but, with decisions on strategy and planning, degrees of vulnerability and the extent to which a risk might affect project outcome, some may require further analysis so that the problem can be avoided or managed.

Strategic projects such as the nuclear waste disposal project in Chapter 2 are obviously very sensitive to political opinion and technological feasibility. However, the long-term nature of the growing nuclear waste disposal problem and the very high level of funding would, no doubt, be factors in Pangea's decisions to proceed.

Factors for analysis in other forms of project might range from regional economic instability to political unrest. Detailed issues bearing on financing and implementation, such as fluctuating exchange rates, variations in labour, material costs or transport costs (where these constitute a major item of expense) or, in revenue producing projects, fluctuations in demand, can be analysed to determine how great a variation the project can tolerate without failure and the extent of any budget provisions required to cushion the effect of the risk.

For many projects an analysis of the different effects of likely cost fluctuations in an estimated range of, say, ±10 or 15 per cent will be sufficient to indicate financial impact. Other issues may be more complex, involving the use of computers for linear programming problems, and a number of programs are available to assist with risk analysis techniques.

3.19 MANAGING THE RISKS

It is always cheaper to 'plan out' risks than leave them to be addressed during project implementation.

3.19.1 Deal with severe threats first

Priority 1 risks pose the most severe threats to the project; they are of two kinds, those with the most severe damage potential, and others, individually less traumatic but more numerous and having a high probability ratio whose combined consequences might impact badly on the project outcome. In dealing with these threats, consider:

- a change of strategy to reduce probability or soften their potential impact (for example, move to a BOT agreement in which much of the risk is borne by the contractor);
- contingency plans to deal with the consequences if they occur;
- arranging plans so that foreseeable problems emerge early in the project life cycle when they can be rectified most easily and at least cost;
- special measures to provide early warning of the danger;
- allowing extra time to accommodate the consequences of variance.

3.19.2 Reduce the lower-level threats by planning

With priority 2 risks, minimize the threat in the planning stage by eliminating those that can be removed at moderate cost. Those that cannot be easily eliminated should be dealt with in the contingency plan.

3.19.3 The small problem areas – priority 3 risks

If it is not contained, the cumulative effect of many low impact difficulties can become quite serious. Many of these will have common factors or stem from the same source. Make allowance for monitoring and correction during implementation.

3.20 ANTICIPATING THE EXTERNAL RISK

Internal projects for reorganization, introducing new methods or routines, are often susceptible to unexpected resistance on the part of employees or employee organizations who anticipate a threat to employment, working conditions or personal routine.

Those conducting logic-based studies should therefore be aware of possible sources of opposition and the need for consultation with potential stakeholders (possibly on a broad front). If difficulty is anticipated, it may be a good idea to include a generalist or public relations adviser to assess any external threat and advise on measures to forestall misinformed comment, avoid apprehension or combat opposition.

THE REFORESTATION PROJECT

The aim of the project was to enhance the beauty of a tract of land between some old slag heaps and a stretch of deteriorating woodland on the fringe of an industrial city.

The intention was to combine the commercial advantages of timber production with provision of an attractive recreation area and enhance the local landscape. The trees, it was argued, would also benefit the ecology and the initiative appease local environmentalists.

Because the proposals had been raised by, and extensively discussed with, Forestry Commission experts and government funds allocated, local government officials considered a feasibility study inappropriate and unnecessary.

The grant-aided plan enjoyed favourable media coverage in its initial stages. Work on clearing the land occupied by old slag heaps went without incident. On completion of this task, work continued on the stretch of woodland where a number of old and rather unattractive trees were to be removed to make way for the mechanized planting of saplings.

At this stage, the project met with unexpected opposition from a number of the people it had set out to placate. Members of environmentalist groups picketed boundaries, blocked entrance gates and chained themselves to some of the trees that were due for removal and replacement.

These activities attracted a rash of vociferous comment and unfavourable press coverage in which the government, as project sponsors, were depicted as environmental vandals and destroyers of century-old trees.

Forestry experts explained that the trees were not as old as people claimed; they had no particular merit, beauty or significance; they were generally in poor condition and unlikely to outlive the new growth that was to replace them. Ecologically, they argued, there was no difference between a young tree and an old one, but these arguments held no sway with the demonstrators who became increasingly militant and threatened to sabotage the entire project.

To resolve the conflict, an independent mediator was brought in. A compromise was eventually reached whereby, at additional expense, a selection of old trees were marked for retention and part of the woodland cleared of other growth. A new planting pattern was then devised to permit the use of about two-thirds of the designated area.

The project went ahead 12 months behind schedule but its scope and its commercial and goodwill value were compromised.

▶

This case illustrates one of the many problems that might have been forestalled with the benefit of a stakeholder and sociological assessment during, or resulting from, a feasibility study.

Scientists, forestry officers and other officials perceived the issues in terms of science and logic as they had come to know it. Regarding themselves as environmental experts, they displayed a fine disregard for the opinions and feelings of other stakeholders, namely the public at large (however misdirected public reaction may have been). They failed to anticipate and forestall the frustration and depth of emotion, fuelled by rhetoric, that can occur when someone's habitat is felt to be threatened or whose interests are perceived to have been ignored.

Where there is a lack of understanding, comment on public issues is often dictated by emotion rather than logic. As feelings become more deeply entrenched, recourse to logic is progressively difficult.

Lessons of the reforestation project are:

1. Consider all who might have an interest in the project (stakeholders).
2. Be aware of the need to keep people informed – all who might become directly or indirectly concerned.
3. When in doubt over public concern, consult, explain and (if possible) involve potential stakeholders in the discussion.

3.21 STUDY TEAMS FOR NEW CONCEPTS

The feasibility of a proposal for work that breaks new ground or calls for the development of new concepts or untried methods deserves detailed and informed scrutiny. Even with the aid of specialized modelling techniques, risk assessment of development and strategic projects is problematical.

Highly trained professionals and specialists are often called to advise on implementation, predict costs and outcomes and assess risk, but however expert their opinions, feasibility will inevitably depend heavily on professional opinion and judgement. Achievement of results will be more difficult to predict, and estimates of time, costs and outcomes will be less reliable than in the case of a logic-based project that is reliant on well-tried processes and recorded data. The study team should feature the best available professional expertise.

case study

THE ROLLS-ROYCE EXPERIENCE

The name Rolls-Royce is known throughout the world for high quality motor cars and the design and manufacture of a famous breed of aviation power units.

The RB211 was an ambitious turbo-fan design concept remembered for a traumatic outcome which temporarily brought this proud company to its knees. ▶

A contract for design and supply of engines for the Lockheed Tristar was signed against strong pricing competition and a fixed price agreed for development and supply of RB211 power units. When the contract was signed, important design details and some essential processes still had to be resolved so the project involved high levels of technological and financial risk.

Development costs had been unrealistically assessed at between £60 and £70 million and specific completion dates were subject to heavy penalty in default.

As time went on, development fell seriously behind schedule and, by the mid-1970s, costs are said to have soared to nearly £170 million. More money was badly needed and the limited help obtainable from government and the banking sector was insufficient to finance project completion, Rolls-Royce were set to lose heavily on the development and late delivery would incur yet more penalties. Losses in the region of £100 million were predicted and, on government advice, the company filed for bankruptcy, voiding the Lockheed contract but, of course, incurring considerable displeasure and loss of prestige. Parts of the Rolls-Royce empire were then nationalized.

Four of the many lessons to be gained from this high-risk project include the following:

1. Be aware of the dangers of market expediency.
2. Do not confuse technological possibility with practical feasibility.
3. Whenever possible, adopt an alternative approach to reduce the risk.
4. Set realistic time limits and use penalty clauses.

case study

THE ROLLS-ROYCE EXPERIENCE PART II: RETURN TO BEST PRACTICE

With the passage of time, significant advances were made and Rolls-Royce regained supremacy in engine manufacture. Lessons learned in the course of the RB211 failure were put to good use.

Rolls-Royce regained its reputation and dominance in the aviation industry, with power units such as the massive Trent 800, unrivalled by contemporary competition.

A benchmark project

The decision to establish world leadership in turbine blade machining was taken in October 1997 when a proposal to build, equip and establish an entirely new machining facility was approved. The facility was designed to lead the world in

▶

terms of technology, manufacturing methods, product cost and customer satisfaction.

The HP Turbine Blade Machining Facility is a good example of a complex, well-planned and effectively managed project that meets the success criteria described in Chapter 4.

> The intention is to achieve a 50% across the board reduction in machining cost, a 75% reduction in non-conformance on start up and continual improvement. A lead time of 10 days from casting receipt to dispatch equating to an 80% reduction in inventory. (M. Hullands, Project Manager, 1999).

> A combination of effective planning at all levels, technological expertise, good communication, teamwork and people management enabled the project to be completed on target. The new facility was opened a mere 326 days following the Ground Breaking Ceremony. (A. McLay, Programme Manager, 1999)

Continuing Market Success

British Airways favoured the RR Trent for their 17 new Boeing 777s as these engines could deliver extra power and, by early 1999, the higher thrust capability had attracted other customers, including Cathay Pacific, Singapore Airlines, American and Delta.

As RR built its market share with lower pricing, General Electric and Pratt & Whitney were reported to be pressing Boeing for exclusivity to protect their investment.

For them, the cost of development and certification of such an engine was said to

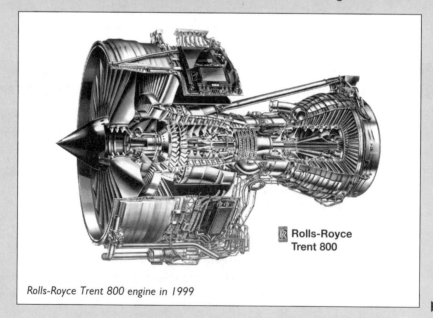

Rolls-Royce
Trent 800

Rolls-Royce Trent 800 engine in 1999

▶

exceed $1 billion. And RR's competitors feared that their market share might not be large enough for them to recover costs. Engine manufacturers then faced the dilemma of possible loss of sales for their lower powered engines used on B777 standard models (Thomas, 1999).

Rolls-Royce has bounced back to supremacy and displayed a new refinement in project skills. The high cost of development in such complex areas highlights the need for accurate forecasting, far-reaching decisions on technological capability, pricing, market positioning, careful analysis of financial risk and the availability of funding to cover all eventualities.

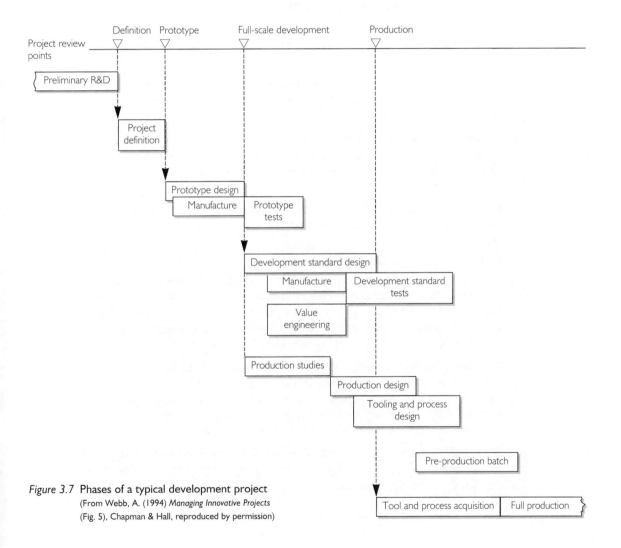

Figure 3.7 **Phases of a typical development project**
(From Webb, A. (1994) *Managing Innovative Projects* (Fig. 5), Chapman & Hall, reproduced by permission)

3.22   PREDICTING SUSTAINABILITY

The likelihood of residual and prolonged benefit resulting from a costly development is of constant concern to national and international aid donors painfully aware that benefits of projects in developing countries are, all too often, short-lived. Sustainability is thus an important consideration for inclusion in feasibility recommendations and may call for careful strategy formulation to ensure lasting project benefit.

---

case study

LOCALIZING AVIATION MANAGEMENT (FEASIBILITY AND SUSTAINABILITY)

The management of an airline or a civil aviation authority calls for the highest international standards of managerial and specialist ability in a combination of complex technical, legal and operational functions.

Aircrew duties, air transport policy and planning, air traffic control, landing, terminal and aviation safety facilities must be conducted to approved international standards.

Faced with an acute shortage of trained people, many developing countries are obliged to employ expatriates in these senior positions. This situation is costly and often politically unattractive.

On gaining independence, Papua New Guinea was heavily reliant on Australian expertise. Most senior aviation appointments were occupied by expatriates who were, in addition to their day-to-day duties, nominally responsible for 'coaching' appointed local 'counterparts'.

In a few cases, a senior 'national' appointee would be 'assisted' by an expatriate who, in reality, often took much of the responsibility for decisions and did most of the work.

With the exception of Aerodrome Maintenance and Air Traffic Control (areas successfully covered by the provision of an effective and well-conducted Aviation Training College), little progress in the localization of some key jobs was made for several years. Very few 'nationals' became competent in high-level jobs and those who did so tended to move elsewhere to even more lucrative fields of work, leaving the Civil Aviation Authority again bereft of high-level expertise.

The combined efforts of international aid agencies resulted in a programme of overseas training at approved foreign venues. These ICAO-approved training measures were generally successful and a number of posts were successfully localized. Although the new incumbents lacked experience they knew the rudiments of their jobs and an initial improvement was noticed.

But the improvement was not sustained. Within two years, many of the newly trained executives had either resigned or, because of demonstrated ability, been promoted to other departments.

This case led to the following conclusions:

1. Ability in complex managerial situations is usually the result of a combination of training and experience of the work over a period of time. This is the basis of personal development.

2. In the absence of clearly defined goals for individual progress, 'counterpart' or 'nominal' appointments (in which the actual work is done by someone else) are of very limited value.

3. Effective measures can be taken to accelerate the development of senior managers but training a small selection of incumbents will only lead to temporary improvement.

4. Sustainable improvement would necessitate a staff succession and development programme – a long-term project to train and guide the development of an adequate number of managers at each level through the ranks and enable them to qualify for successive promotions to senior positions. There was no point in promoting a manager competent in a present job if the promotion caused a serious management vacuum at a lower level.

5. A 'sufficiency of management capability' in both senior and subordinate positions was required.

6. To allow for natural wastage and accelerated progression, at least three possible incumbents for key positions at each level had to be identified and trained for the eventual assumption of each more senior appointment.

REVIEW AND DISCUSSION QUESTIONS

1. What is the value and purpose of an initial project proposal?
2. Explain the difference between a preliminary project proposal and a feasibility study report.
3. How might the composition of a feasibility study team for a logic-based proposal differ from that of a new or innovative project?
4. What instructions would be of prime importance in briefing a feasibility study team for a large development project?
5. List important sources of project risk and discuss how these might be identified
6. Discuss appropriate means of risk analysis in different kinds of project.
7. Construct a simple example to show the cost of 'crashing' to shorten the duration of activities on a project's critical path.
8. Consider the circumstances in which it would be appropriate to use a decision tree and expected values in reaching an estimate of project risk.
9. Consider a project to introduce new work methods, total quality control (TQC) and/or just-in-time (JIT) methods into a manufacturing company and list the nature and possible consequences of such a change and how its feasibility might be assessed.

4 AVOIDING MANAGEMENT PITFALLS

Work on a successful project can be a stimulating and rewarding experience but not all projects reach a satisfactory conclusion. Sadly, many ambitious projects, conceived in an atmosphere of hope and enthusiasm, end in partial or complete failure despite valiant efforts on the part of able, dedicated project teams and the infusion of vast sums of money.

4.1 WHAT IS PROJECT SUCCESS?

There is some divergence of opinion on the constituents of project success but the criteria that we should employ in project management and evaluation are:

1. Concept
2. Objectives
3. Quality of result
4. Cost
5. Time

Using these criteria, critical evaluation of the outcomes of a typical sample of 100 projects might produce the results shown in Figure 4.1.

Failed, abandoned or only partially completed projects*	37%
Projects completed but with modified objectives, reduced quality, additional time and/or cost overrun	34%
Satisfactorily completed projects	29%

* This group includes projects in which a result differing from the original intention was publicly represented as satisfactory ('whitewashed projects')

Figure 4.1 Breakdown of project results

4.2 WHY PROJECTS FAIL

Projects fail or are abandoned for a variety of reasons, and many result in only partial success as objectives are not achieved on time, costs escalate beyond acceptable limits, or stipulated levels of quality or achievement are compromised.

Large projects of the past were notoriously risky. Failure to provide an outcome consistent with expectations or to end the project on time and within budget were common, and the larger the project, the greater the fear of cost escalation. Many ambitious ventures were abandoned at great cost and after prolonged effort;

others were completed at a much greater cost than their original budget (for example, the Sydney Opera House and the Channel Tunnel) and some projects were abandoned within an ace of completion as enthusiasm for the concept dwindled or a sponsor became unable to finance spiralling costs (UK AEW System, Rolls Royce RB211, and so on).

Nevertheless, one cannot overlook the fact that many strategic and visionary projects that were widely perceived to be great follies in implementation are now acclaimed to be fine achievements; cases in which a combination of vision, concept and design were powerful enough to override planning, management and fiscal deficiencies or political pressure.

In recent years, important lessons have been learned and great strides made in project management techniques and training for project managers. Better feasibility assessment, risk analysis, planning methods and the use of sophisticated control systems contribute to a dramatic improvement in success rates but these lessons are not always applied. Consider the following example of an ill-fated public project.

---

case study

DOWNMARKET CITY PARK

Downmarket is a thriving city of one million inhabitants. City finances are recovering from excesses of a previous administration when little was done to maintain or enhance the city's attractiveness.

Many council staff are long-term employees, promoted from the ranks of clerical or minor administrative jobs by virtue of time and experience.

The City Engineer, for example, started as a road foreman and his job grew with the administration. He now commands a large staff and enjoys a substantial salary. His management style is autocratic, confrontational and overbearing and he is at loggerheads with the Finance Department over queries about payments to contractors and suppliers.

The City Treasurer is a recent appointee who has attracted animosity for tightening financial controls. His Chief Finance Officer is a young accountant, ill at ease with the engineer and older members of the executive.

The new administration has voted a number of civic improvements in a bid to revitalize the city and restore some of its former beauty. One of these is a project to convert derelict industrial sites into a pleasure park, scenic recreation ground and play area for children.

An environmental artist and a landscape gardener submitted detailed proposals and an attractive plan was accepted by the council. Proposals included extensive terraced lawns, limestone walls, replanting a grove of fully

▶

grown palm trees (professionally moved from another site), and a vast prefabricated metal and concrete sculpture, a dual-purpose attraction, to provide a focal point of attention and to double as an adventure site and climbing apparatus for children.

The park area was to be bordered on two sides by a limestone wall; an impressive entrance with ornamental gates would open on to a main thoroughfare.

Under the chairmanship of the City Engineer, a committee was convened to control and direct the project. Members included the Chief Finance Officer, the Superintendent of Parks & Gardens and an administrator.

At the first meeting, the possibility of appointing a project manager was broached. This suggestion was ridiculed by the City Engineer who claimed that it would be costly and unnecessary. He said that, to contain costs, development work should be done by his staff assisted by contractors with whom he was acquainted.

The environmental artist was responsible for prefabricating the massive sculpture and superintending its erection on a concrete base to be provided at the site.

Day-to-day control of work was then assumed by the City Engineer who scornfully rejected requests for plans and schedules, claiming them 'a bureaucratic waste of time for men who knew their jobs'.

To maximize political advantage and consolidate public image, the Lord Mayor and council encouraged publicity for the project and fixed the date for an elaborate opening ceremony on the day after that scheduled for project completion.

The park was bounded by main roads leading to the city centre and passers-by watched progress with interest. Limestone walls and the massive entrance occasioned favourable comment, as did areas of turf that were laid and regularly watered.

Then, for some weeks nothing seemed to happen and it soon became known that the project was not progressing as intended.

The next event was something of a surprise. The elaborate entrance was partially demolished to allow access for large transporters carrying fully grown palm trees. The ground, well soaked by rain, was soft and the new turf was destroyed by vehicle movement and digging equipment. Brick pathways were also damaged but this was insignificant compared to what was to come.

The entrance gap had to be made even bigger so that the prefabricated work of art could be delivered. Because of its weight and size, positioning the

▶

sculpture posed further difficulty. The concrete base was inadequate and had to be relaid. This took two weeks while the sculpture hung in readiness between two mobile cranes.

Opening day drew near but the entrance could not be rebuilt while the cranes remained inside the park. Landscaping and other work was also delayed.

An animated and very public altercation between the environmental artist and City Engineer ensued. The artist claimed breach of contract, saying his requirements had been ignored, a proper foundation for the sculpture had not been made and, until this was done, it could not be erected.

Information 'leaked' to the press brought forth accusations of inept management, escalating cost, negligent estimating, and failure to provide a site for the sculpture.

The engineer contrived to disguise some excess costs by diverting labour from other services but by then, the project had become a major source of embarrassment and council members were under pressure to apportion blame.

The opening took place four months late, in bad weather. It was not well attended.

How does this project score against success criteria and what can we learn from it?

1. Concept – despite political overtones, the concept appears sound.
2. Planning – planning and implementation were *ad hoc*. There was no clear definition of objectives and related activity plans.
3. Quality – apart from initial difficulties, standards for the park itself seem to have been achieved. The desired element of public approval, however, was seriously compromised.
4. Cost – budgeted and actual cost figures are not available, but there is no doubt that estimates were exceeded, due particularly to inefficient use of labour, reworking tasks, prolonged crane hire ($2000 per day) and the implications of late completion.
5. Time – haphazard management practices and an absence of planning resulted in major delay and late completion.

Those accustomed to good administration will question the credibility of this unfortunate account. But it is a fact that, while some public projects are well conducted, others are tackled unmethodically and encounter serious difficulty, so let us analyse the ills of the City Park Project and see how such a simple endeavour might have been better managed.

1. Project management structure

- There was no logical management structure, definition of responsibility or accountability.
- Management by committee and loosely defined responsibility seldom result in a satisfactory project outcome.
- Day-to-day control (such as it was) was exercised by the City Engineer, a man untrained in project work and not subject to supervision in this task.
- The participation of other managers, on a part-time basis, was unsatisfactory. Their competence and commitment to project work were unclear and their minimal activities uncoordinated.

2. Planning and scheduling

The engineer's 'hands-on' approach and confrontational style were inappropriate to a project of this nature. He ignored the need to consult others, such as the environmental artist and tree specialist, coordinate their contributions or agree how their work would be done. He did not estimate the duration of each activity or work out a logical sequence of events.

The use of programme evaluation and review techniques (PERT) would have clarified the sequence of events, and facilitated communication, control and project management.

3. Costs and financial control

It was assumed (without investigation) that the use of council employees and contractors would reduce overall costs. These people were paid from public funds on a basis of regular need, that is, the work from which they would have been diverted, so the real cost of this labour is difficult to assess. Calls on their time were certainly more than expected, to the detriment of routine work. So cost items that could not be disguised and were not featured in the budget included labour, materials, and the hire of cranes and other mechanical equipment for extended periods.

4. Conclusions

- A combination of ill-defined management structure and part-time participation makes for poor coordination and difficulties of control.
- With competent management, the project could easily have been completed on time. The cost of employing a competent project manager and a properly contracted workforce would have been less than that achieved by the *ad hoc* use of council employees.
- Had the project been properly planned, managed and financed, use could still have been made of any spare capacity in the council workforce for clearly defined tasks.

4.3 AD HOC MANAGEMENT AND REPETITIVE PROJECTS

Advocates of *ad hoc* management rely heavily on process familiarity and specialist competence in routine work to see them through a major project, often with minimal preparation and few of the basic steps of systematic planning and control (as illustrated in the Downmarket City Park Project).

Owners and managers have been known to base quite large ventures on flimsy or incomplete information, hoping to tackle situations as they arise and 'play it by ear'. In defence of their actions, such people claim the success of ongoing operations or work on repetitive projects with only a few predictable variables or those that have been developed over time and learned by rote, for example established packages in construction, franchising or exploration geology.

Other 'ad-hocists' cite the performing arts, including film making, as examples of projects that consistently deliver on time without recourse to traditional project techniques. In fact, there is strong evidence to suggest that these industries would benefit from a more systematic, project-based approach, but despite the artistic and scenic differences, most big productions such as 'blockbuster' films made on a grand scale have common factors of routine, similarity and repetition.

Another factor is the deeply ingrained tradition that surrounds the financing, venue, casting, design, production of scenery and sets, rehearsals and all the other details that go into the final production. The script and cast may be different, but from a managerial viewpoint, one play or one film is often very much like another.

It has been observed (by Hartman, Ashrafi and Jergeas, 1998) that those involved in the performing arts are linked by culture, motivated by tradition and well schooled in their roles and duties.

Stakeholders (including the audience) are emotionally involved and, within broad bands of rejection or acceptance, expectations are predictable and comparison of traditional project practices and those of the live entertainment business suggests that 'alignment of participants' is an important factor.

4.4 OTHER CAUSES OF PROJECT FAILURE

Some of the factors said to be common to project failure in the USA include:

- ineffective coordination of resources and effort;
- poor human relations.

Listed project failures in the United Kingdom point to somewhat different problems. These include:

- poor performance related to part-time project management in client, consultant or contractor organizations;
- inappropriate organization – common to unsuccessful projects, when the roles, responsibilities and scope of key participants' contributions is not clearly defined;

- decisions on contract strategy taken too late (restricting alternatives);
- failure to assess feasibility, assess risks and make contingency plans;
- cost escalation resulting from poor control, failure of uncontrolled schedules or unplanned expansion of tasks.

Some North Sea oil-related projects are well known for management inadequacies leading to delay in completion and heavy costs. These include:

- management and logistics for complex technical operations;
- ill-defined organization structure, unclear areas of responsibility, limits of authority and the different management structures used by contractors;
- inadequacies in planning, budgeting and control;
- conflict and interpersonal problems caused by ill-defined boundaries and poor work organization.

Many overseas projects get into difficulty because expatriate managers and project contractors do not understand local customs and attitudes to time. Surveys of project failures in Saudi Arabia, for example, list 14 contributory factors ranging from low profit margins to unexpected bad weather and control by 'a certain nationality' (Osama Jannadi, 1997). Opinions, sought from both legal accountants and contractors, varied in ranking some of the factors but in each case the first six included:

- bad judgement;
- difficulty in acquiring work;
- low profit margins;
- difficulty with cash flow;
- lack of experience in the firm's line of work;
- lack of managerial experience.

After fixed capital in construction had peaked at SR 90.2 billion, a number of contractors in the industry were hit by the 1983 recession. This led to many financial problems for contractors that were prejudicial to the conduct of their projects. It became clear that the administrative practice of awarding a contract to the lowest bidder did not always produce the best outcome. To generate urgently needed cash flow, some contractors were forced to cut their profit margins to win a contract, often with disastrous results.

A survey of delay in public utility projects in Saudi Arabia (Al-Khalil and Al-Ghafly, 1999) showed that delays were frequent in both short- and long-term public utility contracts for water and sewage projects. Owners and consultants blamed contractors, while contractors placed blame on the owner. This tendency is partly influenced by local attitudes, but it nevertheless points to problems of communication and contractual agreement.

Occasionally, a project will fail or be abandoned because of external circumstances which could not reasonably have been foreseen and the project management could not hope to control.

Projects in politically unstable areas are particularly vulnerable to changes of government policy or, sometimes, physical security. Most problems of this kind can be anticipated and the project cushioned or underwritten against such eventualities.

Inappropriate objectives, lack of feasibility, poor organization structure, unsound or inadequate planning, ineffective control, poor human relations and similar symptoms of managerial ineptitude are common in both home and overseas projects and since a sound basis of feasibility and structure is fundamental to rational progress, management failure in the initial stages is particularly damaging. Unless errors or omissions are corrected at an early stage, it will become increasingly difficult to redeem an unfeasible or badly structured project.

Some of the many areas of failure which may occur singly or in concert are listed below.

Concept phase

By project sponsors, and owners:

1. Failure to devote enough time and resources to a proper feasibility study
2. Imprecise or unclear terms of reference or briefing for the feasibility study
3. Inadequate research and risk assessment at the feasibilty study stage
4. Failure to secure the cooperation of all stakeholders and the agreement of public bodies or individuals who may subsequently oppose or hinder the project
5. Inadequate management backing and/or specialist capability in the initial stages

Planning phase

By owners, sponsors or advisers:

1. Invalid project purpose, for example private agendas on the part of politicians, contractors or others to promote the project for publicity or personal gain
2. Inadequate planning capability, badly defined objectives and lack of activity planning
3. Inappropriate management structure; ill-defined delegation of authority
4. Failure to consult those directly involved with the processes, think through processes, events and timings, and plan accordingly
5. Failure to consider possible impediments, analyse risks and formulate contingency plans
6. Failure to provide adequate finance, budget and cash-flow forecasts, make effective resource plans or properly specify technical and quality requirements
7. Poor contract negotiation

Project execution/implementation

By sponsors, manager and team leader:

1. Poor selection of specialists, team leaders and managers
2. Inappropriate leadership styles

3. Inadequate monitoring and control by managers and team leaders
4. Poor coordination of activity, and inability to achieve full cooperation of project personnel and/or contractors
5. Inattention to training and team development needs
6. Poor resource provisioning; late delivery of essential materials or equipment
7. Materials or equipment not up to technical or quality specification
8. Failures in communication of reporting procedures
9. Reluctance to take remedial action when actual results fall short of planned targets
10. Failure to conduct regular reviews and (where necessary) project revision
11. Meddling or interference by politicians or senior members of the owner's organization

Termination phase

By senior project personnel:

1. Failure to complete on time
2. Failure to reach required quality standards
3. Inadequate handover arrangements
4. Inadequate project evaluation and follow-up
5. Lack of sustainability for project objectives

4.5 PROBLEMS OF DELAYED IMPLEMENTATION

Some big projects suffer considerable delay in the early stage. In the case of large public sector and international projects, delay in acceptance often occurs between completing the feasibility study and project implementation because of complex approval procedures. Other causes of delay are difficulty in reaching final agreement, acceptance and gaining the commitment of interested parties, budgetary cycles, political wrangling or a requirement for modification to some aspect of the proposal.

Good ideas that were not taken up on an initial proposal but were later resurrected, and projects that have lain dormant for a considerable time, deserve close scrutiny for continued relevance and feasibility.

Checks have to be made to ensure that the financial and technological bases and their related objectives remain valid and viable. In particular, one should consider:

- *Project need.* Does the same need still exist?
- *Changing circumstances.* Has any part of the project been overtaken by time?
- *Technology and specification.* Are all specifications still up to date and appropriate? Have new methods, cheaper or more suitable equipments been developed or become available? (Particularly important in high-technology projects using rapidly developing processes)

- *Project finance.* Are cost estimates still valid? Are resources still available at previously quoted prices and are other costs (including salaries, allowances and expenses) still realistic? Are funding arrangements still effective and will there be delay in reactivation or making funds available?
- *Timetable.* Are new dates for commencement and completion realistic and feasible?
- *Objectives.* Have the objectives been modified? If so, what effect will the changed objectives have on project plans, budgets, staffing and project costs?
- *Recruitment.* Is the lead-time for recruitment and training adequate?
- *Availability of expertise.* Are key personnel still available?

It is important to identify planning redundancies or unworkable proposals at the outset and update plans before implementation as corrective action will be increasingly difficult and costly as the work progresses.

4.6 ANTICIPATING EXTERNAL CHANGE

Many long- and medium-term projects are susceptible to external change but, in most cases, changes that are likely to have a serious effect on the project outcome can be anticipated.

Project agreements should make allowance for identifiable risks and also stipulate that revisions required by sponsors or customers, for example to scope, specifications or completion dates, will be negotiated, mutually agreed and fully funded by them.

4.7 OPPOSITION, POLITICAL CHANGE, AND ACTS OF GOD

Careful reconnaissance of project environments prior to the initial proposal and during the feasibility study will usually disclose the possibility of industrial dispute, or opposition by individuals or groups who may feel their interests to be, in some way, prejudiced by the project. These possibilities can usually be assessed. Where special circumstances apply, the less likely effect of political unrest, earthquake, freak storm and the like will be considered in the risk analysis.

To foresee opposition or dispute unrelated to the project is more difficult. In areas where the political, environmental or industrial relations climate is sensitive, or those with abnormally high rates of violence or crime, agreements usually make blanket provision for foreseeable risks.

4.8 SUCCESS FACTORS AND BEST PRACTICES

A range of studies in the USA indicate that most successful projects had these factors in common:

- adequate and suitable organizational structures;
- adequate planning and suitable control mechanisms.

In the United Kingdom, common factors recognized in successful projects include:

- commitment by parent organization, client and project manager to:

  1. established activity schedules and control procedures;
  2. established budgets and control of expenditure;
  3. technical goals and milestones linked to time and cost;

- organization structures suited to the nature of the project;
- team participation in planning and determining methods, schedules and budgets;
- absence of legal encumbrances;
- minimizing the number of bureaucratic public or government agencies involved;
- enthusiastic public support.

In addition to qualities important in the developed countries of the western world, projects in foreign environments call for much more than a superficial understanding of local conditions, language, customs, attitudes and philosophies. The need extends to an understanding of the abilities and motivations of local and, sometimes, non-indigenous workforces, for example in the Middle East and the Arabian Gulf where foreign workers are routinely employed in many kinds of work.

4.9 A FORMULA FOR SUCCESS

A sometimes quoted formula for success in project ownership and management is:

$F(P + S) \times (C\ C\ L)$ or

Feasibility of objectives, Planning & Scheduling $\times$ (Leadership, Communication, Control)

Success calls for feasible objectives, appropriate organization and managerial skill, especially in planning, control and leadership. Unlike the managers of ongoing routine work, project managers cannot hope for good fortune or rely on 'gut feelings' for there are no short cuts in project management.

Team leaders must combine good leadership with the right administrative systems and routines to progress, stage by stage, between project milestones and reach objectives.

The manager who applies the formula effectively is likely to succeed. Do not forget the importance of a well set up and effective reporting system! Without this essential tool, it may become impossible to manage progress.

4.10 BEFORE THE ASSIGNMENT – THE FIRST QUESTIONS

Finally, before accepting assignment to a project that has already been specified, consider the answers to these questions:

1. *Concept.* Is the concept good? Has the project a valid purpose and is it feasible?
2. *Objectives.* Have the objectives been made clear and unambiguous?
3. *Structure.* Is the management structure appropriate and workable?
4. *Planning.* Has the project been properly planned in outline and detail?
5. *Scheduling.* Have all activities been scheduled and resources planned?
6. *Monitoring and control.* Will all activities, events and expenditure be constantly monitored?
7. *Competence.* Is the project team competent, committed, motivated and well led?

REVIEW AND DISCUSSION QUESTIONS

1. Why and on what grounds do some professionals reject systematic project management concepts? Suggest instances when *ad hoc* projects would have benefited from a systematic approach.
2. What criteria should be adopted in evaluating the likelihood of project success?
3. What common causes of project failure were identified in the USA and the UK?
4. What common factors were identified with successful projects in the USA and the UK?
5. What problems are often associated with part-time management of projects?
6. What special consideration would you give to a project proposal that had experienced delay between feasibility assessment and acceptance?
7. List some special demands of projects in developing economies.
8. Consider a project of your knowledge that has experienced difficulty or failure, and discuss the reasons for its problems and how these might have been avoided.

5 PROJECT RESOURCES

We could have saved sixpence. We saved fivepence. (pause) But at what cost?

S. BECKET

5.1 THE LIFEBLOOD OF A PROJECT

Efficiency in providing and managing resources is fundamental to project success. Each project will demand a unique combination of type, quality and volume of resources. Some projects are obviously capital intensive while others rely heavily on technology, new processes, equipment or the application of specialized knowledge and expertise, but whatever the project orientation, resources remain the project's lifeblood; they must be carefully chosen, accurately specified and their acquisition carefully planned.

They must be available where and when required and their use properly controlled. Fortunately, the nature of project management implies accuracy, focus and a limited life cycle; all factors conducive to clarity in specifying and predicting project needs.

Over-resourcing is wasteful and results in an unsatisfactory outcome. It invites resource imbalance, overspending, poor control and, sometimes, fraud. Other consequences include diminished cost-effectiveness and, sometimes, delay in project completion. Under-resourcing, on the other hand, will strangle the project and a shortage of essentials may lead to total failure.

Resource management will not be effective if it only concentrates on the project's most complex or dominant resource to the exclusion of less obvious but essential items which, though small, are nonetheless vital to the process.

As the project develops, control decisions will be influenced by the availability and use of resources in relation to considerations of cost, time and quality. Proper inclusion of all resource needs at the planning stage will obviate many possible difficulties of project implementation.

5.2 LISTING THE RESOURCES

In the interests of simplicity we can marshal project resources into a few general categories (the 7-Ms of resource management):

THE SEVEN RESOURCE GROUPS

Money – Finance for the project and its supporting activities (all projects)

Materials – Raw and manufactured materials (most projects)

Merchandise – Manufactured goods of various kinds, including food (many projects)

Machinery – Including equipment, either part of the project outcome (where the project specification includes the supply or installation of equipment), or for use in the course of project work, for example infrastructure, construction, engineering and some technical projects

Manpower – People with appropriate levels of skill to develop, design or perform specified work (not confined to labour-intensive projects)

Management, Professionals and Specialists – To manage the project, lead activities, provide specialist expertise and advice or carry out work on sensitive or complex project issues (all projects to varying degree)

Movement – Transportation, of people, machinery and equipment, materials, mail, and other essentials, to and from the project site(s) and within the project area – not commonly included in business resource planning but, none the less, important in project and resource planning

Every project has its own unique needs; some resources are dominant because of their quantity or technical complexity. Any shortage or late delivery of key resources will usually result in project delay, cost increase or even failure. Examples of dominant resource needs are shown in Figure 5.1.

Resource group	Construction projects	Technology transfer	Attitude or behaviour oriented	Relief projects	Training projects
Money (Finance)	×	×	×	×	×
Materials	×			×	
Merchandise/ Foodstuffs				×	
Machinery	×				
Machinery – special equipment	×	×			
Manpower	×			×	×
Management and specialists	×	×	×	×	×
Movement	×	×	×	×	×

Figure 5.1 Dominant resource needs of a selection of project categories

5.3 PROJECT MANAGER'S RESPONSIBILITY FOR RESOURCING AND PROVISIONING

Resourcing and provisioning functions by project managers usually include:

- determining needs, quantities and required delivery dates (what is needed and when);
- defining and confirming technical and quality specifications;
- determining the best source of supply, method and terms of purchase;
- contracting and agreement, prices and terms;
- arranging transport and storage;
- confirming deliveries (quantities, quality, condition and so on);
- payment authorizations;
- control of use, stores accounting and security;
- disposal of surplus and used items no longer required.

5.4 ESTIMATING RESOURCE NEEDS – HOW MUCH AND WHAT WILL IT COST?

When project scope and objectives have been proposed, it is possible to consider what resources would be required, where and how these could best be obtained and how much they would cost. This is the prelude to a more comprehensive resource plan. The first estimate is usually made during the feasibility study. It will take into consideration most of the likely decisions on ways, means, methods of operation, availability and sources of supply, the relative advantages of costly machinery over labour content, and so on. Initial estimates of labour and management costs will be made with the aid of simple formulae that include allowances, travel, overtime payments, accommodation, and so on. Potential suppliers may be called on to offer quotations based on initial specifications for equipment, goods and other services.

5.5 THE FINANCIAL RESOURCE – A BALL-PARK ESTIMATE

The first reasoned approximation of resource needs and their costs is calculated during feasibility consideration. When essential items, their specifications, price and availability have been established and manpower requirements considered, it will be possible to reach a 'ball-park' estimate of total cost. In reaching this assessment, it is usual practice to add a figure to cover detailed and unforeseen expenses and, in the case of a lengthy project, a further margin to allow for inflation or cushion variations in monetary exchange rates.

5.6 WHEN THE PROJECT BEGINS

When the project has been given the go-ahead, further planning will offer more and more detail on each main resource need. Details of specification, quality, availability, required delivery time, transportation and storage will become clear and can be accurately assessed, tenders invited and evaluated and contracts negotiated.

5.7 FINANCE AND CASH FLOW

As the picture of material, machinery, merchandise and the labour requirement develops, finance needs are brought into sharper perspective.

Decisions on needs, when (at what dates and project stages) costly items will be required and development of provisioning, manpower and transport plans provide a basis on which to review expense estimates and arrive at more accurate figures of resource costs, and the total finance need, cash flow, interest charges or credits, customs duties, taxation (if applicable), and so on.

A review of other aspects of the master plan, the project's activities and the methods to be used will help to confirm major expenses and finance estimates, details of which will themselves form a major section of the master plan. Figure 5.2 shows the layout of a typical pro forma used to illustrate this process.

Resources list	Project activity No. 234 Repeater station	Duration .... weeks Earliest start .... Latest start .... Latest completion ....

Week	1 2 3 4 5 6 7 8 9 10 11 12 13 14 15 16 17 18
Details of resource	
Consultants	xxxxxxxxxxxxxxxxxx xxxxxxxx xxxxxxxxxxx
Technicians	xxxxxxxxxxxxxxxxxxxxxxxxxxxxxxxxxxxxxxxxxxxx
Operators	xxxxxxxxxxxxxxxxxx
Labour	xxxxxxxxxxxxxxxxxxxxxxxxxxxxx xxxxxxx
Electrical	xxxxxxxxxxxxxxxxxxxxx xxxxxxxxxxxxxxxxxxxxx
Transmitter	xxxxxxxxxxxxxxxxxxxxxxxxxxxxxxxxx
Materials (specify)	
1	xxxxxxxxxxxxxxxxxxxxxxxxxxxxxxxxxxxxxx
2	xxxxxxxxxxxxxxxxxxxxxx xxxxxxxxxxxxx
3	xxxxxxxxxxxxxxxxxx
4	xxxxxxxxxxxxxxxxxxxxxxxxxxxxxxxxxxxxxxxxxx
Merchandise	
1	xxxxxxxxxxxxxxxxx
2	xxx
3	xxxxxxxxx xxxxxxx
Other ABC	xxxxxxxxxx
Finance ($000) Stage cost	3.5 1.7 14.1 0.3 8.3 1.6 3.8 2.1 1.1
Cumulative ($000)	3.5 5.2 19.3 19.6 27.9 29.5 33.3 35.4 36.5

Figure 5.2   Summary of resource needs pro forma

5.8 CONCURRENT RESOURCE PLANNING

Initial stages of activity scheduling and resource planning can usually be developed concurrently.

As we work through the plan and schedule each activity, its resource needs will be disclosed; they can then be programmed and their cost estimated. So in the planning of each activity, resource lists, quantities, specifications and schedules are developed.

Project stages and tentative dates when each item will be required are established and lead times for order and delivery or replenishing the resource can be estimated. An easy way of doing this is to endorse master and activity charts with the estimated total costs of each activity. (Activity plans can be similarly endorsed to show major deliveries.) Figure 5.3 shows an example of this method.

Figure 5.3 Flow chart annotated with resource costs

Figure 5.4 shows the layout of another simple pro forma listing the specialist and resource needs of a project with dates and duration of need.

5.9 THE RESOURCE SCHEDULE

Having established the main resource needs, a schedule listing each item, its expected cost and required delivery date can be drawn up. The schedule is updated as each item is requisitioned, ordered, delivered and paid for. Although some costs will have been underestimated, these may be balanced by savings made on others. Figure 5.5 shows an example of a section of a project provisioning schedule also used as the basis for an equipment status report.

5.10 INVENTORY CONTROL

Project inventory control is concerned with cost-efficient provisioning to meet material resource needs. It means knowing where, when and how to order so that the project always has enough, but not too much, of the right things, accounting for their use and maintaining security over them.

Some form of formal inventory control procedure will be required for projects that take up large quantities of materials and/or costly resource items but, with no

Project Implementation Schedule
PNG Civil Aviation Assistance Project

No	Activity	1986	1987	1988	1989	1990	1991	1992	Remarks
01	Project approval by ADAB & PNG								
02	Select & appoint Managing Agent								
03	Agent managing project								
04	App Team Leader & A/way Advr								
05	Team Ldr/Proj Mngr Famil & Brief								
06	Specify Basic Equipment								
07	Obtain quotations & order equip.								
08	Equip manufact & deliv PNG store								
09	Rad/Elect Advrs to PNG–Prep Prog								
10	Radio & Electrical Installation Prog								
11	Team Lead to PNG Estab Proj Off								
12	Project Admin Officer to PNG								
13	App AFM.Mtce Stds.Draft Advrs								
14	AFM.Mtce Stds & Draft to PNG								
21	Appoint radio & elect instructors								
22	Radio & electrical instructors PNG								
31	Appoint ATP, P & S advisers								
32	ATP, P & S advisers PNG								
41	App Manag Trng & Dev advisers								
42	Manag Trng & Dev advisers to PNG								
51	Short-term Eng Trng advisers								
52	Short-term ops Trng advisers								
53	Short-term manage Trng advisers								
61	ATC & Radar System specialists								

Figure 5.4 Human resource needs – example of project resource forecast

PROJECT EQUIPMENT

Equipment item	Req'n no.	Purchase order no.	Cost		Date of delivery		Status/ remarks
			Budget US $	Actual US $	Scheduled	Actual (Est.)	
(a) Frequency & time standard quartz oscillator (Item 1) (b) Flange unit		001700 08/07/91	15 000	(a) 10 300 (b) 75	1991	1991	Received: saving $4625
Passenger cars × 3 (Item 10)		–ditto–	33 000	21 250 (1005)	1991	Nov 1991	Received: saving $10 745
Minibus (Item 11)		–ditto–	16 000	26 850	1991	Nov 1991	Received: over by $10 850
Bubblejet printers × 2		011294 31.01.92	- - -	645	- - -	Mar 1992	Received
Notebook computers × 2		011312 31.01.92	- - -	5 876	- - -	Mar 1992	Received
Whiteboard	911105	020460 14.02.92		350	1992	June 1992	Received
Photocopier heavy duty × 1 (Item 8)	911102	020462 14.02.92	4 000	12 025	1991	June 1992	Received: over by $8 025
Cable & auto sheet feeder for Bubblejet printer	920533	20521		159	April 1992		Received
(a) Dictating machine, desktop × 1 (b) Dictating m/c, hand-held × 2	920555	020646 22.05.92	- - -	257 297 (110)	1992	Aug 1992	Received
Desktop publishing systems × 3 (Items 6 & 7) 3 × computer 386/25, 168Mb h/d 120Mb tape backup 3 × Laserjet printer III 3 × Deskjet 500C (Colour) 3 × UPS 3 × Scanner Scanjet IIc 3 × lots of software 9 × cables 3 × manual data switch 6 × memory chip 3 × mouse shipping	911101	020583 (Rev'd) 03.08.92	48 000	 15 366 5180 2368 2782 4570 5182 60 187 1025 263 4033			Received: saving $9545
1 × A/C 2 ton split unit 2 × A/C 2 ton window unit 1 × 5 cubic ft refrigerator	920579	020726 07.08.92		1480 1220 430			Received Received Received
2 × Word Perfect 5.1 reference manual		020727 15.07.92	- - -	133			Received
1 × photocopier		020754 03.08.92	- - -	2920			Received
Telephone answering m/c w/fax	920574	020776 07.08.92	- - -	535 (180)			Received
Books: 'The New Mager Six-Pack'	921014	020807 04.09.92			Oct 1992	Feb 1993	Received
2 × training video tapes	921051	020867 06.10.92	- - -	1252 (158)			Received
Software: 'OmniPage Professional'	921063	20888					

Figure 5.5 Example of equipment provisioning schedule and status report (sheet 1)

direct historical data on which to base decisions, project inventories can seldom benefit from the quantitative inventory control tools and mathematical models available to ongoing operations for establishing lot sizes, economic order quantities, replenishment cycles, and so on. So the nature of project work usually dictates a non-quantitative approach to inventory control.

Simple but effective control and accounting arrangements should be decided in the planning phase and introduced prior to project implementation.

Large project inventories are difficult to control because many of their assets are portable and some will be subject to decisions by a range of people, some of whom may be locally employed contractors or temporary project employees. A minimum requirement will be to check and record receipts, deliveries and storage details, and to control and record materials consumed. These records must always be up to date for costing and accounting purposes, and, most importantly, to enable replenishments to be ordered within the required lead time.

Regular attention to inventory levels and a working knowledge of lead times for order and receipt of regularly used items are important.

5.11 INVENTORY SECURITY AND ACCOUNTING

Project property is particularly vulnerable to loss, theft or misuse, and the effects of loss are likely to exceed the cost of replacement by far. Loss not only wastes administrative time and causes additional work in investigation and replacement of the missing items, but loss of resources may seriously delay completion of an important activity, disrupt the critical path and even jeopardize the whole timetable.

Even more serious are the consequences of slack administration and its effect on staff attitudes and morale, while the stigma of suspicion can be highly detrimental to teamwork and motivation.

Allegations of corruption or nepotism against project managements are not uncommon and the nature of the work sometimes attracts suspicion. To avoid conflict of interests, clear agreement on the extent and limitations of a project manager's authority to disburse funds and enter into purchasing agreements and a clear understanding of guidelines or mandatory purchasing regulations should be reached before the start of project implementation.

So accounts of expenditures, issues, supply movements and usage are essential safeguards against false allegations, fraud, loss, misuse and non-availability of supplies. For the benefit of all project employees, these accounts should be regularly checked and audited.

5.12 THE COST OF LATE DELIVERY

Delay in delivery of equipment or materials is a common cause of cost escalation caused by disruption of project time schedules. For this reason, suppliers of key resources should be scrutinized, not just for technical competence but for reliability, financial capacity and performance capability.

Not all resource failures can be laid at the door of a contract supplier. Project administrations or finance departments occasionally withhold or delay payments to suppliers for their own reasons and failure to remit moneys when they are due is a common cause of suppliers' reluctance to provide good service.

5.13 LEAD TIMES, ORDER CYCLES AND BACKLOGS

Lead time reflects the total time between transmission of the original order and the point in time when the goods are received. Administrative lead time, on the other hand, begins when need is established within the project. It may include the specification, search for or selection of a supplier, contract negotiations, conditions of payment, agreements, transport, shipping and so on.

Backlog is the time it takes the supplier to obtain or produce the goods. This can be a few days or many months. Project managers and purchasing or supply managers working in an unfamiliar field or foreign territory do well to confirm the supplier's ability to meet delivery dates and deadlines. It is worthy of note that order cycle times will lengthen as the vendor's sales increase.

During a downturn, order cycle times will decrease. Trade magazines in purchasing provide useful information on lead times for different industries (Cavinato, 1984).

5.14 HEDGING

Hedging involves currency negotiation, purchasing futures and similar tactics to minimize pricing risks.

Long lead times sometimes involve a risk of heavy cost increase. This can affect either the project manager or the supplier. The four most common ways of avoiding price risk are:

1. buying the goods and storing them until they are needed;
2. contracting for a fixed price; in this case, the vendor takes the risk and may add a percentage to the price by way of insurance against extra cost;
3. contracting the purchase price in US dollars or some other stable currency;
4. hedging – using a commodity exchange to transfer forward buying risks to other parties.

case study

THE AIR NAVIGATION PROJECT

The costly Air Navigation Project was designed to modernize and re-equip a national system of flight safety, provide better navigational aids and a new system of air traffic control. The purpose was to achieve a safer, faster and ▶

less cumbersome system as a prelude to reorganization of the country's air traffic services.

The project involved the choice and installation of new and sophisticated equipment, support services, training for operators, technicians, maintenance staff, and changes to the Air Information Service publications.

The project was scheduled to last 12 months, by which time the new system was to be fully operational and the new Air Navigation Instructions would be operative. A panel of experts was formed to investigate developments, best practices and sources of equipment supply, decide the disposition of installations, design the new system and draw up technical specifications.

Their recommendations resulted in a system that conformed to international standards and was well received by the aviation industry.

The carefully decided choice of equipment was to a specification that was available only from one, well-regarded, European manufacturer. A price for the required package was negotiated, taking into account necessary modifications, reliability guarantees, delivery dates, service facilities, availability of spares and replacements, and operator and maintenance training.

Contracts were exchanged and the project seemed to be well on the road to success.

Complications began during the implementation phase with intervention at parliamentary level. A parliamentary question cast doubt on the motives and competence of the project panel, and alleged infringement of government purchasing regulations which required three quotations from potential suppliers.

The questioner, who had no technical or aviation experience, was not satisfied by assurances that no comparable and cost-effective alternatives were available and, despite the fact that their system differed from the one chosen by the expert panel, claimed that a United States company, also of international repute, should have been invited to quote.

After a long and costly delay, a compromise was reached in which the original contract was renegotiated and a hybrid system developed to accommodate some equipment supplied by each company.

It is difficult to establish the origins and true motivation behind the intervention into the affairs of this project; however, the consequences are easily recognized. They include:

1   introduction of a less effective, hybrid system not favoured by the experts;
2. delay in project implementation and completion;

3. substantially increased project cost due to renegotiation of the original contract, higher installation costs, a requirement for two ranges of spares, operator and maintenance training on two sets of equipment and increased cost of installation;
4. adverse effect on staff morale due to reduced confidence in management.

Lessons to be learned from this case are not confined to the need for project managements to take into account established (even inappropriate) purchasing and supply procedures. The vulnerability of project work and the effect of critical supply stoppages extend to a wide range of materials and services and every precaution has to be taken to avoid costly stoppages from whatever cause.

Lack of autonomy in project management has already been cited as a major ingredient in project failure and/or cost overrun. When purchasing responsibility is shared between project personnel and the procurement department of a project owner's organization, conflict of priorities can frustrate the project manager's freedom of action and be highly detrimental to efficiency.

At the time of their appointment, managers, contract managers and purchasing officials should:

1. make themselves familiar with any existing regulations that might have a bearing on the conduct of the project, and
2. establish the extent of *actual authority* which should be clearly defined in terms of reference by way of an unambiguous statement of the extent and limits of delegated authority to commit the organization, for example to make commitments, purchases and so on, without incurring personal liability for financial or other matters.

5.15 ACCURACY OF SPECIFICATIONS

It is essential to specify resources in terms of performance, capability, quality, delivery places and dates, price and technical requirements. For key items, penalty clauses may be justified to safeguard against project delay or cost overrun. These should be sufficiently demanding to offer real protection against failure or late delivery.

Specify:

- all key items – technical specification, quality, delivery date, price and terms of payment;
- all contract work – extent, quality, completion date and price;
- all technical support – nature, extent, quality and cost;
- all key posts – duration of work, responsibilities, capability, qualifications, experience, renumeration;
- all training for project employees (including training to be provided by manufacturers as part of a re-equipment programme) – number of trainees and the standards of competence to be achieved;

- standards of serviceability for leased or contract-serviced machinery and equipment;
- minimum standards of maintenance to be provided for purchased machinery or equipment.

5.16 CONTRACTS FOR THE SUPPLY OF RESOURCES

Contracts for the supply of resources often follow an 'Invitation' or 'Request to Quote' (RFQ) or a 'Request for Tender' (RFT). Depending on the way in which it is framed, a request for tender may incur legal obligations and care should be exercised in initiating the tendering process (for example, the Canadian Law of Tender – Jergeas and Cooke, 1997).

The guidance of an expert in contract law and practice and customs regulations in the country where the project is to be conducted and, in the case of overseas purchasing, the country of origin is strongly advised.

A contract is a legally binding agreement (*Oxford Dictionary of Law*). The law of contract varies between legal systems. In many countries, a contract must satisfy six criteria:

1. manifestation of intent, that is offer and acceptance, some form of agreement;
2. consideration – some form of payment or reward;
3. capacity to contract – legal capacity and authority;
4. reality of intent – freedom of error, or duress;
5. legality of purpose – the contract cannot be for an illegal act;
6. the agreement must comply with any formal legal requirements, for example common law, statute law (in the USA, the Statute of Frauds, and so on).

Most contracts for project supply are based on one of two propositions. These are:

1. fixed price;
2. cost plus.

5.16.1 Fixed price contracts

Fixed price contracts, probably the more common, are particularly suitable for supplies or tasks that can be clearly specified before tenders are invited.

However, the tendering process can take some time to complete and once the contract has been awarded, the contractor will be more concerned with saving money than time.

Although a good price may have been negotiated, the contractor may be expected to maximize profit on the total range of work at his disposal. This may lead to concentration on the most profitable contracts, neglect of less remunerative ones and possible delay in delivery or completion.

Safeguards in the form of penalty clauses can be written into the contract but these may not make for project success and, in any case, they may be difficult to apply before the consequences of delay are felt.

Stringent penalty clauses, on the other hand, may only serve to deter a good contractor from tendering or cause him to increase the quoted cost substantially as an insurance against unforeseen difficulty. An unscrupulous contractor, on the other hand, may not be deterred by penalty clauses, gambling that they will not be applied in practice.

Another consideration is that changes to resource requirements due to project revision are likely to involve extra payment to the contractor.

5.16.2 Fixed price incentive contracts

This is a variation of the fixed price contract in which both parties agree on target cost and the contractor's target profit. The figures are linked to a ceiling price and a formula for adjustment, for example:

Target cost $500 000
Target profit $50 000
Ceiling cost $600 000

In this example, it has been agreed that:

- if the cost is less than $500 000 the contractor is paid 30 per cent of the saving;
- costs in excess of $500 000 will be 70 per cent financed by the customer, 30 per cent by the contractor.

5.16.3 Cost-plus contracts

Cost-plus contracts reimburse the contractor for work done.

Payment usually includes both direct and indirect costs incurred and a margin of profit.

The contractor's profit can be calculated either as a fixed sum or a percentage of total cost.

Tendering for this type of contract may take less time than would be the case in a fixed price proposition and the result may be beneficial when project needs are not fully determined but the contract has to be let without delay. Another advantage is that the contractor's profit can be easily set; however, the cost ceiling may be difficult to determine and it may be more difficult for the customer to enforce some performance details and ensure an acceptable result.

To prevent price escalation and safeguard the outcomes of cost-plus contracts, strict monitoring procedures should be agreed between both parties and carefully observed.

5.17 TERMS OF PAYMENT

Terms of payment may follow a variety of agreed rules. Smaller contractors making regular deliveries may seek payment within 30 days of each delivery, but for larger commitments, such as structural work or the manufacture or supply of heavy machinery or special equipment, stage or progress payments to an agreed schedule may be requested and some contractors may seek payment of 'front-end costs' to cover expenses related to 'setting up' or preparatory work done to obtain the contract.

Terms of payment should follow a legally approved form and be set out in the contract.

5.18 BALANCING THE ALTERNATIVES

Decisions on project resource needs are more complex than simple comparisons of, say, the cost of manual labour with that of expensive equipment, the speed of available machine alternatives or the quotations of potential suppliers. Some project managers will be faced with a range of possibilities offered by the manipulation of multiple activities to achieve the most beneficial and cost-effective results from combinations of machinery, equipment and human resources, and considerations on the relative merits of purchase or leasing capital machinery.

Assumptions, established practices and local experience of work in developed countries are not always applicable to best practice in developing countries or even in developed areas with substantially different conditions and labour costs.

5.19 PROVISION OF MACHINERY AND EQUIPMENT

Decisions relating to combinations of machinery and labour costs call for information on:

1. initial cost of equipment;
2. length of useful life;
3. estimated resale value;
4. maintenance and repair costs;
5. machine operating costs;
6. labour costs for the activity;
7. cost of special training related to the machine or method.

Examples of two alternative propositions calculated in £ sterling are shown in tables A and B in Figure 5.6 on the following page.

Of course, these examples do not take into account reliability or the quality of work produced by the machines, resale values of the machines, or the effect of tax allowances for depreciation which might apply in some cases.

Although many decisions on the acquisition of machinery and equipment rely on simple financial considerations, life-cycle costing is used increasingly to obtain the best financial result from a transaction. This is particularly applicable to multi-project companies and project contractors who seek to maximize the value of a physical asset over its total life. Project managers are advised to familiarize themselves with this approach (Woodward, 1997).

Table A

Equipment ABC – Project duration 5 years

Initial costs (GBP)

Purchase price	800 000
Installation costs	25 000
Operator training	15 000
	840 000

Labour and operating costs

	Year					
	1	2	3	4	5	Totals
Labour (increasing @ 0.5% p.a.)	20 000	21 000	22 050	23 152	24 312	110 514
Fuel, oil, etc	1000	1050	1102	1158	1215	5525
Repair & maintenance	4000	4200	4410	4630	4860	22 100
Totals	25 000	26 250	27 562	28 940	30 387	138 139

Grand total (GBP)   978 139

Table B

Equipment XYZ – Project duration 5 years

Initial costs (GBP)

Purchase price	210 000
Installation costs	12 000
Operator training	5 000
	227 000

Labour and operating costs

	Year					
	1	2	3	4	5	Totals
Labour (increasing @ 0.5% p.a.)	50 000	52 500	55 125	57 880	59 330	274 835
Fuel, oil, etc	800	840	882	926	972	4420
Repair & maintenance	1000	1050	1103	1157	1215	5525
Totals	51 800	54 390	57 110	59 963	61 517	284 780

Grand total (GBP)   511 780

Figure 5.6 Equipment cost comparison

5.20   LEASE OR BUY DECISIONS

Leasing is often an attractive alternative to purchase as a means of obtaining costly project equipment.

Decisions will be based on:

1. whether funds are available for purchase;
2. the cost of financing the purchase (interest on borrowed money or how much the funds could earn if otherwise invested);
3. the useful life of the machine;
4. the cost of possible breakdown and/or maintenance (particularly when the leasing contract provides for free replacement and/or maintenance);

5. in cases where the project produces revenue, the earning potential of the asset and the relative effects on taxation (depreciation of purchased assets, machinery interest payments and so on);
6. present values of future payments;
7. likely resale value of the asset when the project is completed.

When costly machinery or equipment is required for limited periods, leasing may be a sensible option. A simple comparison of lease and purchase cash flow might look as shown in Figure 5.7.

Year	Unaffected by tax		When tax advantages are applicable	
	Purchase Cash flow	Leasing Cash flow	Purchase Cash flow	Leasing Cash flow
0	200 000	50 000	200 000	50 000
1		50 000	(20 000)	40 000
2		50 000	(20 000)	40 000
3		50 000	(20 000)	40 000
4		50 000	(20 000	40 000
5		—	(20 000)	(10 000)
Totals	200 000	250 000	100 000	200 000

Figure 5.7 Comparison of lease and purchase options

Of course, actual costs and taxation rates would have to be applied and calculations could well also take into account interest on money borrowed or the present and future values of capital required to buy the equipment.

5.21 PRESENT VALUE CALCULATIONS

These useful tables are used in buy or lease decisions to calculate the effects of inflation, value of interest on money, depreciation, and so on (Figure 5.8).

For financial investment analysis, the three key items are initial capital cost, the annual net benefits and the present value rate. Many long-term projects take place in a non-profit environment where questions of income and taxation do not apply but the present value of money is relevant to machinery and technical equipment decisions.

Life-cycle costing can help in selecting the best alternative when the equipment is to be used for several years, initial cost is high and the item is expensive to run.

Yr	Interest rate 1	2	3	4	5	6	7	8	9	10
1	0.9901	0.9804	0.9709	0.9615	0.9524	0.9434	0.9346	0.9259	0.9114	0.9091
2	0.9803	0.9612	0.9426	0.9246	0.9070	0.8900	0.8734	0.8573	0.8417	0.8264
3	0.9706	0.9423	0.9151	0.8890	0.8638	0.8396	0.8163	0.7938	0.7722	0.7513
4	0.9706	0.9238	0.8885	0.8548	0.8227	0.7921	0.7629	0.7350	0.7084	0.6830
5	0.9515	0.9057	0.8626	0.8219	0.7835	0.7473	0.7130	0.6806	0.6499	0.6209
6	0.9420	0.8880	0.8375	0.7903	0.7462	0.7050	0.6663	0.6302	0.5963	0.5645
7	0.9327	0.8706	0.8131	0.7599	0.7107	0.6651	0.6227	0.5835	0.5470	0.5132
8	0.9235	0.8535	0.7894	0.7307	0.6768	0.6274	0.5820	0.5403	0.5019	0.4665
9	0.9143	0.8368	0.7664	0.7026	0.6446	0.5919	0.5439	0.5002	0.4604	0.4241
10	0.9053	0.8203	0.7441	0.6756	0.6139	0.5584	0.5083	0.4632	0.4224	0.3855

Yr	Interest rate 11	12	13	14	15	16	17	18	19	20
1	0.9009	0.8929	0.8850	0.8772	0.8696	0.8621	0.8547	0.8475	0.8403	0.8333
2	0.8116	0.7972	0.7831	0.7695	0.7561	0.7432	0.7305	0.7182	0.7062	0.6944
3	0.7312	0.7118	0.6931	0.6750	0.6575	0.6407	0.6244	0.6086	0.5934	0.5787
4	0.6587	0.6355	0.6133	0.5921	0.5718	0.5523	0.5337	0.5158	0.4987	0.4823
5	0.5935	0.5674	0.5428	0.5194	0.4972	0.4761	0.4561	0.4371	0.4190	0.4019
6	0.5346	0.5066	0.4803	0.4556	0.4323	0.4104	0.3898	0.3704	0.3521	0.3349
7	0.4817	0.4523	0.4251	0.3996	0.3759	0.3538	0.3332	0.3139	0.2959	0.2791
8	0.4339	0.4039	0.3762	0.3506	0.3269	0.3050	0.2848	0.2660	0.2487	0.2326
9	0.3909	0.3606	0.3329	0.3075	0.2843	0.2630	0.2434	0.2255	0.2090	0.1938
10	0.3522	0.3220	0.2946	0.2697	0.2472	0.2267	0.2080	0.1911	0.1756	0.1615

Figure 5.8 Present value table – value of $1 over time

The analysis takes into consideration:

1. purchase price;
2. length of useful life;
3. maintenance costs;
4. operating costs;
5. resale or salvage value;

Figure 5.9 shows the comparison between two possible choices of equipment.

5.22 PREDICTING MANPOWER NEEDS

The availability, quality and cost of manpower varies greatly throughout the world and within countries by trade, attitude, reliability and expectation.

Project managers are advised, wherever possible, to go for the best quality and smallest workforce able to accomplish the job within planned time limits. Always allow adequate lead time for recruitment, testing, selection and training, for a hastily recruited workforce may incur major difficulties.

Time allowances may be needed if the workforce is subject to trade union agreements on hours or conditions of work, or if other legal regulations apply. The cost of special work conditions, limitations or restrictive practices has to be brought into planning and the budgeting equation.

Equipment X – useful project life: 5 years

Inflation 8%
Yearly cost increase 5%

Year	0	1	2	3	4	5
Purchase ($)	160 000					
Instal. cost ($)	20 000					
Training ($)	5 000					
Operating ($)		40 000	42 000	44 100	46 305	48 620
Fuel & power ($)		20 000	21 000	22 050	23 152	24 310
Maintenance ($)		12 000	12 600	13 230	13 891	14 586
Total cost ($)	185 000	72 000	75 600	79 380	83 348	87 516
@15% PVF	1.000	0.926	0.857	0.794	0.735	0.681
Total present value cost ($)	185 000	66 672	64 789	63 027	61 261	59 598	500 347

Equipment Y – useful project life: 5 years

Inflation 8%
Yearly cost increase 5%

Year	0	1	2	3	4	5
Purchase ($)	200 000					
Instal. cost ($)	10 000					
Training ($)	4 000					
Operating ($)		45 000	47 250	49 612	52 093	54 698
Fuel & power ($)		10 000	10 500	11 025	11 576	12 515
Maintenance ($)		6 000	6 300	6 615	6 946	7 293
Total cost ($)	214 000	61 000	64 050	67 242	70 615	74 506
@15% PVF	1.000	0.926	0.857	0.794	0.735	0.68
Total present value cost ($)	214 000	56 486	54 891	53 390	51 902	50 664	481 333

Figure 5.9 Comparison of the cost of two items of equipment at present value

5.23 INITIAL STEPS OF MANPOWER PLANNING

As resources lists are made for each activity, overall manpower needs become apparent. *Ad hoc* decisions on the relative merits of using machinery to limit labour costs can be re-examined, and draft manpower needs estimated and coordinated, allowing time for recruitment, selection training (if required) and familiarization.

If the project is located in a remote area or in extreme weather conditions, recruitment incentive payments may be necessary and extra time allowances made for travel or acclimatization. A pro forma is used to summarize initial estimates of manpower needs, as shown in Figure 5.10.

Activity numbers cost (per person)	Category	Total man/days	Daily cost (per person)	Estimated cost
21 to 34, 36	Building workers	110	30.00	3300
26	Plumbers	10	90.00	900
33	Electricians	5	85.00	425
36	Installation mechanics	4	180.00	720
etc.				
Total number of people		**Estimated total cost**		

Figure 5.10 Summary of manpower needs

5.24 SMOOTHING THE MANPOWER REQUIREMENT

Considerable savings can often be made by rescheduling labour-intensive activities so that tasks can be run consecutively. This reduces the need to dismiss satisfactory members of the workforce when one activity is completed, only to employ and train similar people a short time later.

Alternatively, some advantages may be found in prolonging tasks that are not on the critical path to reduce the number of people needed. If this can be done without prejudice to the project completion date, those employed may be able to move directly from one task to another, minimizing severance and recruiting, familiarization and training costs and improving employee stability and motivation. A manpower activity diagram is helpful in reaching these decisions (Figure 5.11).

Figure 5.12 illustrates the effect of rescheduling some non-critical tasks and activities to eliminate peaks and troughs in the activity of certain categories of project worker.

5.25 COMPUTER ASSISTANCE IN SCHEDULING MANPOWER AND OTHER RESOURCE NEEDS

The process of listing manpower and other resource needs can be assisted by means of one of the user-friendly software programs that are readily available. One such program is Microsoft Project which offers a facility for resource scheduling linked to the activity list.

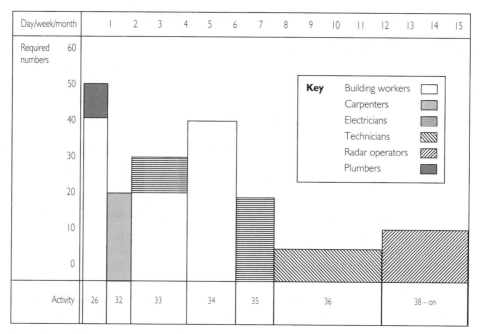

Figure 5.11 Manpower activity histogram

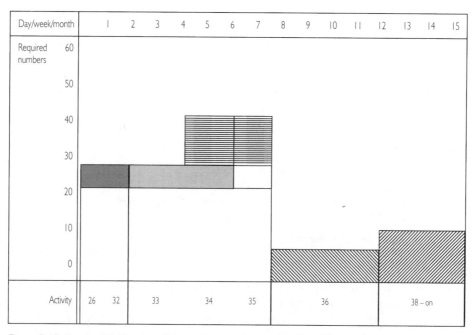

Figure 5.12 Rescheduled activity histogram to reduce peak demand for manpower

5.26 EFFECT OF THE LEARNING CURVE ON MANPOWER NEEDS

Manpower calculations for a workforce to perform repetitive operations usually take account of the progressive increases in the quality and speed of production that should occur with practice based on frequent repetition of the proper way to perform an operation. The learning curve phenomenon is based on 'Wright's Law' which illustrates the relationship between repetition, speed and the way in which production increases with practice (Figure 5.13). This is a routine consideration in assessing manpower requirements and labour costs in engineering production, building and many other situations in which speed of output is a significant factor, but learning curve theory is not confined to long production runs or repetitive manual operations. Its effects can also be seen in a range of scientific, clerical and administrative tasks where familiarity and practice result in a reduction in the time required for an activity or an operation (Hirschmann, 1964).

Expectations of learning and speed of operation for repetitive or frequently performed tasks may be based on historical data relating to similar operations but it is important to remember that valid conclusions can only be drawn from the results of a **comparable** workforce **using the same methods and operating under similar working conditions**. Another consideration is the level and validity of training because this will have a decisive effect on the build-up of operating speed.

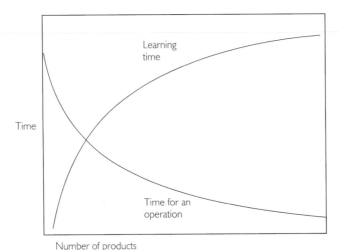

Figure 5.13 The learning curve

Extensive use of learning curve theory is made in estimating the manpower needs of some projects but it important to bear in mind that these calculations may become invalid with a disruption of activity, such as a client-inspired change, and projects involving production runs are vulnerable to any unexpected alteration in methods which may invalidate learning speed calculations.

The effect of disruption on the planning of development projects can be seen in many large project undertakings, for example in defence, aviation and major infrastructure. An analysis of the experience of a contractor for one of the major projects for the Channel Tunnel is described by Eden, Williams and Ackermann (1998) in 'Dismantling the learning curve: the role of disruptions on the planning of development projects'.

5.27 ALLOWING FOR LOCAL CONDITIONS AND MANPOWER CHARACTERISTICS

The availability, quality and cost of manpower varies throughout the world, within countries and by trade, attitudes, reliability, work practices and expectations. Project managers are advised, wherever possible, to go for the best quality and smallest workforce able to accomplish the job within planned time limits.

In project work, lead time for recruitment, testing, selection, training and familiarization is frequently underestimated. A hastily recruited or inadequately trained workforce can lead to delay and far-reaching project difficulty.

Employees of projects in remote areas may need special allowances for travel, acclimatization, settlement, medical attention and recreation, all factors which bear on effective time on the job, and the size and cost of the workforce.

Sections of the workforce governed by trade union agreements or government legislation, for example on hours of work or health and safety, may need special treatment and the cost or limitations of restrictions brought into the budgeting and planning equation.

As a resources list is made for each activity, broad manpower needs become apparent. *Ad hoc* decisions on the relative merits of using costly machinery to limit labour costs can be re-examined, and draft manpower needs coordinated.

REVIEW AND DISCUSSION QUESTIONS

1. List the categories of resource needed for completion of a typical project of your knowledge and specify dominant needs.
2. Discuss and list causes of 'stockouts', late delivery or materials shortages.
3. Explain the terms 'lead time', 'administrative lead time' and 'backlog'.
4. Discuss the effects and possible causes of inventory shrinkage.
5. Discuss the relative merits of fixed price and cost-plus contracts for the provision of resources to a project of your knowledge.
6. Prepare an activity and resource list for a typical project operation (this may be done manually and/or with the aid of a computer program).
7. Consider circumstances in which manpower calculations, adjusted for speed of learning, might prove incorrect and delay project completion.

6 PROJECT MANAGEMENT STRUCTURES

A good organization tends to simplicity ... SIR ARTHUR HELPS

6.1 MANAGEMENT INADEQUACIES LEAD TO FAILURE

Adequate and appropriate management structures are fundamental to project success. To establish a proper organization structure is an obvious preliminary to the implementation of any project but surprisingly, many ambitious and costly undertakings are set in motion without the benefit of clear decisions on management responsibility, lines of communication or delegation of authority.

The deficiency is not confined to large projects. For every major project deficient in this respect, hundreds of smaller but, to their sponsors, equally important ventures begin without proper management arrangements. Most of these fail, are abandoned or return mediocre performance despite feasible objectives and individual effort well worthy of success.

6.2 FACTORS IN PROJECT FAILURE

Studies in the United States show prime factors in project success to include 'an adequate and appropriate organizational structure'. United Kingdom studies found problems such as part-time management, inappropriate organization, and lack of direction and control amongst the principal causes of project failure and high-lighted the importance of 'a clear and logical organization structure'.

Many examples have been found in which 'inappropriate organization' was a prime cause of project failure. Some North Sea oil projects, for example, were prone to problems with general management, administrative support and coordination – glaring inadequacies, when viewed against the scale, cost, working conditions and complexity of the operations.

The Arabian Gulf has been a region of intense project activity, particularly in the field of construction and civil engineering, but cultural differences and attitudes of project owners and expatriate workforces are often disregarded or misconstrued in the formulation of management hierarchies and in the leadership styles of overseas consultants and contractors.

Western project managers and contractors who adopt a formal and inflexible structure seem to encounter frequent instances of delay in securing important decisions and obtaining action at successive levels of the hierarchy due to differing attitudes to time and communication. The nature of the labour force may also present problems deserving of consideration in the organization structure (Loosemore and Al Muslmani, 1999).

In Saudi Arabia, failures in management by both project and construction managers have been identified as contributory factors in the failure of construction projects in the Eastern Province (Osama Jannadi, 1997).

Transitional economies face difficulties in establishing effective project structures as a result of rapidly changing attitudes and needs. Structure and characteristics of the project environment are seen in Russia as being of vital importance in developing project managements in that region (Voropajev, 1998).

Difficulties of control tend to complicate the organization of projects that require the detailed contributions of a number of major contractors. Each contractor will have its own project structure, priorities, communication routine, managers with differing responsibilities, expectations and style. The problem can be somewhat reduced by stipulating organizational requirements as a condition under which the contract is awarded. In some cases, a senior contractor representative, acceptable to the project management and with agreed levels of authority over his/her contractor's personnel, can be seconded to the project management structure to facilitate control and provide necessary coordination between project and contractors' activity.

6.3 THE ORGANIZATION STRUCTURE

An organization structure maps the management hierarchy, shows reporting channels and formal communication networks and forms a guide to parallel and coordinating functions. It also indicates areas of delegation or cooperation, and links between the external and internal structures and managerial elements, extending from the project sponsors, owners, guarantors and financing organizations to the project manager and leaders of specialist functions or activities.

6.4 DEVELOPMENTS IN PROJECT ORGANIZATION

In recent years, significant changes in living standards, behaviour and expectations have had a marked effect on the behaviour of people in organizations. Widespread adoption of worker empowerment principles has resulted in an increased use of individual initiative in problem solving, a tendency for people to establish more productive lines of unofficial communication and cooperate more readily in the achievement of common goals. In practice, this means that while formal lines of communication are better understood and respected, both formal and informal networks are strengthened and more effective and the employment of a good workforce results in a very different outcome from similar management structures a few years ago.

Another outcome of this evolutionary process is a revival of some of the simpler formal structures that were previously abandoned. With hindsight, their form is once more recognized as having been effective because new management, employee attitudes and behaviour have overcome many erstwhile problems.

6.5   THE EXTERNAL AND INTERNAL ORGANIZATIONS

Project organization takes place on two levels, external and internal. The external organization is concerned with the *management of projects* as opposed to the more specific *project management.*

In the case of a small, in-company project the external element might be confined to the board of directors or company chief executive. A more sizeable project will usually have an external group consisting of sponsors, financing organizations and, possibly, advisory boards to whom the project manager also has a responsibility. Multi-project organizations like some agencies of the United Nations, on the other hand, will have large and complex structures, as do major national and international enterprises.

Most external structures are formed by circumstances beyond the control of the project manager, who is largely responsible for linking both structures. His or her primary concern, however, is to design and develop the internal structure which deals more immediately with the operation of the project itself.

The form of the internal organization structure depends on such factors as:

- project nature;
- project size and complexity;
- technology, processes or procedures involved;
- geographical locations of project elements;
- maturity and nature of project personnel.

6.6   TYPES OF MANAGEMENT STRUCTURE

Most project structures fall into one (or a combination) of the following groups:

1. differentiated and dedicated structures;
2. hybrid structures;
3. matrix structures;
4. modular structures;
5. flat structures.

Different projects call for very different structures, attitudes and styles of leadership. Large and complex construction and engineering projects, for example, tend to have rather formal, differentiated management structures and many favour somewhat autocratic and confrontational styles of management. Research and development projects, on the other hand, may use a formal organization at higher levels combined with semi-autonomous work teams, technology-based leadership and high levels of coordination at activity level.

From the project manager's point of view, the task force or dedicated project team has the advantage that people and resources are allocated to the project on a full-time basis and the manager has full authority over them (Harrison, 1981).

6.7 DEDICATED FUNCTIONAL MANAGEMENT STRUCTURES

For uncomplicated projects with their own staff and resources, a simple differentiated structure is usually adequate and most effective (Figure 6.1). A few years ago, in connection with ongoing activities, these simple 'line and staff' structures attracted adverse criticism amongst 'management experts' but most of their shortcomings were related more to morbidity of attitude, ingrained behaviour and lack of management flexibility than faults with the organization structure itself, which remains well suited to a great deal of project work.

The essential advantages of a functional structure are simplicity, logic and independence. In many project environments these goal-oriented management structures make for effectiveness, control, good communication and coordination of effort.

One contention is that, by presenting fewer opportunities for economy of scale, they are not always cost-effective in the use of services and resources because they require facilities which are not shared. So, though 'self-standing' project organizations structures are usually desirable, they entail the full cost of management and resources, factors that may seem hard to justify in very small projects.

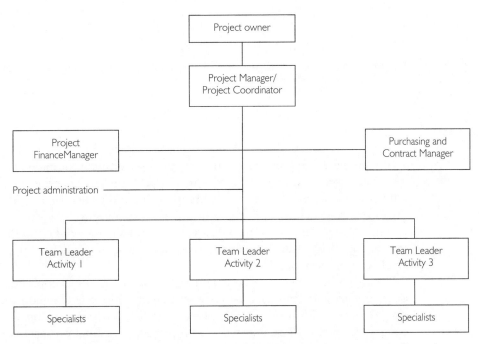

Figure 6.1 Simple differentiated structure in a project embracing three activities

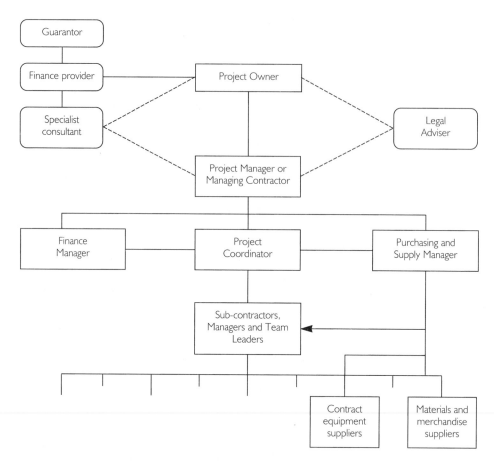

Figure 6.2 Differentiated management structure, showing the relationship between external and internal levels of management

In Figure 6.2, the guarantor, who may be a government or international body, and the project owner have access to advice from an independent consultant who would work in close collaboration with the manager. Although the organization structure appears somewhat rigid, most of the formal lines of communication are at senior levels and, under the right conditions and management style, productive teamwork and close coordination at operational levels can be developed.

In cases where there is a large contracted procurement or supply requirement, or a contractor is employed to conduct major work, it is common practice for the contractors to appoint a manager in their own organization to run their company's contribution, and work with project personnel on matters related to the contracted responsibility.

6.8 HYBRID STRUCTURES FOR INTERNAL PROJECTS

The 'internal hybrid' structure is often used for in-company projects. In these cases, a project manager is usually appointed. Although he or she may have some staff fully employed in project work, the manager has to rely on permanent company employees, departmental and line facilities activities for much of the important project work in areas where they can provide specia;ist assistance.

Hybrid structures are common in internal projects where the scale of operation does not seem to warrant use of external facilities, and in setting up internal projects, sponsoring managers tend to rely on these arrangements in the expectation that they will offer economic use of functional departments within the organization.

There is nothing wrong with these structures in internal or in-company projects, but results are reliant on the availability of services and the levels and extent of cooperation between managers.

The success of projects using these structures relies heavily on the willingness of line managers to cooperate and accept accountability for their timely contributions to a company project, the quality of their cooperation and the degree of authority delegated to the product manager to command appropriate performance from contributing departments. The example in Figure 6.3 shows the structure of a typical in-company project in which staff, functional managers and subordinates provide services in support of the project. In this case, the main activity is performed by personnel allocated on a full-time basis but some essential activities and services are provided by the parent organization.

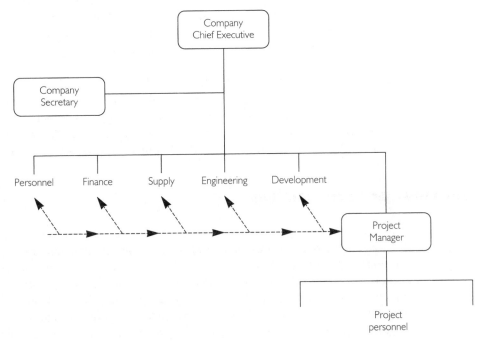

Figure 6.3 Example of a simple hybrid structure

Difficulties of cooperation are partially overcome when the project manager is given a free hand and full control of expenditure. The project can then act as a 'client' of selected internal departments which contract to conduct activities for payment within agreed specifications, time and cost.

6.9 PART-TIME MANAGEMENT IN HYBRID AND MATRIX STRUCTURES

Amongst smaller projects a common cause of failure is linked to the involvement of part-time managers and specialists, particularly those without project training or clear instruction on the conduct of their project work, priorities and the scope of their part-time responsibility.

In larger companies, responsibility for a range of projects with conflicting needs is also closely linked to project failure.

6.10 MATRIX STRUCTURES IN MULTI-PROJECT ORGANIZATIONS

Matrix structures come in several forms. The two most common to project work are:

- the functional matrix; and
- the project matrix.

Many large, multi-project organizations successfully employ a matrix organization (Figure 6.4). This makes for economic use of scare or costly resources and know-how, as these can be shared amongst a variety of projects.

Matrix structures are widely used but they do entail some problems which may lead to difficulty unless they are addressed at an early stage of project development.

Most common amongst the problems are those brought about by conflicting priorities, and the availability of special equipment, professional expertise and skilled labour. Financial constraints can also lead to delay in implementation if the organization is over-committed or lacks the resources to support a number of projects as they go through high-cost development or production cycles.

6.11 MULTI-PROJECT CONTRACTORS

Project contractor organizations tendering for work on major projects such as design, engineering, construction and so on tend to maintain high levels of specialist expertise, equipment and capability for the performance of large projects in their fields of work. Such companies are often organized on a matrix system, simultaneously conducting a number of projects using their resources of skilled staff and development or production capacity to carry out specialized functions. It is normal practice for each project to have its own manager or coordinator although some of its personnel may be shared. Functional managers are in charge

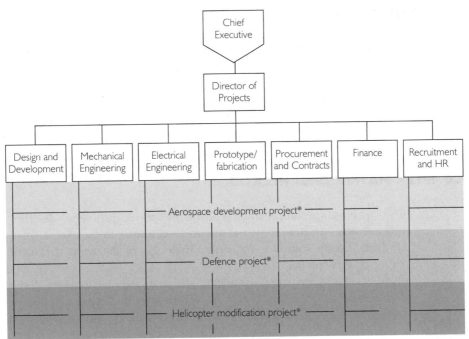

* Note: Each project has its own project management and coordination team

Figure 6.4 **A project matrix structure in a multi-project organization**

of the work of specialist activities. One obvious advantage of this type of organization lies in the opportunity for economy by sharing scarce or highly specialized resources. Another is that high levels of remuneration can be sustained to allow specialization and world-class expertise. Specialists can be shared between several projects and many projects can be undertaken at one time. Estimates of savings achieved by resource sharing vary, but claims of up to 40 per cent saving in labour and 15 per cent in materials costs are common. Work priorities and workloads for each function or department have to be carefully scheduled to avoid delay as a bottleneck in progress on one project can be detrimental to several others. Because of efficiency in the availability and use of consultants and special resources, contractors using this type of organization are much favoured by government and international project owners, financiers and guarantors.

In theory, the system should result in the provision of cost-effective service. In practice, it is sometimes less effective than one might expect. Specialization and difficulty over the recruitment of enough top-level project managers and coordinators sometimes result in a costly and disappointing outcome. The example in Figure 6.4 shows a typical project contractor matrix in which each project has its own manager, expert advisers and coordination team. Specialist departments are managed internally.

6.12   THE PROJECT MATRIX

The project matrix is favoured by many large project organizations. Its main advantage over the functional matrix is that authority and responsibility for all project work rests with the project manager, functional managers acting as advisers, providing technical expertise, and, in many cases, as suppliers of specialist personnel. Given the right calibre of specialists and managers, this structure retains the advantages of the functional matrix and overcomes many of its disadvantages.

6.13   COMPLEX MATRIX ORGANIZATIONS

The increasing complexity of projects poses problems in the design of management structures. Matrix structures continue to be extensively used, many of them linking complex, functional, modular or flat team structures within the larger project sphere.

An outline matrix structure related to aerospace development, linking a variety of essential and complex functions, is illustrated in Figure 6.5. Complex versions of this basic configuration are used in many military and space programmes.

6.14   MODULAR STRUCTURES

Modular project structures are used in situations where small groups with special expertise can be developed to deal with special, limited, tasks involved in the achievement of a larger project objective, such as setting up a project in advance of the arrival of its manager and experts, establishing a management decision-making laboratory, software adaptation, and so on. Although modular teams would nominally be subordinate to the project manager or project coordinator, their special responsibility and team expertise usually endow advisory status and considerable practical autonomy. A modular system is often used in projects based on concurrent engineering principles, for example to provide the functional components of an internal development project.

6.15   FLAT STRUCTURES FOR RESEARCH AND PROFESSIONAL WORK

Figure 6.6 illustrates a simplified form of 'flat' or team structure in which participants determine many details of their workloads, operate under minimal day-to-day supervision and interact closely with one another as a team having a common purpose.

Loosely defined structures this sort of require considerable maturity and high levels of professional motivation on the part of individuals and teams, high levels of expertise, reasonable internal harmony and strong dedication to project objectives.

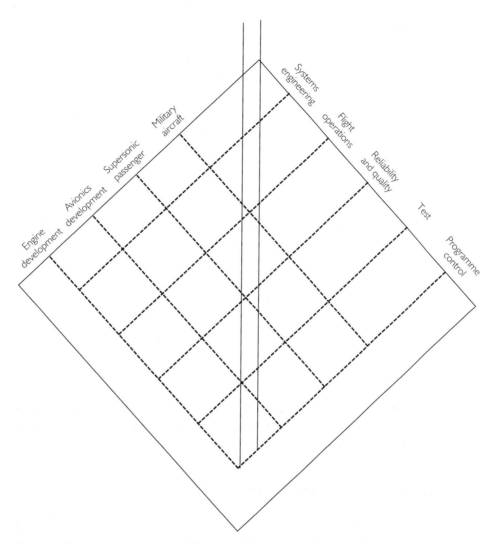

Figure 6.5 Complex matrix structure similar to that used in a space programme

In addition to professional, liaison and support roles, the project team leader plays a vital part in defusing conflict and maintaining team morale and work momentum in time of difficulty. He or she must not only exert considerable influence as leader within the group, but may also be required to act as senior expert or adviser.

Not all well-motivated professionals work well under this type of arrangement. Empathy with objectives, the team leader and other team members are essential ingredients of success.

One of the most difficult structures to establish, for scientific work or work of high complexity, teams of this nature can neverthelessbecome extremely productive.

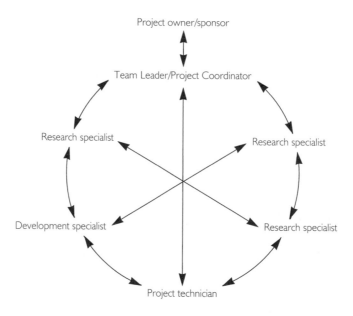

Figure 6.6 Flat team structure for a simple research project

Flat structures are sometimes favoured in simultaneously engineered projects, particularly in areas of product development or research, where the team is closely coordinated and staffed by well-motivated specialists.

6.16 GLOBAL PROJECT ORGANIZATIONS

Global projects embrace and coordinate the work of a variety of consultants, contracting organizations and public utilities in a complicated matrix of activity, some operating under very different constraints and conditions. Some projects extend the scope of products or services to a wider range of people, others combine knowledge and facilities for greater efficiency in research or production and many establish health or safety standards on a worldwide basis, for example for sea or air travel, international search and rescue, and so on.

Foremost among project organizations are the agencies and organizations of the United Nations, many operating highly successful multi-project structures (Figure 6.7).

6.17 TECHNICAL COOPERATION PROJECT ORGANIZATIONS

Figure 6.8 shows the organization of the International Civil Aviation's Technical Cooperation Bureau in 1994.

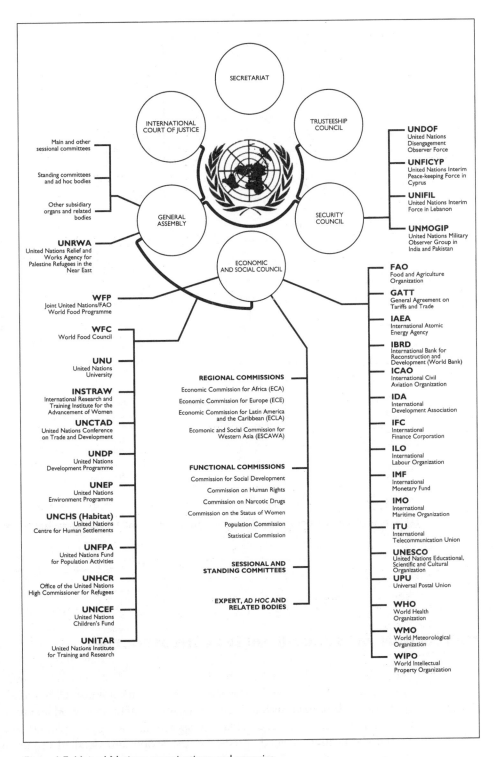

Figure 6.7 United Nations organizations and agencies

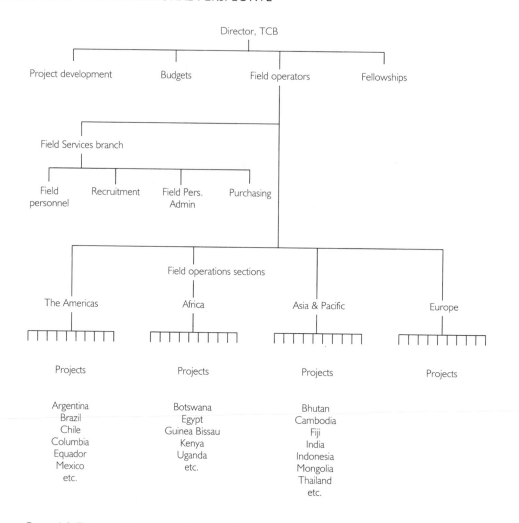

Figure 6.8 Technical Cooperation Bureau – International Civil Aviation Organization 1994

6.18 MAKING MANAGERS ACCOUNTABLE IN THE STRUCTURE

Project owners and sponsors should have clear expectations of managerial performance. A structure is only as strong as its weakest constituent and allocation and acceptance of responsibility are key factors in achieving workability from any management structure. Broad areas of responsibility are easily plotted (see Figure 6.9) but clarification is needed to show the scope and detailed requirements of each job.

Responsible for	Project Manager	Team Leader A	Team Leader B	Admin. Supervisor
Master plan	A	C	C	C
Activity plan A	C	A		C
Activity plan B	C		A	C
Resources plan	A	C	C	C
Finance plan and cash flow	A	C	C	C
Monitoring and control	A	A*	A*	C
Contracts	A			C
Local purchase	A	A*	A*	C
Hire of plant	A	C*	C*	C
Daily reports		A*	A*	C
Periodic reports	A	C*	C*	C
Project review and revision	A	C	C	C

A = Accountable; C = Contributor; * = accountable for work related to own activity

Figure 6.9 Team members' responsibility chart

Particular care must be taken to avoid gaps in coverage, and when overlapping responsibility is inevitable, areas of joint responsibility should be clearly understood.

To achieve realistic standards, it is necessary to supplement clear objectives with adequate and well-defined limits of authority and accountability (usually set out in the project document and the job specification) and supplement the information with detailed briefing on special tactics or methods of operation (if important to the project owners), mandatory reporting routines, and so on.

Other important considerations, such as a need for industrial harmony, requirements for preservation of public image or avoidance of political enmity, may have be defined.

6.19 HOW DO PROJECT MANAGERS SPEND THEIR TIME?

For many, a principal attraction of the job is the variety of work and the diversity of the daily challenge.

The work of the manager of a major construction project is clearly quite different from that of the leader of a pharmaceutical research project; that of the coordinator of a famine relief project bears little outward resemblance to space research, and so on. But all have one thing in common: they manage a unique operation calling for professional skill, initiative, flexibility and leadership.

A DAY IN THE LIFE OF A PROJECT MANAGER

William Howe was Chief Technical Adviser and Project Co-ordinator of an Aviation Development Project in Pakistan. The International Civil Aviation Organization (ICAO) project is funded by the United Nations Development Programme (UNDP). It has a high technology content related to Air Navigation Systems, Civil Aviation Safety Procedures and Aviation Management techniques. Implementation relies on the work of 21 specialists ranging from an air space management adviser, aerodrome engineers, an adviser on navigational aids and airworthiness, and a management and organization consultant.

Bill Howe is a professional airways engineer with post-graduate qualifications in management and air transport economics. His mother tongue is English; he speaks some French and understands a little Urdu.

The project is based in Karachi. Locally recruited project staff include an executive assistant and two drivers. Other clerical and maintenance staff are supplied by the Government of Pakistan through the Civil Aviation Authority in whose premises the project is housed. Three cars and a passenger bus have been purchased from project funds.

Following a feasibility study, a period of time elapsed before funding became available and the project agreement between the Government, UNDP and ICAO was completed. Some project revisions were made to update scope, objectives, structure and technical specification.

Other considerations included the effect of new developments in air navigation systems technology, growth of regional air traffic between Pakistan and the Central Asian States and the impact of the new Jinnah Terminal at Quaid-E-Azam Airport.

The carefully planned project extending over a three-year period was to provide advice and some re-equipment to help the 12 000-strong Pakistan Civil Aviation Authority (CAA) which sets standards of air navigation and safety in line with world criteria. The work of each expert was phased in to a schedule designed and agreed by ICAO and Pakistan CAA experts.

Project advisers were internationally recruited by ICAO, Montreal, approved by the host nation and allocated to the project for the duration of their assignments. Some were required for periods of two or three months, others, like William Howe, were in office for a period of several years.

Experts on short-term assignments were usually housed in one of the excellent local hotels; medium and long-term professionals, accompanied by their wives and families, rented houses for the duration of their stay.

▶

Fortunately the project was well planned because the Project Coordinator performs a dual role; as Chief Technical Adviser to the Director of Civil Aviation and other senior officials, he is required to liaise with UNDP authorities in Islamabad, speak at international level on project matters, provide advice to technical suppliers, administer the project and its funds, whilst providing constant leadership and support (including administration, and the induction of individual project experts).

This is a typical working day:

05.00   The working day begins when Bill Howe is awakened by a telephone call from Montreal clarifying details of a desktop publishing system to be obtained by local purchase for use by CAA Human Resources Development Branch.

07.20   Driving to the office, he negotiates Karachi traffic to call at city hotels for two short-term experts who have no personal transport.

The remainder of the day goes something like this:

07.30   'Morning prayers' – Start of the day meeting with project experts – informal discussion on plans, progress, tactics and experts' needs preceded by the introduction of a newly joined Flight Safety Adviser.

08.00   Induction, briefing and administration for new expert.

08.40   Administration – daily update, check and deal with faxes, e-mail, and returns.

09.21   Introduces new adviser to Director General, CAA, senior directors and officers; arranges familiarization visits to International Airport and other key locations; initiates enquiry for family accommodation.

10.00   Telephone discussion with budgets officer, UNDP, Islamabad Office on project revision.

10.20   Calls local supplier about software purchase, also orders computer hardware for project.

10.55   Deals with international and local mail, drafting replies on urgent matters.

11.20   Interviews driver about motor accident involving project car. Driver, who appeared unblameworthy, was detained overnight at remote location and released on intervention of CAA Legal Director. Arranges legal representation for driver's court appearance.

11.50   Receives information from Indian boarding school on a problem relating to a consultant's children; talks to consultant, arranges emergency leave and air travel.   ▶

12.40 Visit of United States aviation expert.

13.10 Sees CAA Director of Security to arrange new 'Airside' passes for expert advisers.

14.45 Travels to airport for Director, Airworthiness' conference on non-destructive testing.

15.55 Chairs (as acting chairman) meeting of UN Staff Security Committee in Karachi, to discuss a dacoitry and armed vehicle theft, from lady employed by another agency of the UN.

17.50 Counselling visit to project finance adviser, resident in a Karachi Hotel (the adviser was reported to show signs of nervousness and reluctance to move about the city); enlists support of colleagues for reassurance to this adviser.

19.00 Returns home.

19.40 Home security guard requests leave and assistance with air fare for travel to Kashmir for funeral of sister, killed in border dispute.

19.55 Dinner with wife.

21.00 Long telephone call from ICAO, Montreal about project revisions and budget.

23.00 Power failure cuts out air conditioning and lighting.

The influence and professional standing of the project manager is vital to project success. Much of Bill Howe's long working day seems to be spent on relatively minor details of welfare and administration. Should he be doing all these things, and what level of support should project staff be able to expect?

With careful delegation, a manager engaged on a technical or research project located at the sponsor's premises in his/her own country might expect to devote up to 60 or 70 per cent of project time to work of a technical nature. However, managers of overseas projects involving a variety of professionals in cooperation with national counterparts can seldom find it possible to concentrate so much time on technical matters. Support and coordination of experts' activity is an essential aspect of team leadership in the field and many tasks cannot be delegated without loss of staff confidence. Unless these are done or arranged by the manager in person, a loss of individual confidence may result. The demands of team leadership call for the manager's personal attention to many apparently minor details. In this situation, his concern for the working conditions and welfare of experts is germane to good leadership.

A Pareto-style selection of management inputs, suggesting that 20 per cent of inputs result in 80 per cent of technical impact and, conversely, that 80 per cent of activity results in only 20 per cent of impact, might be applicable in this case (Figure 6.10).

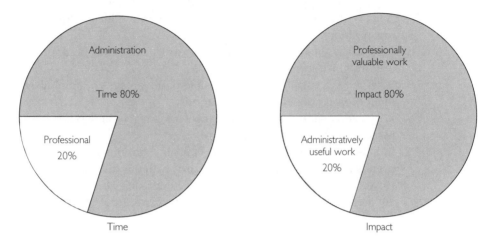

Figure 6.10 Typical breakdown of project manager's time

So however skilled in self-organization a manager may be, he/she may expect to devote time to welfare and team support. Bearing in mind that the project coordinator/manager is one person facilitating the work and results of many, this situation may be well justified.

The sort of things a project expert might reasonably be able to expect from his/her manager include:

- regular briefings on scope, objectives and progress, liaison with clients and other stakeholders;
- clear agreement on results (deliverables) required from each activity and 'yardsticks' against which they will be measured;
- conditions under which they can work effectively, without hindrance;
- team coordination and effective leadership;
- protection from bureaucratic or political interference;
- best possible conditions of work, personal and family safety (within reasonable limitations of the locality, situation and prevailing conditions in the project area);
- provision of project resources to specification as, and when needed;
- personal support in project work, and in project and personal administration;
- security, safety, health protection and welfare support;
- efficient personnel management, payroll administration and the provision of a workforce with the required skills.

REVIEW AND DISCUSSION QUESTIONS

1. What difficulties might the part-time manager of an in-company project face when he/she must rely on contributions from line and functional departments for work on the project?

2. What are the disadvantages of part-time management?

3. What are the advantages and disadvantages of a self-standing (separate) project organization?

4. Consider a situation in which a 'flat' structure would be appropriate and the way in which it might be established.

5. What are the advantages and possible disadvantages of employing a specialist, multi-project contracting organization?

6. What steps should be taken to make managers and other key project staff accountable?

7. In a project with which you are familiar, consider how the project manager spends his/her time, how this compares with the case study account of William Howe's day, activities that might be better delegated, and activities, though apparently insignificant, that ought to be carried out by the project manager.

7 BUILDING THE PROJECT TEAM

Lead, follow, or get the hell out of the way – UNITED TECHNOLOGIES
CORPORATION STAFF MESSAGE

Much of this text is devoted to the essentials of planning, budgeting and control – all activities that are fundamental to project success. These are the tools of administration and leaders must be skilled in their use. However, this chapter deals with the project's most vital ingredient – the people who plan the work, contribute professional expertise and lead it to a successful conclusion – specialists, team leaders, project coordinators and managers, their attitudes, skills and management styles, and how these affect the project team.

A project team has a good deal in common with an orchestra – each member plays a well-defined and rehearsed part and contributes to a result much greater than the sum of each contribution. An orchestra is highly dependent on its leader whose talent and behaviour can lead to harmony or discord.

7.1 INDIVIDUALS IN THE PROJECT TEAM

Teams are sensitive to discord and key players must be compatible if the project is to prosper, so what sort of people make up a good project team and how should we go about the task of selecting and training them? Four important considerations are:

1. *Sensitivity.* First and most importantly, we must remember that teams rely more heavily on control and leadership than do players in ongoing operations. They are more sensitive to, and reflect more acutely, the styles and attitudes of the project manager, coordinator and other key people.
2. *Individual capability.* Because a project is a team effort with limited resources, it is essential that each member be fully capable to contribute his or her area of responsibility, and equally ready to integrate his or her contributions with those of other team members.
3. *Teamwork and cooperation.* Team play calls for more than mere integration of effort. It requires initiative and leadership on the part of all members in a variety of situations, some of which are peripheral to the individual's prime task, that is, a contribution to team management and a role in team success.
4. *Compatibility, empathy and mutual respect.* While team members will have differences of attitude and background, there must be a measure of mutual understanding, a willingness to cooperate and a degree of mutual respect.

The choice of project team members is dictated by such factors as the nature of the project, its technology, complexity, the expectations of the profession or discipline, the make-up of the project team and the conditions under which it will have to work. Coordinating a humanitarian project in Panama, for example, would call for somewhat different qualities than a university-based project in pharmacology or an internal project to re-engineer company organization.

The list of desirable manager characteristics in Chapter 1 is a start but it is too superficial for purposes of selection and training and we need more on which to base successful selection and team development.

7.2 UNDERSTANDING TEAM ROLES

Many specialists and administrators, selected on the basis of their professional knowledge, adapt readily to project conditions and a team environment. This is just as well because there is usually very limited time in which training and team development can take place. As the team develops, individuals, in addition to their special area of expertise or responsibility, assume a variety of roles in the team itself. Individual characteristics and circumstances combine towards role adoption.

They are variously identified and grouped, for example by Margerison and McCann (1990) as:

Creator-innovators, Explorer-promoters, Assessor-developers,
Thruster-organizers, Concluder-producers, Controller-inspectors,
Upholder-maintainers and Reporter-advisers.

Belbin (1981) on the other hand uses somewhat different descriptive groupings:

Plant: a good ideas person, innovative – may lack attention to detail
Resource investigator: enthusiastic, good problem solver
Coordinator: mature and confident, defines goals, uses skills of team members
Shaper: courageous: dominant task leader – may provoke others
Monitor evaluator: the group analyst – sober and judgemental, good at detail – may be uninspiring
Teamworker: people-orientated, a good mediator and motivator
Implementer: conservative, practical, inflexible, meets deadlines
Completer: task-oriented and conscientious, intolerant of casual work attitudes
Specialist: committed to narrow skills and specialization

Parker (1990) favours a model made up of only four roles:

Contributor, Collaborator, Communicator and *Challenger*

Attempts to classify and identify the individual characteristics of candidates are often made with the aid of psychology-based questionnaires such as 16. PF, Humm-Wadsworth and so on, and most major organizations employ a psychologist to administer one or other form of 'profile' or 'competency model' to help them identify 'tall poppies' for recruitment, development and promotion. But for many selectors, the main value of these instruments is in highlighting areas of uncertainty or special interest to be examined more closely in an interview situation.

7.3 BALANCING TEAM ROLES

John Adair (1986) provides a valuable insight into group, individual behaviour and describes factors leading to high performance in teamwork in his book, *Effective Team Building*.

In practice, project teams seldom employ so varied a balance of personalities as those listed above. But one can seek a range of behaviours that will be conducive to synergy, and assist in task completion and achieving project objectives.

Useful task roles include:

- leading;
- offering ideas and suggesting courses of action;
- building progress;
- seeking data and other information;
- summarizing.

Team maintenance roles include:

- supporting and encouraging;
- defusing tension;
- giving attention;
- gatekeeping (helping to exclude disruptive elements).

In practice, the manager can seldom pick an ideal range of skills and role players for the project team but with careful selection, it is usually possible to choose candidates who are likely to do well, both in their individual responsibilities and collectively as members of the team. Once the team has been selected, the way it develops is largely governed by the training, guidance and leadership exerted by managers and team leaders.

7.4 EMPOWERMENT IN PROJECT WORK

The concept of 'empowerment' is based on research demonstrating an inherent human need for people to control their own environment and important aspects of work (Figure 7.1). Those who can do so are likely to extend themselves more fully, increasingly exercising their abilities and enhancing the probability of success. It is particularly useful in improving quality and overcoming unforeseen difficulties.

Self-determination has long been a common factor in the management of projects and, unlike many ongoing or routine operations, the job needs and expert status of key team members make for success in the empowerment of project workers.

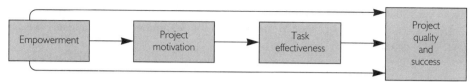

Figure 7.1 Empowerment in a project environment

Even limited degrees of self-regulation may have a marked influence on motivation and the use of initiative by individuals and teams. The benefits are not confined to specialist teams.

Careful briefing and some training may be needed, but many projects with artisan and largely unskilled workforces manage to instill a considerable interest in the project, and enable workers to identify with project tasks and goals, leading to very positive contributions to the final result.

7.5 THE MANAGER AS TEAM LEADER

Even in these times, some sources describe aggression and confrontationalism as attributes of a good project manager but there is very little evidence that, even under extreme circumstances, these attitudes and qualities have any real merit. An authoritative approach, on the other hand, may be very important. Perseverance, stamina, self-reliance, decisiveness and assertiveness are certainly valuable qualities. Management styles and the effect of power on leadership are discussed later in this chapter but the ability to recruit and motivate capable individuals and, with very little time, mould them into effective work teams must be paramount. It is usually best achieved with a participative leadership style based on a mixture of trust and respect for both the individual manager and his/her competence in the job.

In project work, managers and team leaders must be competent in all aspects of teamwork, meeting the needs of the project and the task in hand, the individual(s) responsible for doing it and the success of the team as a whole. This demands flexibility of approach and a variety of roles, showing influence, leadership and control from whatever point in the team structure it will be most effective. Figure 7.2 illustrates the dynamic relationship between individual members and the team as a whole in relation to the common task. Successful completion or excellence in an individual's contribution is of litle value unless it contributes to team success in achieving the required objective.

Figure 7.3 shows alternative positions from which team leadership may be exercised. The 'hub' provides overall coordination, a central source of information and reference; the specialist role provides for the introduction of expertise and the orbiting situation provides support, coaching and the maintenance of individual morale.

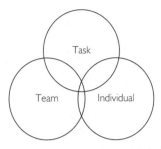

Figure 7.2 The three elements of teamwork

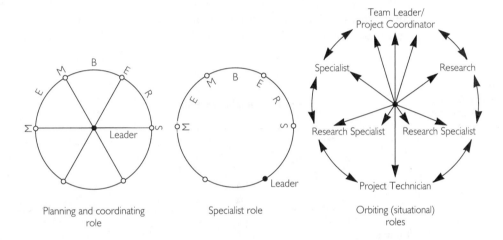

Figure 7.3 Alternative leadership positions in teamwork

7.6 MANAGEMENT STYLES

Much has been written about leadership, management styles and their effect on motivation and productivity. Opinions differ as to the style of leadership that a project manager should adopt.

Various combinations of theory traceable to interpretations of early, but nonetheless valid management theory, such as McGregor, Maslow, Herzberg, Blake, Mouton and many others, point to the essential truth that there is no sure way of encapsulating the notion of a typically successful style for a project manager or team member.

7.7 LIFE-CYCLE LEADERSHIP

In practice, management behaviour tends to change with circumstances, the nature of the task, the maturity of team members and the way in which the team itself develops. Situational leadership models developed in the 1970s (Hersey and Blanchard, 1977) illustrate how effective leaders balance their levels of concern for team relationships and task achievement to achieve effective delegation, acceptance of responsibility and control. A similar model can be related to the project life cycle which dictates changes in management preoccupations as the project progresses, the team matures, develops capability and becomes more self-reliant.

These situational changes are illustrated in Figure 7.4, which shows that during the planning phase, managers tend to concentrate on issues of technology, process and detail. As the project progresses through implementation, greater attention is directed to human resource issues such as recruitment, selection, training, team building and morale. As team capability increases, coordination and control assume greater importance.

Figure 7.4
Management behaviour and the project life cycle

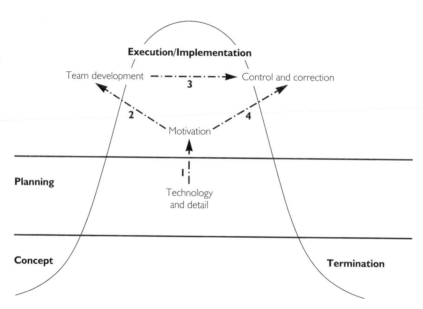

case study

THE DYNAMIC PROJECT MANAGER

With a budget in excess of US$ 8.5m the 24-month aid project was aimed at modernizing electronic communications in a rapidly developing area of SE Asia. Project planning was completed prior to the selection of a project manager who would assume overall control.

▶

The choice of a US national, Joseph K. Bolz, was based on his experience as Vice-President (Administration) of a leading developer and manufacturer of telecommunications hardware.

Bolz interviewed well and left an impression of being a decisive and capable manager.

For personal reasons, Bolz did not take up the appointment until the project was into its sixth week. By this time, five expert advisers had arrived and, despite a lack of basic project facilities, commenced work on their assignments.

Bolz took another two weeks to settle in, leased a large house and dispensed lavish hospitality to local dignitaries and project personnel alike.

In the office, Bolz was critical of the work that had been done in his absence and changed the direction of some activities. His initial briefing left no one in any doubt of the high performance standards that he required of the team members. Since each one was an acknowledged expert in his or her field, this pronouncement was received with a measure of reserve.

With the passage of time, Bolz adopted an increasingly dictatorial and hectoring attitude, criticizing experts' judgement and calling for repeated revision of reports and recommendations on matters of technical detail (much of which he did not fully understand) or English usage.

His insecurity was manifested in a tendency to over-supervise. This led to further resentment and awareness of a lack of professional trust. By the time that a total of eight experts were in place and working on the project, progress was seriously behind schedule and morale had reached an all-time low.

Jealous of their professional reputations, advisers knew that premature resignation would be harmful to their careers, and incur disappointment, inconvenience and financial penalties.

Three months into the project, the matter came to a head when Bolz reported adversely on his experts, blaming them for the lack of progress which they, in turn, attributed to him. As the position became untenable, the experts orchestrated a protest.

Seven of the eight specialist advisers simultaneously tendered their resignations with the result that Head Office suspended activity and conducted an enquiry.

An unrepentant Bolz blamed his staff of expert advisers, claiming that they could not cope with the necessary pressures of work, up-to-date methods and American standards of efficiency. This notwithstanding the fact that three of his strongest critics were, themselves, US citizens. It was significant that, in the interviews, none of the experts expressed personal animosity towards Bolz or his

▶

> behaviour. Their expressed concerns were centred on the adverse effect that he was having on the project itself.
>
> Bolz's contract was terminated and management of the project was reluctantly accepted by a member of the existing team who was seen, in discussions, to be influential and well respected.
>
> Project revisions were made to allow for changes in timings and budget and to permit a new start.
>
> Under new leadership, the project made good progress. Despite inauspicious beginnings, due to the efforts of the team it reached a successful conclusion, on time and within budget.

To avoid a repetition of this unhappy saga, the project sponsors held an internal investigation into selection procedures. This confirmed a good record of success in forming project teams but reached these conclusions:

1. Scrutiny of Bolz's background had failed to reveal the significance of his experience being limited to long-term progression within one company.
2. With hindsight, it was clear that his previous appointment, though senior, was the result of manipulating internal politics and the use of power bases rather than technical and managerial ability.
3. Power, position and autocratic management styles, sometimes adopted in construction projects, are not conducive to effective leadership of self-motivated professionals or team development.
4. Professionals working in teams will accept monitoring and coordination but do not react well to over-supervision.
5. The selection process was restricted to scrutiny of credentials and a series of interviews. There was no opportunity to observe candidates in action or in interaction with others in a team situation.
6. In project work the consequences of bad selection are costly in terms of money and reputation. This justifies more detailed investigation into the suitability of all candidates for key posts.

7.8 MANAGING THE EXPERT PROFESSIONAL

Contemporary managers are now routinely called on to manage and coordinate the work of specialists whose activities and levels of knowledge do not fall within the scope of their own expertise. This requirement is common in project work where managers, coordinators and team leaders must have respect for the professional knowledge of other team members, taking on trust their judgements and their ability to produce the right results.

The dynamic manager case study offers an example of the consequences of mistrust on the part of an insecure manager whose supervisory style was inappropriate to the needs of a professional team. His attempts to become involved in the detail of professional activity led to antagonism and diminished respect.

Of course, limited knowledge of a professional area does not excuse abdication of responsibility, failure to coordinate activity or exercise proper control.

In complex technical areas, the manager should concentrate on resources, timing, sequence and results. Guidelines for managing specialist professionals might include:

Inter-disciplinary understanding

1. Establish mutual understanding and respect between disciplines and levels of activity.
2. Develop an overview of the specialist aspects of the project, particularly their implications, realistic time scales and resource needs for their activities, possible problems or areas of difficulty and indicators of success.
3. Involve the experts in planning, activity timing and scheduling; get their advice and commitment to quality levels and the use of resources.
4. Learn the meanings of technical jargon.
5. Agree reporting procedures and the nature of expected results.
6. Have regular discussions on activity, methods, professional needs, and progress and support the reasonable needs of the professional.
7. Focus on needs, targets and results – avoid interference in professional detail.
8. Give positive feedback – acknowledge progress and success and keep them well informed of overall progress and project status.

7.9 POWER AND LEADERSHIP

Your power never gives you the right to command ... DAG HAMMARSKJOLD

Since management and specialist knowledge endow a measure of power, we should be aware of the significance of power in both leadership and team formation.

Power is derived from a variety of sources:

1. *Expertise.* Common in project work, expert power is derived from the possession of special skill or knowledge deserving the respect of others and influencing their behaviour.
2. *Positional power* (sometimes termed legitimate power). This is power vested in a manager or commander by virtue of his or her rank and position. Its potency

is largely confined to subordinate positions and those involved in the same structure or organization.

3. *Power of leadership.* The ability to influence the behaviour of others by behaviour and ability, building confidence, admiration and respect. It induces a willingness to comply, usually without fear and often without reward. Not conferred by position or decree, leadership power can only be earned by its holder.

4. *Information power.* Based on the holder's possession of, or ability to access, information, this form of power is often encountered in the political arena or at high level in some types of organization.

5. *Connection power.* This is based on the holder's familiarity with influential people and/or institutions. Encountered in politics, financial circles and some government circles.

6. *Reward power.* Important in (but not confined to) situations based on reward motivation, for example employment of casual labour and local staff, especially in developing countries.

7. *Coercive power.* This is power based on fear of punishment or the consequences of failure to comply. The nature of fear may be extreme, for example fear of physical attack, starvation or bankruptcy, or in less extreme cases, loss of bonus, promotion or punishment in the form of a loss of status.

A project manager will usually begin with positional and, possibly, expert power. With the passage of time, the team will develop and he or she will, hopefully, rely less on positional power, which will have been largely displaced by the more effective combination of leadership- and expertise-based power.

However, in dealing with stakeholders, there may be many situations in which a combination of expert and information power is of telling importance and in dealing with some contractors and temporary employees, the importance of reward power cannot be ignored.

7.10 THE SECRET OF GOOD SELECTION

The keys to selection are understanding and judgement – a good appreciation of three areas: the job, the nature of management and specialist skills, and the ability and attitudes of a candidate to do the work and fit into the project environment (Figure 7.5).

Figure 7.5 Understanding job needs

7.11   ESTABLISHING JOB NEEDS

This is done by a process of job analysis and recording. Both tasks can be combined into a single operation by the use of a pro forma like the one illustrated in Figure 7.6.

For the layman it provides a useful aide-mémoire and working record. It is easily modified to meet the special needs of each project.

PROJECT POSITION ANALYSIS / JOB SPECIFICATION

PROJECT TITLE

POSITION (JOB TITLE)   DATE

GRADE / LEVEL   SALARY SCALE

JOB LOCATION   LANGUAGE(S) IN USE

MAIN PURPOSE OF THE JOB (CONCISE DESCRIPTION)

RESPONSIBLE FOR (BRIEF DESCRIPTION OF RESULTS)

EXTENT AND LIMITS OF JOB AUTHORITY

EXTENTS AND LIMITS OF JOB AUTHORITY

REPONSIBLE TO (POSITION OF PROJECT SUPERIOR):
JOB INVOLVES LIAISON AND / OR COOPERATION WITH:

REQUIRED CONTRIBUTION TO PROJECT TEAM

EXTENT OF PROFESSIONAL OR OPERATIONAL SUPPORT TO BE PROVIDED

SPECIAL DEMANDS OR DIFFICULTIES TO BE OVERCOME (IF ANY)

SUPPORT OR SPECIAL TRAINING TO BE PROVIDED

KEY RESPONSIBILITIES	TASKS AND PROCESSES INVOLVED
(ESSENTIAL AREAS OF WORK IN WHICH	EACH KEY AREA OF WORK
PERFORMANCE MUST BE SATISFACTORY)	
1.	
2.	
3.	
4.	
5.	

Figure 7.6(a)
Project position
analysis/job
specification
pro forma
(page 1)

Figure 7.6(b)
Project position
analysis/job
specification
pro forma
(page 2)

PROJECT POSITION SPECIFICATION, PAGE 2

OTHER ACTIVITIES (USEFUL BUT NOT ESSENTIAL)

SUITABLE BACKGROUND FOR THE JOB

TRAINING, EXPERIENCE, EDUCATION

INTERESTS

LANGUAGES (USEFUL OR ESSENTIAL)

ATTITUDES AND BEHAVIOUR

SPECIALIST SKILLS AND KNOWLEDGE

ADMINISTRATIVE SKILLS

ABILITY TO COMMUNICATE

INTERPERSONAL SKILLS

LEADERSHIP SKILL AND STYLE

OTHER USEFUL PERSONAL ATTRIBUTES

FAMILY RESPONSIBILITIES (IF THESE HAVE ANY BEARING ON SERVICE WITH THE PROJECT eg. IF OVERSEAS RESIDENCE IS INVOLVED)

7.12 UNDERSTANDING THE REQUISITE SKILLS

The first step is the realization that projects are not conducted by individuals working in isolation. They are carried out by teams of competent, well-motivated people who are committed to work together for project success. This implies that each team member must be:

- expert in his or her specialist area, able to contribute to project control and administration;
- able to work under prevailing project conditions, that is pressure for results, speed and excellence, climatic conditions, unfamiliar environments, remote locations, using inexperienced labour and so on;
- acceptable to, and able to work in harmony with, other project personnel;
- reliable, self-reliant and able to work with minimal supervision.

7.13 THE SKILLS OF A PROJECT MANAGER AND TEAM LEADER

A good project manager will have appropriate knowledge in three overlapping areas. We might label them Organic, Professional and Administrative – three broad areas of behaviour, experience and ability that make up a pattern of competence and acceptability in project situations. Figure 7.7 shows a breakdown of the three areas.

Figure 7.7 **Project management skills and knowledge**

7.14 ORGANIC SKILLS OF MANAGEMENT

We all have some skill in this area but in some people the organic skills are better developed and more effective than in others. For team leaders and managers, organic skills are the most important but also the most difficult areas to define and assess. They include:

1. Inter-personal skills (skill with people)
   - Leadership, the ability to inspire, motivate and influence others
   - Communication skills, the ability to send and receive information and stimulus in acceptable ways
2. Personal skills and attributes
   - Courage and fortitude
   - Perseverance
   - Determination
   - Self-respect and assurance
   - Behaviour patterns
3. Conceptual skills
   - Spatial skills (ability to visualize physical relationships, positioning, and so on)
   - Imagination, vision and foresight

Ability in each of the organic skills is needed for all project work but the third area (conceptual skill) is particularly important during the concept development and planning phases, while the first and second (skill with people, behaviour and so on) are vital to the implementation phase when the behaviour, attitudes and styles of managers and team leaders are crucial to a successful outcome. Behaviour patterns and leadership styles must be compatible with project needs and circumstances and effective in control while also being acceptable to other members of the team.

7.15 PROFESSIONAL AND SPECIALIST SKILL AND KNOWLEDGE

Specialist experience is often an overriding consideration in the recruitment of a project manager. Requirements are usually well defined but assessing candidates' ability to apply them may not be easy. Specialist knowledge is often assessed by way of academic record which, if valid, provides evidence of study and ability to pass examinations or complete academic projects but not all 'well qualified' candidates perform well in the field and, to the layman, academic records are sometimes misleading. For this reason, assessments of professional skill are often based on past achievement in work of a similar nature to that of the project. Confirmation of successful achievement is advisable.

7.16 MECHANISTIC SKILL AND KNOWLEDGE

These are the skills of administration, the mechanics of planning, scheduling, purchasing, financial and operational control. They involve activities sometimes dismissed by professionals as irksome and unworthy of attention but the project will suffer if they are not properly applied. Fairly simple in application, the requirement can be concurrently assessed in several ways. For example, a candidate may offer evidence of the way he or she coped with the demands of a previous appointment, simple tests or selection exercises may be used and finally, discussion with an informed interviewer will reveal a depth of experience, knowledge and ability.

Screening candidates' record of achievement is a telling indicator. But success and reputation should be confirmed by more than one reliable source and, even then, some probing may be justified.

7.17 PROFESSIONALS IN MANAGEMENT

In practice, many top-level professionals adapt well to the business of team leadership. This is apparent when the depth of their professional expertise engenders respect and enthusiasm and motivates others to cooperate and achieve good results. In these circumstances, the choice of an able professional may be preferable to that of an experienced manager, though the professional may need time or training to become familiar with the details of project administration.

7.18 AVOIDING PROFESSIONAL AND PERSONAL PREJUDICE

Some years ago, prejudice between management disciplines was rife. Book-keepers, accountants and administrators were considered, with some justification, to be highly inflexible, restrictive or bureaucratic. They, in turn, saw marketing people as unreliable, democratic leaders as 'soft', and creativity in business as the seed of anarchy.

Happily this disruptive state of affairs is in the past and managers of today are generally well educated and multi-disciplined; a more open-minded and adaptable band but not all perform well under project conditions. Attitudes to social class, race or nationality are obvious indicators, but ideas and attitudes are reinforced or modified by experience and transported from one situation to another. The selection process does well to take account of prejudice that may affect teamwork or project outcome.

The short-term nature of project work leaves little room for error in selecting key people – the choice of managers, team leaders and specialists who will work harmoniously in a closely-knit team has to be right first time, because it is seldom possible to make a second choice.

7.19 ASSESSING CANDIDATES' SUITABILITY

Scrutiny of a candidate's qualifications, references and background is little more than a filter for *prima facie* suitability. In spite of the importance of good selection, processes often rely on screening of qualifications, confirmation of references and one or more interview. Even when the interviews are conducted by panels of trained interviewers, they may fail to show up or clarify important considerations. They seldom disclose the true nature of a candidate or the extent of his/her ability to influence and communicate with others. Properly designed psychological and aptitude tests can be helpful, mainly for screening purposes, where they can eliminate unsuitable candidates in the early selection stages and suggest areas of doubt for clarification in the course of interview and background investigation.

For a better overall picture of short-listed candidates, many selection boards favour the use of simple selection exercises so that candidates can be observed in action. A range of simple and inexpensive exercises is available to meet differing needs. An example of these is the author's mining town exercise described in the next chapter. It enables selectors to observe a candidate in discussion with others, and assess his/her power of expression, reaction to other individuals, ability to contribute ideas and initiatives, ability to exert leadership, and cooperation. This basic exercise can be applied in a variety of forms to fit the project background. Despite the high cost of poor selection, it is surprising that simple expedients of this kind are not more widely adopted.

7.20 SELECTING CONSULTANTS

The selection of consultants is always problematical due to the various personalities, skills and aptitudes of the individuals who make up the practice and the many associates with whom they work.

There is little research into the standard of contributions by consultants to project work but despite many successes, there are other instances in which the consultant contribution is not regarded as having been totally successful.

Specialist consultants in the construction industry come in for a good deal of criticism. In Saudi Arabia, for example, in a survey of responsibility for long delays in water and sewerage projects, in 52 per cent of cases surveyed, owners assigned responsibility to the consultant (Al-Khalil and Al-Ghafly, 1999).

In project work, consultants are found in variety of roles. These include:

1. in the process role – as technical or professional advisers to the external organization, that is, a government body, sponsor, owner, financing organization;
2. in a process role – acting as an agent of change to diagnose problems and help the manager remedy project deficiencies or difficulties;
3. in the resource role – as scientific expert or technical adviser to a technological, training or advisory project;
4. in the managerial role – in which the consultant is engaged by the project owner to manage the project;
5. in a resource role – as project contractor to conduct the project and supply all or most of the key human resources and expertise.

It goes without saying that the criteria for each category will be a little different but a common factor in all cases is the personal capability and quality of each of the individuals who make up the consulting practice and those in their employ.

In recent years, the conduct of large overseas projects has become a major revenue earner for consulting firms, some of whom have become adept in project administration, though they do not always produce the desired results.

Specialist expertise is usually the first essential criterion in selecting consultants but the character and quality of practitioners is next in line, almost of equal significance.

When it is possible to amass the experience of several projects, a state of mutual confidence develops between project sponsors, managers and individual consultants. This is a valuable product of experience, an asset of inestimable value and a step towards future project success.

It is important for a consultant to be respected and acceptable to the project manager and other specialists. In the Sydney Opera House project, for example, it is interesting to note that the consultant was said to have been engaged without consultation with Jørn Utzon, the architect, or the engineers responsible for development and construction of the building. If this is true, the decision may not have been helpful to the conduct and outcome of the project. 'The consultant and the client should feel competent and comfortable with their respective roles' (Kubr, 1986).

The financial standing and ability of a consultant to complete the project assignment is important. In cases of direct appointment to a salaried position on the project staff, expenses will normally be borne by project funds but when a consulting practice is engaged to provide large or more comprehensive assignments, it is prudent to seek evidence of their ability to complete the work under foreseeable circumstances.

Consulting practices engaged in project work routinely maintain resource lists of 'associates' not in their regular employ but who, nonetheless, express willingness to participate in certain kinds of work on a temporary or contract basis. It is important to scrutinize the qualifications, background and suitability of associates put forward under this system, their qualifications and availability.

7.21 LISTING CONSULTANT SELECTION CRITERIA

Where a decision has to be made between the suitability of a number of contenders, a simple pro forma of the kind illustrated in Figure 7.8 may help to assess relative merit.

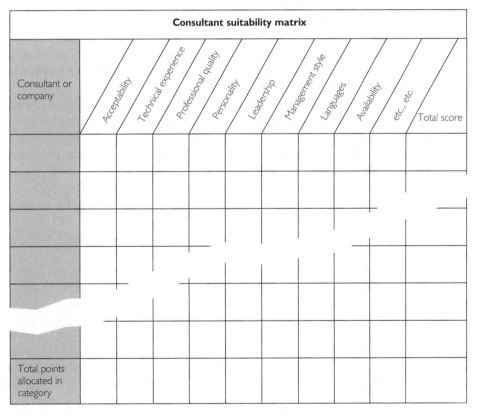

Figure 7.8 Consultant suitability assessment matrix

7.22 SUMMARY

Well led, project experts work well in teams and the outcome of a project depends on the competence and motivation of its people. Managers, team leaders and experts have a crucial bearing on ultimate success. Team leaders, in particular, need the right mix of qualifications, knowledge, leadership style and management skills. Job analysis provides a good insight into job needs for recruitment purposes but mature judgement is also vital if the right candidate is to be selected for each key job and form the basis of a well-motivated team. When team members offer complementary roles, a better level of team synergy can be developed.

The special nature of project work and the limited time-frame in which a project must be concluded make the consequences of incorrect recruitment severe and the penalties heavy. For this reason, selection processes should be designed to provide the highest probability of success in matching candidates to project needs.

REVIEW AND DISCUSSION QUESTIONS

1. Why is good selection of managers and professional specialists so important in project work?
2. What qualities and qualifications are most appropriate to the needs of a coordinator or manager of a high technology project and how might these differ from the manager of a major road or aerodrome runway construction project?
3. How would you explain the kinds of skill needed by project managers?
4. How do the concerns of a project manager change as the life cycle progresses?
5. What kinds of power might be detrimental to leadership and what classifications of power would be beneficial to a manager concerned with effective team development?
6. How are consultants commonly employed in project work, and what problems might one face in selecting the best firm of consultants for a particular job?

PROJECT TEAM SELECTION

8.1 PROBLEMS OF SELECTION

A basic requirement of any major project is an effective and well-balanced team. But recruiting the key players is an inexact science in which mistakes are not easily or cheaply rectified. Team members must work effectively together, each contributing special skill or ability to achieve a common objective.

Careful scrutiny of a candidate's credentials and background is fundamental to all selection procedures but this is no more than a filter to eliminate unsuitable applicants.

People behave differently in an interview situation, and the interviews, even backed by valid forms of psychological assessment, seldom contribute enough insight into the way that a candidate will behave in a group of peers.

This chapter offers an example of one of the many simple activities that can be used to enable the selection panel to exercise their best judgements.

8.2 GROUP SELECTION ACTIVITY

The activity consists of an observed exercise-discussion in which participants are allotted a planning task to be completed as a group effort within a limited period of time. It is usually performed on conclusion of candidate screening and an initial selection interview.

The discussion is based on the planning of a mining town. Participants are not expected to have prior knowledge of open-cut mining operations, town planning or the geographical region in which the scene is set but all participants, observers and assessors should have read the scenario (Discussion and Participant Brief) before a verbal briefing is delivered.

8.2.1 Size of the group

The activity is suited to small groups of between six and eight people. At least three observer-recorders are required for each group.

8.2.2 Observers

Observers do not need special training but they should be carefully briefed on their responsibilities and method of recording.

8.2.3 Materials and equipment

The following items of equipment should be prepared prior to the exercise and available for use.

1. Briefing sheet 'Mt Keel Mines' – copy for each participant and observer.
2. Clipboard with 'instructions for observers' and 10 copies of observation sheet for each observer.
3. Two tables about 110 cm × 150 cm (large enough to accommodate exercise map and town layout chart) for each exercise group.
4. Large-scale map of coastal mining area marked with deep water access, contours, location of the mine site (primary and secondary ore bodies can be added if desired), location of airstrip, transmitter site, reservoir and other features, including the location of any prohibited areas.
5. Paper chart to represent a large-scale map of the chosen town site for the mining town area (minimum size 100 cm × 140 cm) ruled with 5 cm squares but no geographical features.

    This chart is the base on which trial layouts can be tested in discussion. The agreed layout of the town will be indicated by using the model buildings
6. Model buildings or small blocks to represent buildings and mining installations. ('Cuisinaire' children's teaching blocks are easily obtained, colour coded and very suitable.)
7. 'Key' to identify (size, shape, colours) of models or bricks used to represent buildings to be located in the new town.
8. Red board or plastic markers: arrow to show direction of prevailing wind; disc to indicate chosen location for town site. (Other items may be added at the discretion of the directing staff (DS).)
9. Whiteboard or 'flip chart' and felt pens for use at participants' discretion.

<table>
<tr><td>

discussion scenario and participant brief

</td><td>

MOUNT KEEL IRON ORE COMPANY – A MODEL TOWN FOR A MODEL MINING OPERATION

The open-cut mining opreation at Mt Keel is now in its mine development and construction phase.

Mt Keel is situated in a remote, coastal area of Western Australia bordering on an Aboriginal reserve. Mining leases are subject to restrictions prohibiting access to neighbouring Aboriginal reserves and sacred sites.

The area is located within the tropical cyclone belt. There is a 'wet' and a 'dry' season but no summer or winter in the tropics and temperatures in the Mt Keel area range from 33 to 44 degrees Celsius. Daily rainfall of up to 10 cm is common during the wet season.

▶

</td></tr>
</table>

Agreement has been reached to allocate job preferences to indigenous applicants who are qualified and willing to work in any kind of mining job.

Exploratory drilling and feasibility studies indicate sufficient reserves to support mining operations on established ore bodies, continuing for at least 20 years.

The operation involves the removal of topsoil, blasting and collecting ore from benches (terraces) in the production area. The large pieces of ore are loaded onto vast 'Haulpak' trucks and transported to a crusher where they are reduced to smaller pieces for transport to the shiploading area. A secondary crusher is to be installed to further reduce the size of the material which will then be stockpiled for loading into bulk carriers by belt conveyors at the deep water port.

The management cadre includes a general manager, mining manager, geologist, geo-chemist, mining engineer, maintenance manager and an administration manager. There are 250 other personnel. At this stage, non-managerial personnel are employed on a 'fly in–fly out' basis working a two-week shift system of 12 hours per shift. They are housed in temporary, prefabricated air-conditioned accommodation and return to Perth (some 1400 km) by charter aircraft every two weeks. Managerial grades commute by air to the minesite weekly.

Minesite employees perform a range of functions from administrative clerical, maintenance, nursing, construction and engineering to blasting, machine operation and driving the vast ore-moving trucks needed to convey ore from the minesite to the primary crusher. At this stage, all employees are men but, under the company's equal opportunity policy, and as permanent accommodation becomes available, it is expected that a number of young women will be attracted by the high wages, to find employment in professional, heavy truck driving, maintenance, catering and administrative jobs. Experience of other open-cut operations in the area suggests a likely ratio of 70 per cent men and 30 per cent women, perhaps 10 per cent of the latter being dependants of other resident mineworkers.

Most mining towns in Western Australia are reasonably attractive and offer high standards of residential accommodation for married and single employees. Three-, four- or five-bedroomed air-conditioned bungalows are usually provided for families and allotted on a basis of family size, regardless of job status. Accommodation in the form of small flats or 'home units' is provided for single employees. Good recreational, sporting and social facilities are usually available. A mess hall offering, at subsidized rates, good and very plentiful food on a 24-hour basis is the expected norm. Other facilities might include a licensed social club, cinema, church, squash and tennis courts, child-minding centre and kindergarten facilities, infants' school, first-aid and health centre and a small supermarket shopping centre.

▶

This sub-project aims to establish firm recommendations and criteria for the siting and layout of the Mt Keel township which, it is hoped, will become a showplace and model for the mining industry throughout the world.

Under the company policy of consultation, all employees are involved in the decision-making process and your group has been formed to recommend:

1. the location of the township within the area of the mining lease;
2. the layout of the township and the locations of its residential accommodation, main office buildings and amenities.

Discussion will take place in two stages:

- *Stage 1*. During this stage, the group will site the secondary crusher (this reduces the ore to small pieces and can be anywhere between the production and shiploading areas). It is a noisy installation that generates a certain amount of dust.

The group will then decide on the best site for the township. When concensus is reached, the location will be indicated on the map by means of a red circle which is to be placed over the chosen site.

- *Stage 2*. The group will discuss and agree on the best layout of buildings and facilities in the mining town, most suitable sites for residential, administrative and amenities buildings and other facilities.

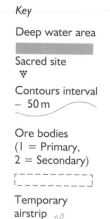

Key

Deep water area

Sacred site

Contours interval
– 50 m

Ore bodies
(1 = Primary,
2 = Secondary)

Temporary
airstrip

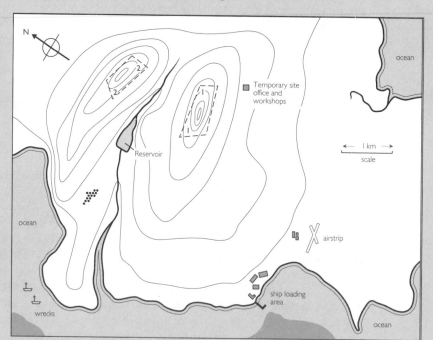

Figure 8.1 Relief map of the Mt Keel mining lease

8.3 CONDUCTING THE EXERCISE

8.3.1 Setting up the discussion area

Two tables hold the map and planning chart, whiteboard or flipchart with felt marking pens for each discussion group.

Chairs are not provided. Participants should be allowed adequate space to move round the tables without difficulty. If more than one group is being considered allow at least 3 m between locations.

An arrow is placed on the map to indicate prevailing wind (varying wind direction will usually alter the final decision).

The correct number and sizes of wood blocks or model buildings are placed on the chart table with a 'key' to identify the nature and size (but not the purpose) of the building represented by each type of marker.

8.3.2 Time allocation

Time allowed for discussion and decision making may be varied to suit the size and nature of the group and the needs of observers. Stage one usually take between one and two hours, although a particularly good group may justify considerably more time. Stage two would normally last for a minimum of two hours.

During the discussion, directing staff may remind the group of elapsed and remaining time but should not comment on individual contributions or progress.

8.3.3 Participants' briefing

The purpose of the activity (but not the means of assessment) is explained to participants who should understand that the exercise is not an examination or test of specialized knowledge.

In reaching decisions on exercise problems, participants are encouraged to seek consensus rather than a majority vote. Time limits for each stage are explained.

Each participant is handed a copy of the background narrative (Discussion scenario and participant brief); the group is invited to view exercise maps and other materials, and put questions to directing staff. Questions may not be addressed to DS or observers after the start of the group discussion.

8.3.4 The basis of observation

This activity is not a test of ability. It provides an opportunity for candidates to be observed in discussion with others. More complex versions can also be used in connection with project management training or as a preliminary to team development.

8.3.5 Briefing the observers

The task of the observers is to record significant remarks, input and behaviour of each participant and responses to the comments of others.

After studying the Mt Keel Discussion Scenario, observers are provided with a clipboard and copies of observation records, and briefed according to observer instructions, Observation Record 1 or 2.

Observers may have move about to maintain good vantage points for their observations.

Each observer concentrates on a particular aspect, as follows:

- Observation record 1 – on this plan, one or two observers record the positions taken up by each participant (Figure 8.2), and the volume and direction of remarks made in the course of discussion.

  Each time a participant speaks, the observer draws an arrow to show the direction of his/her conversation. A similar arrow is drawn from the responder's position. Remarks to the company in general are indicated by an arrow to the centre of the group. (See instructions for observers.) Figure 8.3 shows a completed record.

Figure 8.2
Observation
record 1:
Communication
pattern –
sociogram

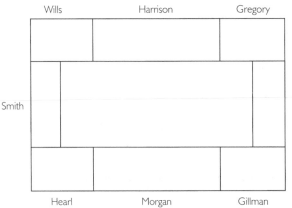

Figure 8.3
Example of
completed record

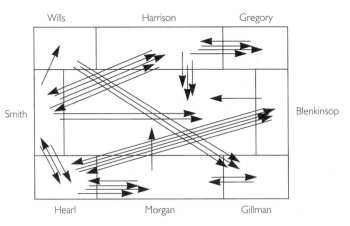

- Observation record 2 (Figure 8.4) shows the number, impact and quality of participants' contributions.

  Participants' names are entered on the form and, as each member of the group makes a comment, a stroke is recorded in the appropriate column to indicate the nature, value and/or impact of the contribution on the group task, or other members of the team and the group as a whole. (See Instructions for Observers – Observation Record 2.)

	High-value contributions	Asking	Information giving	Agreeing/ supporting	Disagreeing/ opposing	Morale helping	Disruptive	
Wills	HHt //	///	HHt	////		//		21
Harrison	//	/		/	///	////	/	12
Gregory	/	////		HHt /	//	/	//	16
Blenkinsop	///	/	////	/	////		///	16
Smith	/	HHt		/	////		HHt	16
Hearl	///	/	////	/	////	///		16
Morgan	////		HHt /	//		///		15
Gillman		//	////	/	/	·		8
Totals	21	17	23	17	18	13	11	120

Figure 8.4　Observation record 2: Quality of individual contributions

- General observations. In addition to the records described above, notes of general impressions, made in note form by the selectors, are important.

8.4　ANALYSING THE RESULTS

Groups should make best use of available time for each task and early decisions are more likely to indicate shallow treatment than high competence.

Observation records are a reminder of what took place in discussion and substantiate conclusions drawn from the assessors' recollections of behaviour, speech and tactics displayed by participants, for example positions taken at the table – a commanding one at the end, a participative one in the centre of the group, a cooperative or confrontational one alongside or opposite a particular member and so on.

Some groups will enter into preliminary discussion (usually at the suggestion of one of the members), clarify objectives and set out time-frames for the task. Others may plunge straight into unstructured discussion.

Voluble candidates do not always offer much in the way of wisdom. The quality and pertinence of effectively stated contributions secure greater effect.

Attempts to take command at too early a stage, followed by flagging influence and subsequent displacement by a less flamboyant but more logical group member, are sometimes helpful in identifying true leadership effectiveness. A confident candidate will get a point across, assume a leading or influential role and contribute to the morale and the effectiveness of the group as a whole. Evidence of teamwork and leadership as opposed to eagerness to impress at all costs is obviously desirable.

On conclusion of the activity, assessors are able to confirm or revise impressions of candidates formed during screening and at initial interview, the way in which they interact with others and the extent of their influence over the group.

8.5 RE-INTERVIEWING CANDIDATES

There are likely to be instances in which a candidate who has interviewed well shows up badly in the discussion and others who were unresponsive at interview but react well to a practical challenge come into their own in a group situation with surprising results, and justify further scrutiny.

Pointers disclosed by candidates in a well-run group exercise invariably provide a fruitful basis for discussion during a subsequent selection interview.

8.6 USE OF THE EXERCISE IN TEAM DEVELOPMENT PROGRAMMES

Exercises of this kind can be extended by making group tasks more detailed and lengthening the duration of work to provide a useful component of team development programmes. They can be helpful in initial stages of team formation when participants are not known to one another and as a basis for brainstorming and decision making or practice in achieving consensus. However, it should be remembered that the results of the activity will be somewhat different in cases where participants have prior experience of working together or are already acquainted.

INSTRUCTIONS FOR OBSERVERS
Observation record 1

Volume and direction of communication between group members

The purpose of this observation is to record verbal exchanges between individuals within the group, the quantity and direction of their remarks.

The observer should take a position from which the whole group can be seen.

When participants have taken up their positions, the observer will note the time on his/her observation sheet and complete the plan by recording names in the positions adopted.

Thereafter, as each person speaks, the observer will draw an arrow showing the direction of the comment, that is, to whom it is addressed. The same procedure is used for any reply that may be made.

When a participant addresses a comment to the group as a whole (or makes a general comment to no one in particular), an arrow is drawn toward the centre of the plan.

If participants change their positions, or the sheet becomes full, start a new sheet showing the time of the change.

Observers are not to comment, answer questions or enter into conversation with participants.

On completion of your observations, submit the observation sheets to the group facilitator and be prepared to discuss the conclusions that you have formed as an observer.

INSTRUCTIONS FOR OBSERVERS
Observation record 2

Quality, significance of contributions, influence and leadership

The purpose of this observation is to record the significant remarks and contributions of each participant. Your task is to list the participants by name, observe what each one says or does and record the number of significant remarks or actions against his/her name.

Each time a participant speaks or takes action in some way, use your judgement in deciding whether the contribution or action is of value to the discussion and whether it falls into one or more of the categories listed on your observation sheet. These are:

1. *High-value contributions* – ideas or remarks of merit that enrich or help the discussion (whether or not they are eventually incorporated in the eventual solution).
2. *Asking* – seeking information from other group members on any subject or clarifying the ideas of other members of the group.
3. *Information giving* – providing factual information or intelligent opinion related to the task or the task environment.
4. *Agreeing or supporting* – expressions of agreement or support for the ideas or proposals offered by another group member or the rest of the group (where a participant continually favours the ideas of one particular group member, this should be noted at the foot of the pro forma).
5. *Disagreeing or opposing* – when a participant expresses disagreement or opposition to an idea or a proposal, enter a mark against his/her name in the appropriate column (if the opposition is frequently or unreasonably directed to a particular individual or topic this should be noted at the foot of the pro forma).
6. *Morale building or helping* – instances of behaviour calculated or likely to reduce tension, maintain or support group morale.

▶

7. *Disruptive behaviour* – remarks or instances of counter-productive behaviour or remarks that are unsettling, cause friction or lower group morale or resolve.

Participants are not permitted to discuss the problem or ask questions of the observers. During the exercise, observers are not to comment, offer advice or enter into conversation with participants.

On conclusion of the activity, submit your completed observation sheets to the facilitator and be prepared to discuss the conclusions that you have reached as a result of your observations.

REVIEW AND DISCUSSION QUESTIONS

1. What useful information or indications of a candidate's suitability might be derived from the mining town activity?
2. What desirable traits of group participation and leadership might a candidate display?
3. In a group problem-solving and planning situation, what practical difficulties may be experienced in achieving consensus?
4. Why should all candidates be re-interviewed after completing an observed activity of the kind described in this chapter?
5. Student exercise – conduct a trial run of the Mt Keel Mining Town Exercise using several independent observers in each observation role. Compare the results of their observations and discuss (a) conclusions reached by two or more observers and (b) differing observations. Assess the value of the exercise in team membership selection.
6. Discuss the value of this exercise as a means of introducing new team members or for initial training of potential project managers.

9 PROJECT PLANNING AND DESIGN

If the trumpet gives an uncertain sound, who shall prepare himself for battle? ...

PAUL

9.1 OBJECTIVES AND PROJECT PLANS

Few projects can survive an inadequate or faulty plan and the annals of failure attributable to planning deficiencies are legion. In past decades, management teaching tended to assume that project work was the province of engineering, construction or sometimes product development and, accordingly, concentrated attention on the essentials of work flow and scheduling, basic activities that were, surprisingly, sometimes disregarded, even in quite large undertakings.

Although essential tools of the planning process, these constitute but two of the many vital stages and processes of a cohesive project plan.

Even the simplest project requires a plan that is workable and effective. The plan is not merely a statement of project activities and their timing, but a progressive statement of objectives, tactics and operations, needed to take the project from start to its successful conclusion. The planning document forms a directory and guide to coordination, telling everyone what to do and when to take action, enabling the project manager to control and coordinate progress as the work moves from one stage to another. It is an essential working tool and a safeguard against chaos that is likely in an unplanned activity (see Maylor, 1996).

case study

THE SYDNEY OPERA HOUSE

The Sydney Opera House is known throughout the world, not only for its idyllic setting and unusual design but for the astronomical cost of its construction.

Apart from the Opera House itself, the buildings include a theatre, cinema and other facilities and it is one of the best publicized and most controversial examples of modern architecture.

Development of the concept began when the Government of New South Wales in 1955 and 1956 conducted an international competition seeking original, innovative designs for an opera house to be built on a peninsular site near the Sydney Harbour Bridge.

▶

An ingenious plan submitted by Jørn Utzon, a Danish architect, was chosen and Utzon was commissioned to lead the project.

Possibly spurred on by enthusiasm and political ambition, the Government of New South Wales agreed to an early start despite the fact that many technical planning and construction problems had not been solved. In 1959, the Premier set the project in motion. An impressive public ceremony marked commencement, when an orchestra played in the background as a fleet of bulldozers moved in unison to begin site clearance.

Contrary to common practice, project engineers (Ove Arup & Partners) were engaged by the Government without consulting the architect. The reasons for this choice are unclear.

As engineers, the standing of Ove Arup is not in question. They were highly competent but it appeared that their experience had not equipped them with the ability to solve the new construction problems in ways that met with the approval of the architect.

Much experimental work was necessary before the complex problems of constructing the shell-like structures could be resolved. After prolonged thought and experimentation, Utzon eventually alighted on the idea of building the huge shells by a modular process as segments of a sphere.

As Utzon strove for perfection in every detail, the need for development at each stage meant that the work proceeded slowly. As time went on, delay attracted a barrage of comment from local architects and opponents of the party in government.

Utzon, who was disinterested in local opinion and sometimes at odds with the engineers, strove resolutely for excellence in every detail. But by 1963, with much of the exterior complete, it was felt in some quarters that the building was taking too long to complete and was costing far too much.

One of the many problems, typical of the situation, concerned the complex interior treatment that involved the use of very large sheets of plywood that could only be produced by one local manufacturer. Utzon encountered difficulties over the purchase and the Public Works Department are said to have caused further delay by demanding that the order be offered to tender despite the obvious absence of any alternative suppliers.

Utzon's vision and much of his development work for the interior as an essential part of the total concept was lost when, in 1965, a Liberal–Country Party government was elected on a platform of 'fixing up' the Opera House and proceeded to exploit perceptions about the cost of construction.

The Minister for Public Works engaged another architect to oversee the project and, in discussion with Ove Arup & Partners, failed to back Utzon. ▶

By 1966, Utzon had resigned and the building had been under construction for seven years, the podium and outer shells were complete and the stage machinery installed. Utzon expected to complete the project within 18 months at a total cost of $22m. A new panel under the direction of the Minister for Public Works then took control of the project.

It was a further seven years before they completed the task at an estimated final cost of $102m (about ten times the original estimate).

What can we learn from this example?

1. The account of building the Sydney Opera House illustrates the danger of uncontrolled concurrency – starting a project without experience in, or knowledge of, the processes to be used and before essential building methods and techniques had been resolved. This, in itself, would have made systematic planning almost impossible. So the Government of New South Wales embarked on this largely unplanned and unstructured project that relied on new and untried methods to be developed as the project took shape.
2. Without Utzon's vision the project would have been doomed to failure but his perseverance and professional brilliance saw it through most of the crucial stages, despite incompatibility with the engineers.
3. The project was aimed at artistic and environmental merit. As with the building of a great cathedral, concept, design and quality were perceived to be more important than time and cost.

Few contemporary projects could be put together or survive in that way. In this case, to commence construction before developing essential techniques and processes may be thought to have been foolhardy in the extreme. Any attempts to reach a realistic estimate of design and production costs must have been well nigh impossible.

4. The project was greatly affected by political considerations. Public opinion and administrative meddling appear to have interfered with progress, carrying the original concept through to its final stages and its eventual success, and led to an enormous escalation in completion costs.

5. The Sydney Opera House project also offers a good example of the relationship between the essentials of quality, time and cost. Balancing the needs of these three considerations are concerns that feature in any project plan and, during implementation, continue to be of major concern to project managers.

9.2 THE PLANNING HIERARCHY

The planning hierarchy is based on mission objectives and begins at strategic levels, proceeds to tactics and then to the grass roots level of operations and activities (Figure 9.1).

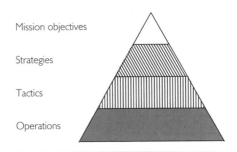

Mission objectives

Strategies

Tactics

Operations

Figure 9.1 The planning hierarchy

9.3 THE LOGICAL FRAMEWORK

A logical framework (logframe or project frame) is a conceptual and analytical tool for sector analysis, project planning and project management, favoured by many international aid agencies and similar project organizations. It usually makes use of a 16-box matrix to describe and summarize the major elements of a project and attempts to integrate planning concepts after data gathering and analysis has taken place, that is, after a feasibility study (Saldanha and Whittle, 1998).

Although the most common form of logical framework has 16 cells, there are several alternative formats. A publication of USAID (1980) showed eight variations of the system formed by the use of extra columns for quantification and verification of assumptions, targets and intermediate outputs. Detail of activities is rightly considered an important ingredient of the logical framework and a Food and Agriculture Organization (FAO) example used a 20-box system formed by the inclusion of an additional row of boxes in which activities are listed between 'inputs' and 'outputs'.

The Asian Development Bank (ADB), as a basis for programme or project design, uses a six-step process of development leading to the development of a logical framework.

The six-step process is:

Step 1 – Sector performance assessment
Step 2 – Identification of sector problems and opportunities
Step 3 – Cause and effect analysis of problems/opportunities
Step 4 – Objectives tree
Step 5 – Alternatives analysis
Step 6 – Project design using the logical framework

Having identified and analysed the cause and effect of problems and opportunities (steps 1 to 3), the process results in an 'objectives tree' which helps to identify alternative actions and their respective impacts which are then subjected to alternative analysis. A graphic example of these procedures is illustrated in Figure 9.2.

The example in Figure 9.3 shows that some organizations have rather different perceptions of planning terminology, but the principle illustrated by the framework is clear. The planning chain is based on a need disclosed in a cause and effect analysis (Step 3), building expectations of results based on a series of 'inputs' designed to result in the achievement of immediate objectives or 'purposes'. These 'purposes' contribute to the longer-term objectives of the project.

The sequence in these cases is, therefore:

INPUTS – OUTPUTS – PURPOSES – GOALS

Progress is monitored at each stage by the attainment of performance and measured against pre-determined 'yardsticks' in the form of 'verifiable performance targets' which are tangible or quantifiable measures of achievement. The 'monitoring mechanisms' are the sources of data used to monitor performance at each level.

Logical framework concepts can be usefully applied in conjunction with other planning routines, for example to record verifiable indicators of progress, 'yardsticks' against which progress may be measured and key assumptions on which planning logic is based. An excerpt from a simple logical framework structure is shown in Figure 9.4.

9.4 PLANNING SEMANTICS

A word of warning! A frequent cause of confusion and misunderstanding is brought about by different interpretations of simple planning terms. In traditional planning, the terms 'strategic' or 'mission objectives' usually describe the ultimate desired result and 'goal' is a term commonly used to describe the desired outcome of a tactical, operational or activity plan.

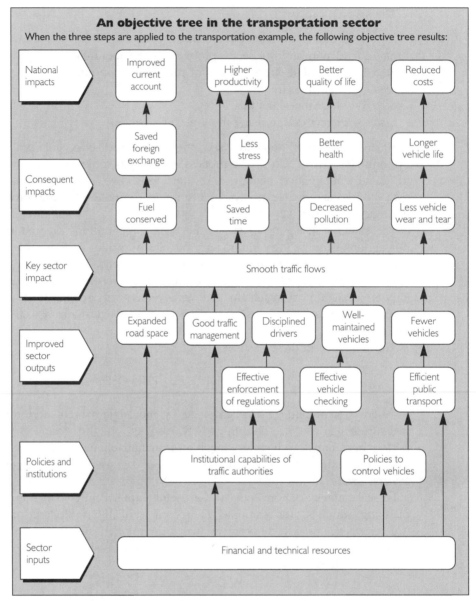

Figure 9.2 The ADB project design process.
Reproduced by permission of the Asian Development Bank

9.5 TRADITIONAL METHODS OF PROJECT PLANNING

Specialized techniques have been developed for certain kinds of repetitive projects but most projects of today are planned with the use of traditional methods. The traditional method calls for:

Design summary	Performance targets	Monitoring mechanisms	Assumptions and risks
Goals (long-term objectives)			
Purpose (immediate objectives)			
Outputs			
Inputs			

Figure 9.3 Basis of the logical framework

- clear definition of scope and mission objectives;
- consideration of activities, sequence and activity objectives;
- preparation of an outline master plan;
- preparation of activity plans;
- preparation of finance and resource plans;
- finalization of master and other plans;
- communication, reporting plans or decisions and review.

Using this method, throughout the hierarchy, plans are adjusted and re-adjusted with the thinking process. Decisions on tactics, method and detail provide further information to progressively modify estimates of cost and time. Computer programs are now extensively used to assist with the task of activity scheduling, resource listing, and estimating cost. The resultant schedules and timetables are integrated into the project plan and provide basic tools for control and review.

The complexity of modern project work has led to refinement and use of a variety of specialized and sophisticated techniques, many of which are effectively incorporated into traditional planning methods.

9.6 COMPUTER ASSISTED PLANNING

The development of user-friendly software has led to widespread use of computers to assist in the mechanics and structuring of project plans, and outlining activities as a series of tasks. The main value of computer assistance is at tactical and operational levels where it can be centred on design, processes, tasks and activities. Thus, within the limits of the software used, the computer can speed the work of integrated planning, scheduling, costing, control and revision. It will

Narrative summary	Verifiable indicators	Means of verification	Major assumptions
Sector goal: To materially assist the PNG Government in providing and operating essential airways and airport facilities and carrying out its responsibilities under the Air Navigation Act and Regulations, for the safe and efficient development of civil aviation throughout Papua New Guinea.	– Accuracy and reliability of air navigation aids. – Effective air traffic services for aircraft movements. – Adequacy and safety of air services. – Compliance with ICAO standards. – Adequacy of airport facilities. – Growth rate of aviation industry.	– Flight checking, outage time statistics. – Delays in aircraft movements. – Feedback from aviation industry. – Public and industry opinion. – Accident and incident statistics. – Comparison with ICAO standards. – Passenger surveys. – Feedback from Air Service Operators. – Aviation statistics.	– That adequate standards of technical, operational and managerial competence can be developed and sustained to enable PMG DCACT to meet national and international criteria in a complex and changing environment. – That essential airways facilities can be supplied and adequately maintained. – That there will be no DCAT organizational changes to the detriment of the Civil Aviation Sector.
Project purpose To enable DCAT to provide essential equipment, specialist and managerial competence for: (a) Efficient policy making and effective regulatory control over aviation industry.	– Quality and adequacy of policy decisions. satisfactory regulatory control.	– Annual review by Project Co-ordination Committee. – Reports from Aviation industry. – Monitoring breaches of Air Navigation Act and Regulations.	– That rapid localization can be achieved with the aid of systematic monitoring of individual performance standards, and effective measures to accelerate specialist training and management development.
(b) The provision and operation of adequate ground facilities to meet the needs of Civil Aviation in PNG.	– Provision of navigation aids and other airways facilities as scheduled. Performance standards of airways facilities.	– Annual review by PCC of completed work compared with scheduled targets. – Flight checking, comparison of outage time with ICAO standards.	

Figure 9.4 **Logical framework structure (excerpt)**

produce tables, charts, precedence networks, calendars and reports, but there is an important consequence. Inexperienced project planners sometimes place too much reliance on the software and centre on its ready-made format, method, detail and process, irrespective of suitability and the extent to which it meets project needs.

Larger issues such as objectives, strategies and tactics must always be paramount and care must be taken to ensure that software frameworks and processes do not dominate or inhibit logical and effective planning.

9.7 SPECIAL TECHNOLOGIES

Complex methodology and modelling programmes have been developed for a variety of needs, such as mineral exploration, oil, petrochemical plants, aerospace industry, and so on.

Cost, time and resources methodology (CTR) was successfully used in a number of North Sea oil projects. The method included the involvement of main project operatives and contractors and provided schedules of the details and extent of their individual responsibilities.

A structured planning methodology known as PRINCE (projects in a controlled environment) is used in the UK by government and private sectors for information technology projects.

The methodology covers all project activity from project board to the final control and audit.

9.8 SCOPE

Project scope is described as 'The sum of the products (deliverables) and services to be provided as a project' (PMI). This implies a clear decision on essential outputs, that is, the extent to which the project will provide 'needs and wants' and which desirable but non-essential deliverables can be included or omitted, leading to clear mission objectives, success criteria, quality cost and duration.

9.9 MISSION OBJECTIVE AND PROJECT MASTER PLANS

The cornerstone of project planning is the mission objective. It sets out in simple terms the purpose of the project and what it is to achieve. All activity is geared to achieving this main objective.

The project master plan will show, in outline, what is to be done to achieve the mission objective. It may include detail on how key activities are to be conducted, when they are to be done, and possibly, who will do them. Details of the plan are usually explained in a project document (the project 'bible') that will also describe subsidiary objectives and detailed plans for each contributory activity and the provision of resources essential to project completion. In this way, the planner builds up a set of closely linked plans leaving no gaps or omissions to prejudice effective management and control (Figures 9.5 and 9.6).

Mission objective .... Master plan ———— (Broad outline)

—— Activity objectives .... Activity plans ———— (More detailed planning)

—————— Resource plans and budgets

Figure 9.5 Sequence of project objectives and planning

9.10 FORMULATING OBJECTIVES THAT WORK

All planning is based on objectives. These must be unambiguous, clearly defined, known and fully understood by everyone concerned with the project, because every project plan and activity will be focused on them. Each objective must be much more than a 'pious hope' or a statement of general intent, if it is to direct activity accurately to the required outcome.

'Woolly' objectives, couched in vague terms like 'satisfactory', 'reasonable' or 'adequate', can be variously interpreted and are an anathema to effective planning and management control.

An adequately defined objective will include (not necessarily in this order):

1 a subject – for example, removal of landmines;
2 a start point (situation at commencement);
3 a target outcome (situation on project completion);
4 a quality result (standards and/or essential ingredients of the outcome);
5 a start date/time;
6 a firm date for completion.

When deciding on the wording of an objective, it is important to focus on the purpose or end result rather than on the method by which it will be achieved.

Here are a few examples:

Mission objective examples

Subject	Mission objective – Bahadabad Airport Project
Situation at commencement	Temporary airport terminal facilities in use as at 30 June 2000 for international and domestic passengers are to be replaced.
Target	The mission objective is to construct, equip and commission an International Airport Terminal Complex for international and domestic passenger and freight traffic.

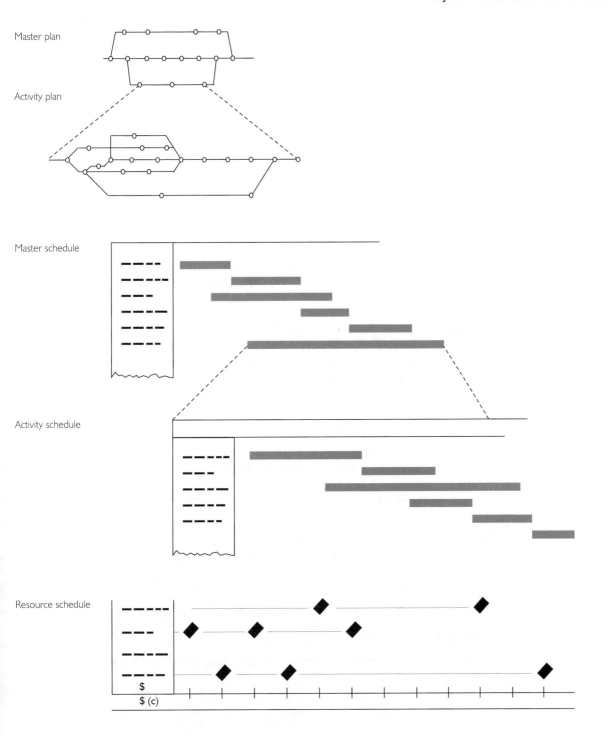

Figure 9.6 Planning diagrams for master, activity and resource planning

Project commencement	Work on the project will commence on 1 July 2000.
Completion date	The project is to be completed and the new airport terminal operational on or before 30 June 2002.
Quality standards and so on	The terminal building, passenger facilitation, aircraft handling and parking facilities are to reflect the best international standards in terms of efficiency and quality as described in ICAO recommendation Noxx and the technical specification at Annex A. Total costs in accordance with the project budget detailed at Annex B are not to exceed (USD) $400 000 000.

Or, expressed in narrative form:

To replace temporary airport facilities in use on 1 July 2000 with a new and fully operational international terminal conforming to ICAO and the attached specifications, by 30 June 2002: cost not to exceed (USD) $400,000,000.

The mission objective in the next example had to be revised, having been wrongly focused on the requirement to set up a training course. Although training is the method by which the objective will be reached, the real objective is the more far-reaching one of health improvement.

Subject	Nutrition Improvement Project – Jampur
Situation	As at 30 September 1998, 76 per cent of the adult population of Jampur suffers from xxxx mineral deficiency. Given community training, the diet of the inhabitants could be changed to overcome mineral deficiency using locally available products. At this time there are no indigenous health workers.
Target	The mission objective of this project is to design and conduct specialized training for 50 health workers, who will advise the population, and lead the conduct of a training programme to secure a sustainable improvement in health standards.
Start date	The project will commence on or before 1 November 1999.
Completion date	The project must be completed by 1 May 2000.
Quality standards and special requirements	1. Instruction to be validated after completion of first training course. 2. Observed feedback to show dietary improvement of at least 50 per cent of inhabitants in each project area by May 2001 when a follow-up review will be conducted. 3. Finance ceiling (USD)$ 400 000.

In narrative form:

To produce a sustainable improvement in the health of Jampur residents through nutritional diet by establishing a cadre of 50 trained health advisers. Budget funding cannot exceed (USD) $400 000. Validation and evaluation will be based on improvement from commencement on 1 November 1999 and completion of the project on 1 May 2000 and a follow-up review in May 2001.

Or an objective for a very simple project:

Subject	Relocation of London office
Start point	Head Office will be vacated on 27 October 1999. Headquarters office will be moved to Brandon House, 167 High Road, Brixton.
Target	The purpose of the project is to ensure a smooth move of personnel, office equipment and documents to the new location within the time limit, without disruption to day-to-day activity.
Start time	The move will begin at 18.00 hrs (6 p.m.) Friday 27 October 1999
Completion time	The move is to be completed in all respects by 08.00 (8 a.m.) 30 October 1999.
Quality	All furniture and office equipment to be damage free and positioned in accordance with the plan agreed by department heads. All internal and external communication systems to be tested and working.

Or:

Between 18.00 hrs 27 October and 08.00 hrs 30 October 1999, to relocate Head Office, all facilities and functions to new premises at Brandon House, 167 High Road, Brixton without disruption to operational routine or equipment damage.

9.11 DEVELOPING THE MASTER PLAN

Planning usually begins with a reappraisal of mission objectives and consideration of the activities that must be carried out to complete the project. Thereafter, it will usually take the form of a series of basic steps:

1. *List.*   List project activities and their duration.
2. *Relate.*   Consider which activities are interdependent.
3. *Consider.*   Rearrange the activities list in chronological order showing those activities that may not begin until completion (or partial completion of an earlier one).

4. *Review.*   Discuss and obtain best information on alternative methods where applicable.

5. *Chart.*   Map out progress, chart the main activities and events; consider and formulate (or reformulate) objectives for key activities.

6. *Describe.*   Support the activity and event chart with written notes where necessary.

7. *Pace.*   Confirm estimates of activity duration and check total duration against project completion dates.

8. *Cost.*   Check initial estimates of resource costs and prepare a rough cash-flow prediction.

9. *Consider.*   If activity times or costs appear excessive at this stage, consider alternative methods, different permutations of activity and event sequences, bearing in mind the relationship between cost, quality and time.

10. *Review.*   Check and recheck the plan for validity and to ensure that no important steps have been omitted.

9.12   PROJECT PLANNING LEVELS

Responsibility for planning at each level is dictated by project scale and the nature of the external organization but whatever the circumstances, a planning hierarchy (however simple) will emerge to deal with each planning level (Figure 9.7).

Project board	Master resource plan	Master activity plan	Initial, end, mid-stage assessments
Project manager	Stage resource plan	Stage activity plan	Regular team meetings
Team leader	Detailed resource plans	Detailed activity plans	Regular team meetings and daily reports

Figure 9.7 Table of planning levels

9.13   ACTIVITY AND RESOURCE PLANS

More detailed than the project master plan, activity and resource plans show the order and methods by which the main activities will be tackled and their resources provided.

Drawn against the background of project objectives and master plans, they are likely to be based on one or more objectives for the activity in question and the provision of project resources.

Activity plans

Not every activity will require a separate plan. However, plans for the complex or difficult activities will include:

- activity description;
- activity objective(s);
- methods and processes to be used;
- sequence and timing of tasks;
- resources (for inclusion in the project budgets and resource plans);
- list of operations, sequence, workflow and coordination;
- limitations on time for completion of the activity and time scale;
- quality standards and requirements;
- control, monitoring and progress reporting;
- links to the resource plan showing provisioning arrangements.

Resource plans

Resource plans form a blueprint for provisioning the project. Resources needed for project administration and to complete each activity are specified, costed and brought into a consolidated list showing both the detail of each requirement and the total resource requirement.

Planning will consider every anticipated project resource, but only the main resources will require a separate plan.

The finance plan

Finance is a resource that features in every project and a project of any size will need a formal plan for it. This will usually cover:

- limits of available finance;
- source and method of securing finance;
- cost of finance;
- project budget;
- cash flow predictions covering the project;
- procedures for controlling project costs;
- procedures for authorization of payments and acquisition of funds;
- accounting procedures.

Machinery and equipment plan

Dealing with major items, this will include:

- machinery and equipment needs;
- specifications and delivery dates;
- costings;
- method of acquisition, for example loan, purchase, lease and so on, and source of supply;

- maintenance service and repairs;
- operator and service training requirements (if any);
- power or fuel needs associated with major equipments;
- disposal of machines and equipment on completion of the activity.

The manpower plan

People and their skills are the main resource of labour-intensive and specialist advisory projects and a major contributor to all others. The manpower plan may contain:

- human resource needs by categories, skills and abilities;
- when and for how long each number and category will be required;
- method of acquisition – casual employment, contract, subcontract, term employment;
- method of recruitment – availability register, international advertising, professional society, consultant, employment agency, local advertising;
- budgeted cost (salary, wages, budgeted overtime, bonus, allowances, incentive payments, accommodation, messing, insurance, gratuities, travel, subsistence, and so on);
- job and recruitment specifications for key managers and specialist members of the project team;
- employment policies and selection methods, for example screening processes, employment of local people, equal opportunity;
- special selection procedures;
- occupational health, safety and welfare provisions.

Materials and merchandise plans

Plans for the provision of materials or purchased goods may include:

- purchasing, tendering and contract policies and timeframes;
- description, quantity and quality specifications;
- transportation arrangements for bulk supplies;
- penalty clauses for late delivery.

Chapter 5 deals with project resources and Chapter 10 provides detail on the tools of project planning and control.

9.14 PLANNING FOR BOT PROJECTS

Build, operate and transfer (BOT) arrangements are now favoured and increasingly used by governments as a means of establishing privatized or commercialized infrastructure facilities.

Advantages of the BOT system lie in the fact that responsibility for initial financing, implementation and much of the risk is accepted by the contractor or consortium responsible for the contract. Examples of BOT projects range from a light rail transit system in the Philippines or the Skye Bridge Crossing in the UK, to a tunnel in Hong Kong or provision of toll roads in NSW, Australia.

Having considered the concept, feasibility, overall objectives and evaluation criteria are agreed by the government department or other sponsor who, after pre-qualification procedures, may issue a request for proposals (RFP).

Planning for BOT projects is similar to that of any other project except that in the early stages, the sponsor, having decided on scope and overall project objectives, is able to solicit proposals from BOT contractors or consortia who, if appointed, will normally become responsible for detailed estimating and activity planning. Planning stages and responsibility are shown in Figure 9.8.

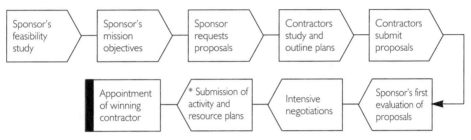

* Contractors and consortia normally prepare plans and schedules for their own use but conditions of contract should include scrutiny and approval of plans.

Figure 9.8 BOT planning stages and responsibilities

9.15 PLANS BY CONTRACT CONTRIBUTORS

When a project owner employs one or more major contractors to manage, conduct or carry out large or complex project segments, the contractors will prepare their own plans.

One should never take for granted the planning capability of even large contractors. Experience shows that contractors' planning routines, and the quality and coverage of their plans, vary a good deal between firms.

Whatever the contractors' standing and credibility, master plans should be prepared by the project manager (in outline at the very least) as a yardstick to verify the adequacy of those produced by the contractor, whose activity plans should be also be checked, approved and regularly updated by the owner's project manager.

A contractor's planning and reporting arrangements will form an important consideration in evaluation of tenders and proposals. Access to contractors' plans and regular progress reporting in an approved form should be a condition of contract.

In their proposals, many major contractors offer details of their planning processes and reporting format as an indication of best practice.

REVIEW AND DISCUSSION QUESTIONS

1. What are the essentials of an effective project objective?
2. What are the basic steps in developing a project master plan?
3. Give three examples of project mission objectives, and test them for effectiveness and ambiguity.
4. Discuss the objectives of a project of your knowledge or experience; consider whether they fall short of essential criteria and if so, how they might be better expressed.
5. List at least six items that you might expect to cover in a resource plan.
6. Explain how the finance plan evolves from consideration of activity and resource needs.
7. What are the advantages of computer assistance in planning and how might over-reliance on software packages inhibit good project planning?
8. Explain the need to check the plans and reporting procedures of a major project contractor and what criteria might be appropriate for their evaluation.
9. Discuss circumstances in which a BOT agreement might be the best way of meeting project needs.

10 THE TOOLS OF PLANNING AND CONTROL

10.1 INTEGRATING THE PROCESS

Planning is essentially a systematic process involving the integration of a variety of activities, resources and spans of time.

In project work, informal planning starts in the initial stages of concept development and extends on a more systematic and progressively accurate basis through to completion. The bulk of detailed planning activity is done before implementation but it does not stop there, for variances, fresh opportunities and new situations constantly call for planning revision.

The nature of project activity makes for the close integration of planning, communication and control of process and their methodology.

The plan is the basis of action, control and the start point for remedial action when circumstances demand, so it is important to employ user-friendly systems that lend themselves readily to these three purposes.

Project planners have at their disposal a useful range of tools. Many facilitate planning, subsequent control and communication. Simple techniques are a valuable aid to establishing:

- logic;
- duration of activity;
- sequence of events;
- coordination of effort;
- communication;
- progress monitoring;
- control and assessment;
- decision making;
- risk analysis and assessment.

These tools include:

1. sequence tables;
2. duration calculations;
3. flow process charts and diagrams:
    - Arrow diagrams
    - Critical path charts (PERT diagrams)
    - Precedence diagrams
    - Gantt and other forms of 'bar' charts;
4. multiple activity charts;
5. decision trees.

10.2 SEQUENCE TABLES

As we think through the events and activities that will be required to complete a project it becomes obvious that some rely on, and cannot start before, the completion of others.

In the construction of a building, for example, foundations cannot be laid until the ground has been cleared, walls cannot be built until the foundations are complete and so on. So the plan of any project activity will be based, not only on how things will be done, but when they may be done; that is, the order in which they must take place.

Deciding the sequence of operations is a matter of simple logic. However, where specialized activities are involved, a clear understanding of each process and the methods to be employed is essential if planning errors are to be avoided.

Projects involving high technology such as aircraft construction, the manufacture of electronic equipment, construction of a nuclear reactor, or building a tunnel beneath the English Channel may offer a permutation of alternative methods and sequences for their activities. Discussion, consultation and specialist guidance would obviously be fundamental to the preparation of a sequence list for their activities. To minimize likelihood of error, the list should be verified and confirmed by project team leaders and the specialists in charge of each key activity before it is finalized.

Even when a master list has been drawn up on the basis of historical data and specialist advice, it is advisable to allow time to confirm the sequence and duration of each activity because the process of 'thinking through' methods and processes, possible delays and problems may bring to light factors unknown or overlooked in drafting the first schedules.

The format of a sequence list should be simple. Requirements are shown in Figure 10.1.

Sequence number	Activity number	Activity description	Depends on (activity no.)	Earliest start (day)	Latest start (day)	Duration (days)	Latest finish (day)
1	1	Prepare ground	0	1	1	6	7
2	2	Dig foundation	1	7	9	9	18
3	8	Pour concrete	2	16	20	2	22
4	10	Build foundation walls	8	18	22	12	34

Figure 10.1 Activity sequence list – example of headings

10.3 ESTIMATING THE DURATION OF AN ACTIVITY

This aspect of programme logic is heavily dependent on good judgement. An expert with valid experience of similar work and a good grasp of project conditions should be able to make an informed guess as to how long each operation or activity will take to complete. In many operations, data on the recorded completion times of similar operations will be available as a useful yardstick of the duration of identical tasks. This results in a range of expected task timings, but when no historical data is available, informed estimates of time have to be made. A simple mathematical model can be used to estimate the probable duration of an activity.

Three time estimates are required to calculate the duration of an activity. They are:

to = the shortest or most optimistic duration

tm = the most likely duration

tp = the longest or most pessimistic duration

The calculation assumes that errors will fall within a normal distribution curve to produce:

te = the calculated estimate of time

The calculation is:

$$te = \frac{to + 4tm + tp}{6}$$

Unfavourable experience by some project sponsors suggests that time estimates have been over-optimistic.

An amended formula can be reached by adjusting the distribution curve to achieve a more conservative approach to the estimating process:

$$te = \frac{to + 3tm + 2tp}{6}$$

Although it is seldom possible to provide an exact estimate of the time required to complete each activity, in practice, an experienced planner will reach a close approximation for at least 80 per cent of tasks, and in many cases, small errors of time will be compensatory, requiring minimal planning adjustments.

10.4 FLOW PROCESS CHARTS

One of the most commonly used planning tools is the process or 'flow' chart. This shows the duration of each activity and logical activity sequences, concurrent activities and the point in the sequence when the activity may begin.

10.5 THE ARROW DIAGRAM

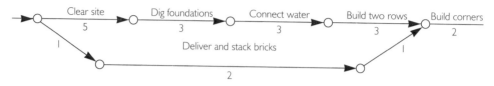

Figure 10.2 Simple arrow diagram

An arrow diagram consists of activities and events. Working from left to right each arrow (or line) denotes an activity, and each circle an event. Activities are arranged in logical sequence; for example, in Figure 10.2, it is necessary to clear the site before foundations can be dug. The nature of each activity may be written above its arrow, its duration below. The diagram is not drawn to scale and the length of an activity line (or arrow) bears no relation to the duration of its activity. Dotted lines on the chart (dummy activities) show points where two or more activities in different streams must be concluded before the next activity in one of the streams can begin. An event occurs when one activity is completed and before the start of another.

Events are usually identified by the allocation of a number related to an 'event and activity list'.

Symbols on these diagrams are known as 'nodes'.

10.6 THE CRITICAL PATH (PERT) CHART

A development of the simple arrow diagram, charts based on critical path methods (CPM) or programme evaluation and review techniques (PERT) include information not only on the duration of each activity, but the earliest and latest times at which it may take place. In diagrams for simple tasks (those without many activities), earliest and latest start times are often shown above the preceding event 'node'. In some charts, these times are written in a space on the node itself. This information is invaluable, not only as a reminder for timing purposes of when to start or finish an activity so that the plan can be completed in the allotted time, but to show which activities are 'critical', that is, those that must be completed exactly within their allotted time frames and cannot be changed without extending the project completion date.

The use of CPM and PERT, once confined to defence, engineering and construction industries, are now not only basic to the planning needs of most projects; they are also useful in analysis, performance evaluation and proof of entitlement in cases of liability claim (Baki, 1998).

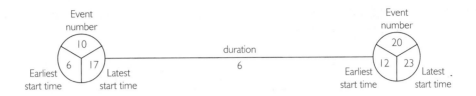

Or in another style:

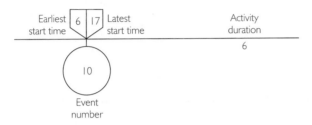

Notes:
1. Event numbers are allocated after the diagram has been drawn.
2. Event numbers only serve to identify the event or point in the sequence.
3. Gaps in numbering permit the insertion of additional activities that may later come to mind.
4. Event numbers in the above example have been set at intervals of 10 to permit identification of activities on a subsidiary (activity) plan which may utilize the intervening numbers.

Figure 10.3 Information nodes

10.6.1 Establishing earliest and latest start times for each activity

Having completed the diagram and verified the length of time required to complete each activity, it is a simple matter to establish the earliest point at which each could begin (EET). Start points can be measured in hours/days/weeks and so on from commencement of the project or, if the project start date has been fixed, they can be given an actual date.

10.6.2 Recording earliest event times

Enter day 1 (or the actual date) as the earliest event time (EET) for the first event and its next activity(s). Follow each sequence of activities, adding the duration of each to produce the EET for entry in each following event node (Figure 10.4).

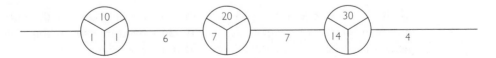

Figure 10.4 Earliest event times (EETs)

Where two or more activities converge on a node, note the total time but do not enter it on the diagram until you have calculated the EETs for all the other paths.

The EET for this event will be the highest number obtained from the longest sequence. (See Figure 10.5.)

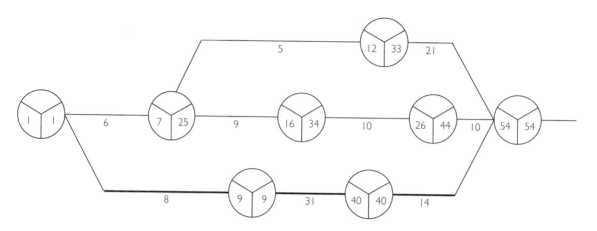

Figure 10.5 Network showing critical path

Reaching the end of the diagram, the highest EET will denote the duration of the project and as this matches the end of the project, it will also be the latest time (LET) for that event.

10.6.3 Latest event times and the critical path

To calculate latest event times (LETs), we adopt the reverse procedure from that used for EETs. In this case, beginning with the last event (whose LET will be the same as the EET), we move back along the activity lines of the diagram, deducting the activity duration from the previous LET, that is, that at the end of the activity.

Where paths converge on the backward track, calculate the LET for each but enter the lowest figure.

10.6.4 Critical activities and the critical path

Where the time required to complete an activity is the same as the difference in time between its two events, the activity must be completed within that time as there is no 'Float' or time flexibility for that activity (Figure 10.6).

The critical path is the route of longest duration through the network. It is often emphasised by tracing on the diagram in red or being marked with heavy lines.

Without a change in the duration of one or more activity on the critical path, the project cannot be shortened.

The EET and LET on the critical path cannot be altered.

10.7 FLOAT (NON-CRITICAL ACTIVITIES)

Non-critical activities, that is, those with different EETs and LETs not on the critical path, may, in times of difficulty, be lengthened or moved within the limits of their start and end events. The difference, or 'slack time', between the EET and LET is known as 'Float'. Float may be calculated for a single activity or the cumulative float calculated for a sequence of activities.

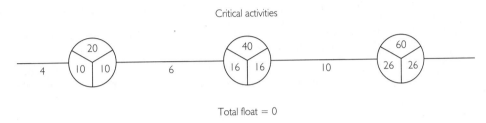

Total float = 0

Figure 10.6 **Zero float between activities on the critical path**

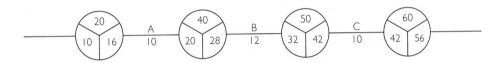

Total float, sequence A B C = 14

Activity A		*Activity B*		*Activity C*		*Sequence A, B and C*	
LET finish event	=28	LET finish event	=42	LET finish event	=56	LET finish event	= 56
EET start event	=10	EET start event	=20	EET start event	=32	EET start event	− 10
Time span	− 18	Time span	− 22	Time span	− 24	Time span	− 46
Less duration A	− 10	Less duration B	− 12	Less duration C	− 10	Less duration A+B+C	− 32
Float	= 8	Float	=10	Float	=14	Sequence float	− 14

Figure 10.7 **Float sequence**

From examination of the float sequence shown in Figure 10.7 it will be seen that there are several types of float:

Independent float – the leeway that sometimes occurs when an activity is conducted between its latest event time and the earliest event time of its successor.

Free float – the leeway between two events. Note: If float is calculated from the earliest event times of each event the figure may differ from a calculation using both of the latest event times.

Total float – the maximum free time between two events when they are conducted as far apart as possible.

Sequence float – the total float in a sequence of events.

10.8 THE USE OF FLOAT

Float is an important planning consideration.

- It enables the planner to level or 'smooth' resource needs.
- It enables the planner to see how far the provision of resources may be deferred to minimize cost and smooth cash flow.
- In project implementation, it helps the manager see which activities may be rescheduled to make up lost time without prejudice to the final completion date.

Postponing resources deliveries may save money, but the resulting lack of freedom to adjust timings on the spot effectively increases project risk by limiting the manager's freedom to take corrective action and make up lost time. It may also leave the project more vulnerable to late delivery or materials shortage.

10.9 CRASHING

Crashing is the process of reducing the critical path, usually by increasing finance and labour or machinery resources, that is, a trade-off between cost and time. Time can sometimes be reduced at the expense of quality or project objectives but such measures would usually necessitate project revision.

An example of the cost of crashing is shown in Chapter 3.

10.10 PRECEDENCE DIAGRAMS

Precedence diagrams are another form of flow process chart. They describe the same sequence and logic as the line and arrow diagrams already described but they are drawn differently. A precedence diagram can also be used to show the critical path.

In an arrow or line chart, the activity is indicated by means of a line, and its start and conclusion are marked by circles known as events. The precedence diagram is drawn to show each activity in the form of a block describing:

1. the activity number;
2. activity description;
3. activity duration;
4. earliest and latest start time;
5. earliest and latest finishing time;
6. total float;
7. (sometimes) resources needed.

Activity sequences and relationships are shown by lines or arrows.

In these networks, arrows leading to the left edge of the activity block indicate a route to the start of the activity indicated. Those leading to the right end of the block indicate a route to the end of that activity. See Figure 10.8.

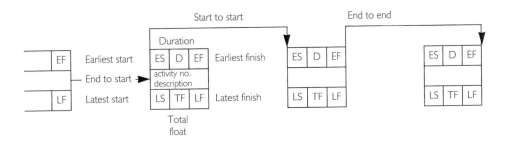

Figure 10.8 Precedence diagrams

Critical activities, earliest and latest start times are worked out in the same way as with an arrow diagram, beginning with earliest and latest start times and float for an activity is calculated by deducting its earliest finishing time from the latest finishing time

10.11 GANTT CHARTS

Gantt charts constitute a valuable aid, not only to planning and communication but also to progress control, since they are easily understood, showing not only the sequence of activities, but when each is scheduled to take place. When a commencement date has been fixed, charts are usually arranged like a calendar to show exactly what should happen and when. After the event, the chart is updated to show progress on any given date. Activities can be linked to show interdependencies and give an indication of float. Although the chart shows sequence, dates and a picture of each activity or task required to achieve project objective(s) it does not lend itself readily to the manipulation of complex tasks and activity relationships or decisions on float.

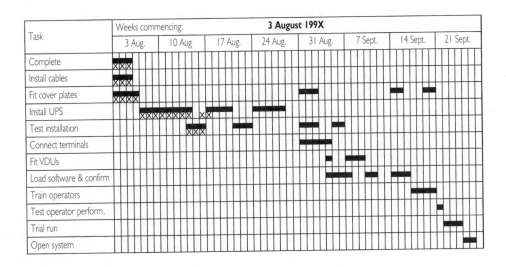

Figure 10.9
Gantt chart
example

The Gantt chart does not replace the arrow or precedence diagram, but it does present a very easily understood picture of task programming.

Figure 10.9 shows a simple Gantt chart in which tasks scheduled to the month of August have been completed on time. Part of another task has been started early and is in progress.

Interdependencies can be indicated by connecting appropriate blocks with a dotted or coloured line.

Figure 10.10 shows a linked Gantt chart.

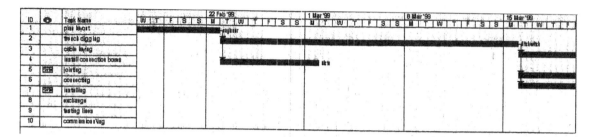

Figure 10.10 Linked Gantt chart (Microsoft Project)

10.12 THE HISTOGRAM

This type of bar chart needs no introduction (Figure 10.11). Histograms offer an easily understood means of graphic illustration for contrasting quantities, peaks, troughs, spans of time and so on.

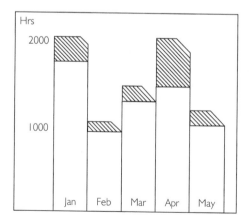

Figure 10.11
The histogram. (Optic cable installation – labour and overtime)

10.13 THE MULTIPLE ACTIVITY CHART

The multiple activity chart is used to assist in optimizing the use of resources such as staff and equipment. Having decided the best combination of activities, the chart becomes a useful aid to communication, showing what is to be done by the respective items at each point in time (Figure 10.12).

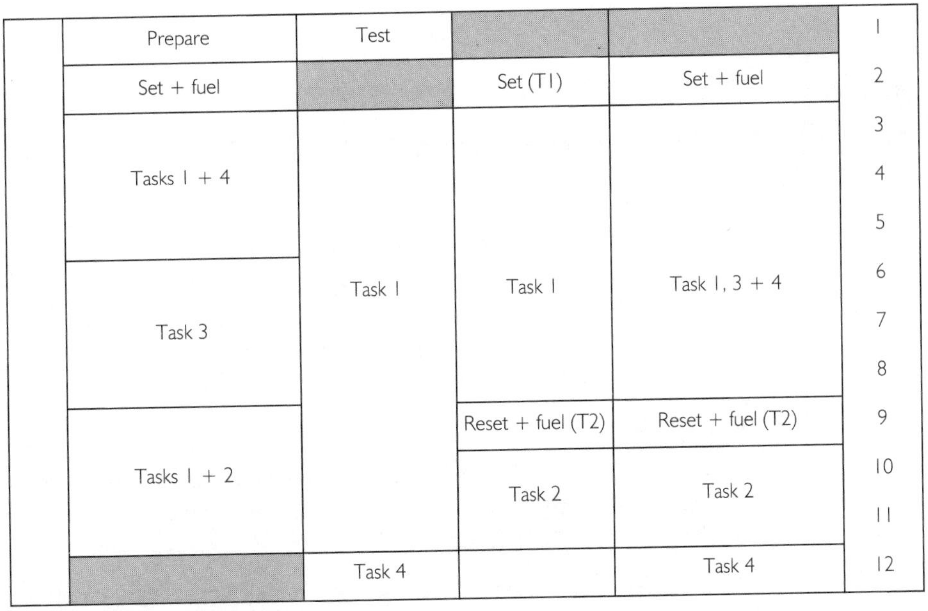

Prepare	Test			1
Set + fuel		Set (T1)	Set + fuel	2
Tasks 1 + 4	Task 1	Task 1	Task 1, 3 + 4	3
				4
				5
Task 3				6
				7
				8
Tasks 1 + 2		Reset + fuel (T2)	Reset + fuel (T2)	9
		Task 2	Task 2	10
				11
	Task 4		Task 4	12

Figure 10.12 Multiple activity chart

10.14 DECISION TREES

The decision tree provides a simple method of systematizing a range of assorted facts, probabilities and chances, the effects of which might otherwise be difficult to manipulate and compare. They can be used in a variety of situations from risk assessment or comparison of alternative propositions to discussion of the results of a brainstorming session. In combination with a bank of established data or computer modelling techniques, sophisticated forms provide a useful tool for analysis. In simple form, the decision tree can bring a measure of logic to the choice of alternative courses of action. The method allows for a mixture of known fact, probability and assessment. For this reason, the quality of any resultant decision will be directly influenced by:

- the accuracy of factual information;
- the quality of individual judgements and assessments;
- probability factors;
- the attitude of the decision maker to risk taking.

Decision trees make use of the following symbols or 'nodes':

☐ Decision

◯ Chance

⬚ Toll   (A cost involved in taking a particular course)

THE PARCEL DELIVERY SERVICE PROJECT – A SIMPLE DECISION TREE

The dilemma

The Ling, Keel Publishing Company have registered a subsidiary company to provide a new fast courier service which will make daytime use of a fleet of vehicles purchased for night delivery of their local tabloid newspaper, 'The Daily Keel'. Marketing Director Harold Glombeck now has to make a final decision on whether or not to launch the new service

The potential

If he decides not to launch the service there will be no cost to the company but if he embarks on the venture and it turns out to be a total failure the company stands to lose about $100 000.

On the other hand, Glombeck is aware that similar operations in other cities enjoy an annual return showing a nett gain in the neighbourhood of $80 000.

Better still, if the service enjoys particular success, the nett return could be as much as $160 000.

The market survey

Glombeck can buy assistance in reaching a decision. At a cost of $6000 he could arrange for a reliable firm of marketing consultants to conduct a market survey. Of course, this would not be infallible but it would provide an indication of whether market conditions are favourable or otherwise.

The decision tree

Glombeck hopes that a decision tree will help him reach the best conclusion. It will enable him to clarify his thinking and allocate probabilities, likely consequences and 'payoffs' at each stage of the process. The first question is to decide on whether he should commission a market survey, so taking a piece of paper, he records the 'start point' and draws lines to map out alternative routes.

▶

In this case, the upper line shows the 'No Survey' path, the lower line denotes the route that will be taken if a survey is carried out.

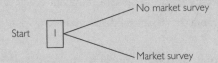

The first decision

If Glombeck decides not to incur the expense of a survey, he must still decide whether or not to introduce the service. If he takes no further action and the proposition stops at that stage there will be no cost and no possibility of profit.

If, on the other hand, he decides to introduce the service without a survey, he could consider three typical scenarios:

1. The service will be very successful.
2. The service will be successful.
3. The service will be unsuccessful.

These alternative positions are mapped on his decision chart (Figure 10.13).

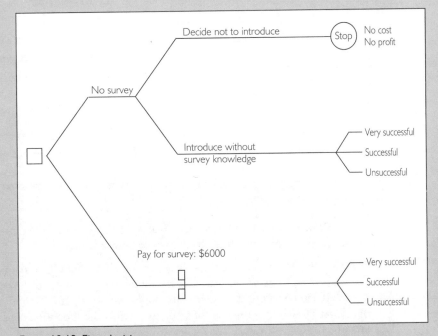

Figure 10.13 First decisions

The alternatives

If he accepts the quotation for market survey, the next question is whether its results indicate a favourable or an unfavourable outlook.

If conditions are favourable, he must still decide whether or not to introduce the service.

If he does not introduce it, the only cost will be the $6000 spent on the survey but no there will be no contribution to company profit. If, on the other hand, he decides to introduce it, he will again be faced with the unsuccessful, successful and very successful alternatives.

Finally, if the survey is unfavourable, he may still decide to take the risk and introduce the service.

Alternative possibilities are again assessed as unsuccessful, successful or very successful.

The main differences in reasoning between the alternatives listed above are in the likelihood, that is, the 'odds' for or against each of the scenarios under consideration.

He then maps out the alternatives as shown in Figure 10.14.

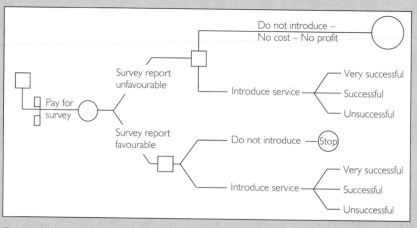

Figure 10.14 Decision tree

Having drawn the diagram, Glombeck will add figures to show his assessment of the estimated payoff and probability factors for each route.

For example, he knows that the survey cost would be $6000, and, if the service proved to be very successful, his estimate of profit contribution is $160 000. He believes that a successful launch would result in a contribution of at least $80 000 but the cost of an unsuccessful operation would incur a loss of $100 000.

Probability factors

From experience and an analysis of similar activities, it is possible to allocate probability factors to each of the three chosen alternatives. If a market survey is undertaken, its results would provide additional information relating to the risk. This would lead to an alteration in the probability factors at each stage.

Glombeck has decided that if the market survey is not carried out, the probabilities would be:

Very successful	20%
Successful	50%
Unsuccessful	30%

But with the aid of a market survey the probabilities would be:

Favourable		*Unfavourable*	
Very successful	30%	Very successful	2.5%
Successful	60%	Successful	40.0%
Unsuccessful	10%	Unsuccessful	57.5%

By calculating the anticipated payoffs or advantages, Glombeck is able to assess the expected monetary value (EMV) of each course of action (Figure 10.15).

Averaging and folding back

To reach an estimated monetary value at nodes C, F and H, Glombeck multiplied each alternative figure by its probability factor before adding the figures to achieve a value for each 'branch' of the tree.

- Without market survey – $42 000
- With favourable survey – $86 000
- With unfavourable survey, loss   ($21 500)

Glombeck is not averse to taking risks and he uses the EMV procedure in reaching his decision, striking a double line through the branches he decides not to take. He believes that the probabilities of a favourable market survey will be 50 per cent and the cost of the survey is $6000 he reasons that the survey would offer a 50 per cent chance of $43 000 (50 per cent of the figure at 'F') less the cost of the survey, leaving $37 000. If, on the other hand, he does not invest the $6000 but still introduces the service, he calculates an EMV of $42 000.

Had he been able to acquire the necessary information from a survey costing say, $1000 or less, it would obviously have been in his interests to reduce the possibility of loss by commissioning the survey. The cost and value of the information are, therefore, an important factor in one of Glombeck's decisions. The expected value is the difference between the EMV produced by following the survey path and that resulting from the no-survey alternatives.

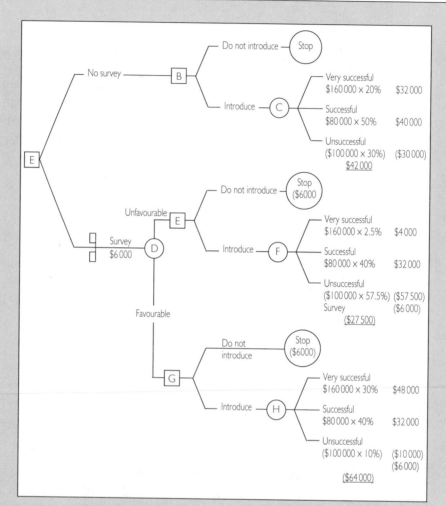

Figure 10.15 Glombeck's decision tree

Attitude to risk taking

Having worked out the possible payoffs, Glombeck's decision will still be conditioned by his attitude to taking risks. If he is entrepreneurially inclined, he will probably make the decision that offers the highest payoff. In the language of decision makers, he would be known as an 'EMVer'. Of course the accuracy of his predictions will depend on the way in which he has assigned payoff figures and probabilities.

Unless his judgement is good, the decision tree will be of limited value.

Decision trees are one of many available aids. Versions are included in some software packages and sophisticated calculating and modelling devices are used for specific decision making in technical and scientific areas.

The effectiveness of decision sequences obviously increases in relation to the accuracy and extent of factual information that can be obtained and the accuracy of assessments.

The decision tree comes into its own where a considerable quantity of data is available. This can be processed electronically, and provide a basis for comparison for a formidable range of alternatives and their respective consequences.

10.15 COMPUTER ASSISTANCE IN PLANNING AND CONTROL

Many planning and control techniques can be effectively and quickly worked with the aid of project management software costing very little or possibly as much as $10 000. A number of popular packages are available but some programs tend to encourage reliance on their design format and all have limitations.

It is important to bear in mind that in project administration and scheduling work, the computer is merely an aid to speed the input, sorting and formatting of information. It can be a tremendous help but a good test to apply is; *'If the operation were being done manually, would I use the same format?'* If the answer is yes, it is likely that the program will help; otherwise, consider whether the program is simply adding unnecessary detail or complicating the system.

10.16 SELECTING A SOFTWARE PACKAGE

Sophisticated techniques may justify the considerable cost of specially designed software for things like design, integration, stress calculations, comparison of complex propositions and so on, but most projects of small and medium size do not need such complexity.

Programs to assist in risk analysis and decision making may be useful but for the many administrative tasks carried out by a project manager, a complex program is seldom required.

A survey of project management tools and their use in the United States disclosed that although most project managers made regular and effective use of their software program tools, much of this use was concentrated on a particular application and there was extensive reliance on 'non-traditional' project management tools, such as Microsoft Excel. For longer-term projects, Artemis Prestige, Primavera Project Planner and Scheduler seem to be favoured (Fox and Spence, 1998).

A 1998 survey of the capability of 18 software packages reported in *Cost Engineering*, May 1998, selected the following criteria:

1. Ease of use and programmability
2. Advanced scheduling and resource management

3. Multiple projects
4. Estimating and cost control
5. Group work and Internet support

With the exception of coverage in advanced scheduling and resource management and some aspects of estimating and cost control, Microsoft Project showed up well in these categories, as did the more costly Micro Planner X (less favoured for group work and Internet support), Primavera, Plan View and ORO (Hegazy and El-Zamzamy, 1998).

Simplicity, speed, ease of training and use in frequently encountered operations are desired and most managers seek:

1. ability to produce charts, graphs and tables, including sequence and arrow diagrams, PERT and Gantt charts, in monotone and in combinations of colours;
2. ability to track dependencies, produce sequence and resource lists, time-related activity schedules and costings, calculate 'float', cash-flow predictions, and comparisons between planned, and actual, performance and costs;
3. ability to produce schedules and reports to the managers' required format;
4. a capability for extracting activities and events or sets of activities and events for analysis, comparison and reporting purposes;
5. provision of reminders and warning of due or overdue items.

Software selection and installation can take several months. Depth analysis of current and future needs will lead to a realistic and cost-effective specification.

REVIEW AND DISCUSSION QUESTIONS

1. How can the critical path be altered and at what possible cost?
2. Discuss the relative merits of arrow diagrams (with information nodes), PERT, Gantt charts and precedence diagrams.
3. In what circumstances would you use each type of chart?
4. Explain how the various planning tools can facilitate communication and progress control.
5. Explain the value of decision trees and prepare a tree to illustrate a project decision involving the use of some available data and a number of probabilities.
6. What criteria would you set and what essential qualities would you seek when selecting a software package to assist in the management of a project of your experience?

PLANNING EXERCISE

Following their experience with the City Park Project (Chapter 4), Downmarket City Council decided to conduct a similar project at a location across the City. Learning from their mistakes, the Council appointed a project manager to carry out a feasibility study to investigate the proposition, consider planning constraints and prepare an estimate of cost. As in the case of the earlier project, an environmental artist was invited to submit ideas and an estimate of the cost of providing a central feature for the park.

The feasibility study recommended that the project should go ahead, offering a 'ball park' estimate of $0.94m. This included the cost of a large metal and concrete feature to be made and delivered by the artist.

The project mission objective was set out like this:

Between 6 April, and 8 June 2000, to establish, complete and equip a City Park and children's recreation area at the site between Nos 147 and 361 City Road, Downmarket, to the layout and standards set out in City planning proposal P/638/2 of 1999, as amended by P/635213. Total cost is not to exceed $0.9m financed from City revenue A/c No. 2.

The Grand Opening Ceremony was scheduled for 12 June, leaving nine weeks for completion of the work.

The project manager called for submissions and estimates from stonemasons and other contractors.

The City Engineer's Department was invited to seek involvement in activities that might enable them to utilize spare capacity in manpower and/or equipment, on payment for work done.

On completion of initial planning, and detailed costings, the project manager came to the conclusion that:

1. there would be a small budget surplus;
2. based on previous timing assumptions, some activities could not be completed, at minimum cost, by the opening date;
3. by bringing in additional contractors, he could allow some activities to be conducted concurrently, and others to be completed more quickly at slightly increased cost.

Following discussion with those involved in the work, the following sequence table of main activities was drawn up:

Serial no.	Activity	Duration (days)	Depends on
1	Clear site	5	–
2	Survey site	1	1
3	Level site and terraces	5	2
4	Install water, drainage and irrigation	5	3
5	Erect rear and side walls	10	2
6	Build toilet block	20	3
7	Partially erect terraces	15	3
8	Excavate and build base for sculpture	5	3
9	Deliver and install art feature	3	8
10	Complete terraces	10	9
11	Prepare ground for planting and turf	5	7
12	Dig holes for large trees	2	11
13	Deliver and plant large trees	3	12
14	Lay brick paving	6	10
15	Install seating, lights and equipment	6	14
16	Complete front wall and entrance	8	9
17	Clean site	2	16

Exercise task

1. Manually or with the aid of Microsoft Project, or similar software, prepare a Gantt chart and a sequence diagram for the project.
2. Calculate earliest and latest times for each activity and any available float.
3. Consider what adjustments and alterations you would make to the sequence in the event of difficulty in completing the project before the opening date.

COMMUNICATION, CONFLICT AND CONTROL

Rude I am of speech. And little blessed with the soft phrase of peace ...
WILLIAM SHAKESPEARE

11.1 THE IMPORTANCE OF PROJECT COMMUNICATION

Communication is fundamental to individual action and concerted effort. It is the nerve system of leadership, teamwork, cooperation and control. It determines the quality of relationships, levels of satisfaction, the extent of our success or failure. Communication breakdown is a prime cause of discord or conflict and good communication the main vehicle for resolving difficulty.

It is widely acknowledged that most of us devote less thought to the way in which we communicate than the way we breathe, only becoming concerned about it when something goes wrong. Communication is an organic skill of management in which many of us are notoriously inept and however hard we try to sharpen our skill, it usually remains the bluntest item in our management tool kit.

In project work, default or lack of attention to communication need is the root of many problems of misunderstanding or conflict but planning and conscious effort can lay the foundations of a good network to avoid or at least cure the serious consequences of breakdown.

A new project begins with no formal, informal or inherited communication systems. The life cycle opens a blank page to present an exciting opportunity for the manager to establish good communication styles, design simple and effective systems, establish new networks and engineer new standards of effectiveness to carry the project to a successful conclusion.

Communication in management offers a vast field of study. In this chapter, we will touch on:

- communication media and the use of graphics;
- interpersonal communication;
- conflict and acceptance of change;
- communicating with the stakeholders;
- the communication plan.

11.2 COMMUNICATION MEDIA AND GRAPHICAL REPRESENTATION

Perceptions and recollections differ between individuals. These differences lead to major barriers to communication and understanding.

Visual communication is an effective and sometimes unambiguous way of overcoming many communication barriers.

Great strides have been made in the development and availability of electronic media and recent innovations are widely used in the course of project work. On-line computing allows almost instantaneous updating of activity plans and schedules; voice mail, mobile radio and cellular telephones speed verbal exchange of information; electronic mail and the fax machine facilitate immediate transmission of plans and documents; global positioning systems enable locations to be pinpointed; video recording and teleconferencing facilitate speed, understanding and decision making. Even in remote project locations, most of these media are available to supplement face-to-face conversation.

Graphical techniques are in common use for presenting and explaining issues to large audiences and in detailed form; they constitute one the best ways of communicating sequences and relationships between plans, activities and time. They illustrate the various aspects of planning, communication and control and are apposite to the needs of almost every project. On an ongoing basis, factual information can be revised and updated with changing situations to show, not only what is planned, but exactly what progress has been made. Useful tools to illustrate the key points of complex narratives, interdependencies and dimensions, they are largely independent of language or culture.

For simple propositions, Gantt charts, histograms and graphs are probably the most commonly used and easily understood form of graphical representations and, for schedule, activity or resource planning, are easily linked to time or produced in calendar form. Activities can be linked to show their relationships and interdependency.

Arrow diagrams, CPM, PERT charts or precedence networks are also a basic form of communication, easily adapted to different languages and unitary systems. Charts of this type are easily produced with the aid of simple planning software. The examples in Figures 11.1 and 11.2 were produced with the aid of Microsoft Project 98.

Opposite page:
(top):   *Figure 11.1* Gantt chart by Microsoft Project 98
(bottom): *Figure 11.2* Section of precedence network by Microsoft Project 98

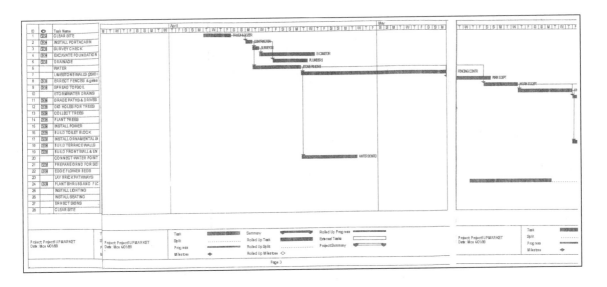

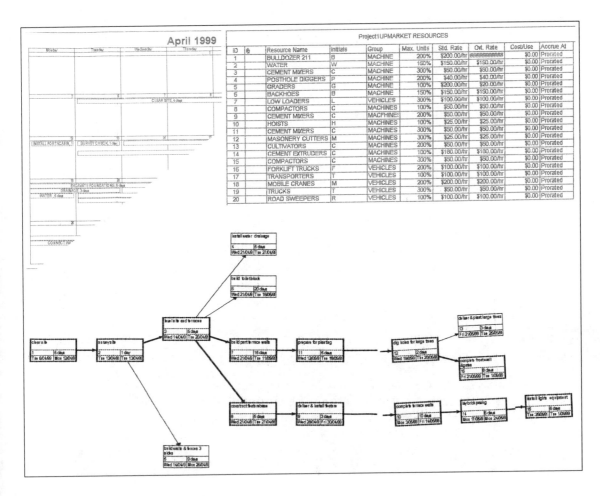

11.3 USE OF MASS MEDIA

To get the message to peripheral stakeholders – interested members of the public or special interest groups – a balanced programme of meetings, press releases, interviews, radio or TV may be required. But in dealing with 'the media' one should exercise caution to avoid the ever-present danger of interviewer or reporter bias, manipulation or selective editing. 'Live' or unrehearsed interviews are notoriously dangerous. Pre-notification of coverage and questions is advisable.

Internet information packages are a popular means of supplementing world-wide project publicity.

One of the most versatile and effective aids to project introduction is a well-prepared videotape or CD-ROM presentation, easily produced with (if necessary) foreign language commentaries.

Offered to agencies on a conditional basis, namely that copyright is subject to screening without selective editing or adverse comment, this ready-made and free programme material may be welcomed by the media. It can present a balanced project image slanted to the interests of the audience, in the desired form, and limit the danger of biased or ill-informed reporting. A good video or CD presentation has many other applications, for example as an introduction to public meetings, finance-raising discussions, briefing new or potential project staff, and so on.

11.4 INTERPERSONAL COMMUNICATION

Projects rely heavily on leadership, teamwork, cooperation and mutual under-standing. Empathy, a vital ingredient of communication, is influenced by the attitude and example of team leaders, project managers and ability in interpersonal communication.

Stress is a common cause of breakdown and since many projects call for team members to work under extreme pressure, in remote and lonely surroundings or under hazardous conditions, the work sometimes involves considerable frustration. Under these circumstances the possibility of discord is very real and harmful tensions have to be defused.

case study

THE COMMUNICATION EXPERT

George Harris was appointed to the Chief Executive position in a small management consulting practice specializing in market research. The overriding consideration that influenced his selection was the quality of his record in data processing and analysis.

▶

Prior to Harris's appointment, the team of research specialists were well motivated and enjoyed agreeable work relationships. Morale was excellent and team members worked closely together.

One of Harris's tasks was to establish an enhanced reputation for accuracy, depth of analysis and incisive judgement. On appointment, a scrutiny of recent assignments led him to suspect that there may have been gaps or deficiencies in the knowledge and experience of his staff and instances of inconclusive investigations or 'short-cutting' assignments.

Harris began by talking collectively with all the firm's employees and then conducted individual interviews to outline and elaborate on his plans and discuss the expectations of each employee. He then assured each of his support and constant availability for advice or guidance.

After the initial takeover, Harris became increasingly preoccupied with establishing a new database, reorganizing input to existing programs and practice administration. This left very little time for team discussion. Consultants, who had enjoyed agreeable and relaxed work relationships, informal and semi-formal chats with the previous CEO, felt unwelcome if they dropped in to Harris's office to find him engrossed in computer work and willing to pay scant attention to them, as he continued to tap on his keyboard and 'gaze moronically at the VDU'.

Work continued in comparative harmony but consultants were bemused by the plethora of written procedures and directives that emanated from Harris's desk. Despite occupying adjoining offices, they discovered that the only way to secure Harris's attention was to put their concerns in writing and send them by e-mail or fax. They could not fault him on the speed with which he answered written messages but the exchanges did nothing to build confidence or empathy.

Team members became disillusioned and there was a noticeable drop in morale as results declined. New recruits to the practice accepted the impersonal and bureaucratic system and seemed to be favoured by the Chief Executive but did not 'fit in' with the rest of the team and became the subject of animosity.

Harris resigned within 18 months of appointment.

This case underlines the significance of personal contact in communication and leadership.

11.5 BENEFITS AND CONSEQUENCES OF ELECTRONIC MEDIA

The many advantages of electronic media are obvious and, unhampered by distance or division, online updating and annotation of plans or schedules can provide an accurate and up-to-the-minute picture of progress in almost every field. Controls can be introduced to prevent unauthorized or inexpert use.

By accelerating the exchange of factual information and data, modern media constitute an invaluable aid to project control but over-reliance may lead to serious repercussions on the total communication process.

With the possible exception of telephone or video conferencing, electronic media can supplement but not replace personal contact which is, all too often, limited by the use of less personal means of communication. Over-reliance on electronic media diverts the manager's focus from the individual to the process itself, keyboard or VDU. There is ample evidence to show that reduced personal contact entails a measure of psychological impact and loss of the interactive aspects of communication, which are so important in the development of empathy, persuasion, influencing opinion and the provision of essential feedback. So the importance of regular face-to-face communication should not be over-looked and adequate opportunity for the exchange of the small but important details, shades of opinion, feelings and understanding feature in any sound communication plan.

Dialogue and personal contact are also germane to motivation and team development. 'Listening to others with perception', 'ensuring good group communication, upwards, downwards and sideways', and 'showing an awareness of non-verbal communication' are important abilities of a leader (Adair, 1988).

'E-mail and voice mail are efficient but face-to face contact is essential to true communication' (Hallowell, 1999). People who feel ignored or rejected or disregarded tend to lose interest, often becoming conditioned to antagonism or a desire for revenge, and conflict is usually preferable to isolation.

This need for personal involvement in communication applies to peripheral and internal stakeholders alike but in the case of project personnel, there is an ever-present need for personal involvement, positive feedback and recognition which are important ingredients of project communication.

11.6 DEALING WITH CONFLICT

Many projects are plagued by conflict. The continuance of confrontational styles of management, once considered synonymous with firm and decisive management and an essential qualification for project work, may be largely to blame.

Happily this preference for confrontation is no longer in evidence but despite careful choice of participants and good leadership, the strain and diversity of project work make occasional conflict almost inevitable and as the project progresses, conflict amongst internal stakeholders becomes more common.

A survey of project conflict intensity published in *Sloan Management Review*, summer 1975, covered the following sources at four stages of the project life cycle:

- conflict over schedules;
- conflict over priorities;
- conflict over manpower;
- conflict over technical opinions;
- conflict over procedures;
- conflict over cost;
- personality conflict.

At that time, a surprising proportion of managers seemed to favour confrontation as the best method of solution but in a contemporary environment the picture would be somewhat different.

Valuable insights into the psychology of communication are to be found in Berne's work as the originator of Transactional Analysis, a process of analysing interpersonal communication and response. This work is commended to project managers who are likely to face, and have to resolve, conflict situations. Thomas A. Harris's (1967) book *I'm OK – You're OK* explains this theory in simple language and identifies the 'ego states' that influence communication. The text likens the brain to a high-fidelity tape recorder using a combination of three programmes in the course of a communication:

1. the Parent;
2. the Adult;
3. the Child.

These 'programmes' shape attitudes, behaviour and communication patterns.

When the ego states of parties to a transaction (communication exchange) are in sympathy, the transaction is likely to proceed in a reasonably harmonious (though not necessarily advantageous) way. When ego states are not in harmony, crossed transactions take place and conflict will result (Figure 11.3).

'Parent' and 'child' programmes are usually less productive than the reasoning logical 'adult' ego state.

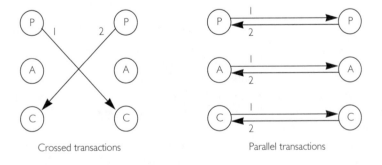

Crossed transactions   Parallel transactions

Figure 11.3 **Crossed and parallel transactions**

For a mutually beneficial outcome – logical, and devoid of destructive emotional overtones – a parallel transaction between 'adult' ego states is usually necessary. Refusal to become embroiled in emotional reactions is essential. With patience, perseverance, and recognition of the other person's concerns, it becomes possible to diffuse the tensions that inhibit an overheated exchange and revert to an 'adult-to-adult' dialogue with advantages to both sides (Figure 11.4).

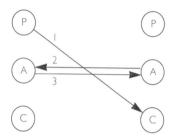

Figure 11.4 Reversion to 'adult' and logical exchanges

Positive emotions and feelings of satisfaction can be beneficial to communication but feelings of anger or anxiety are usually destructive and difficult to diffuse.

A great deal of training on conflict resolution is based on the need for participants to discard or diffuse the emotional overtones and prejudices that pollute effective, mutually beneficial discussion and exchange of views and allow communication to proceed on an assumption of unbiased reasoning, logic and mutual advantage.

11.7 ACCEPTANCE OF CHANGE

A project is an engine of change. As such, it will be welcomed by some but feared and, possibly, obstructed by others, and one can seldom foresee all the consequences of a project or how its implementation would affect every stakeholder.

In addition to being a highway for intelligence and control, communication is the route by which obstacles to change and attitudes based on past experience are overcome to bring about the demise of the sacred cows, so fervently defended by those who resist change.

So, if the project is to meet its objectives the manager must know who the stakeholders are – groups and individuals – and, most importantly, the nature of their different interests, viewpoints and susceptibilities.

11.8 WHO ARE THE STAKEHOLDERS?

Stakeholders are people who are involved in the project and those who may be (or think themselves to be) affected by it. The list may be disparate and considerable. It is important that no one is forgotten as those on it will need adequate, though often different kinds of information. Fortunately, they will not all require the same depth of detail or frequency of attention.

Sponsors	Owners	Financiers
Guarantors	Governments	Neighbours
Local Community Groups	Suppliers	Contractors
Welfare bodies	Environmentalists	Developers
Employees	Functional managers	Unions	Internal organizations
	Political alliances	… and so on

Figure 11.5 Who are the stakeholders?

11.9 COMMUNICATING THE NEED FOR CHANGE

Failure to prepare an effective communication plan is a frequent cause of difficulty in internal projects, for example those involving organizational change. Special action is frequently required to overcome resistance (see Galpin, 1996).

Five main stages in communication for development programmes or projects are listed in Figure 11.6.

Phase	Segment	Background	Intention
1. Information	Peripherals (Copy to internals for info.)	Explain need, how project will impact on stakeholders	Promote awareness and understanding
2. Acceptance	Target peripherals	Feedback on reactions and intentions	To reach concensus or agreement and acceptance
3. Status	Outline to all segments, detail to internals	Objectives, plans, status and review	Explain current situation, progress and way ahead. Explain measures being taken to overcome difficulty or conflicts of interest.
4. Monitoring and control	All internals	Progress and results	To exchange information on progress, compare actual and planned results. Provide a basis for control and coordination.
5. Termination and review	Detailed info. to internals; summary to peripherals	Final report and evaluation	Confirm acceptance of completed project, provide basis for evaluation.

Figure 11.6 Communication matrix – preparation for change

11.10 LISTING THE STAKEHOLDERS

Internal participants include project managers, team members and employees who usually need and also generate much of the detail and the greatest volume of communication. They are easy to identify and their needs require careful consideration.

External participants, for example government bodies directly concerned with the project, guarantors, financiers, bankers or contractors, will also be directly involved but their interests may be more selective and in some cases, the nature and extent of their interest may be less obvious to the project manager.

Participants on the periphery of project activity are sometimes difficult to identify. It is important to find out who these people are at the outset because if their concerns are ignored, some may emerge later in the project with unfortunate results.

11.11 STAKEHOLDER SEGMENTATION

Identifying and grouping stakeholders (stakeholder segmentation) (Figure 11.7) helps the project manager decide on the nature of essential communication (Figure 11.8), how and when to transmit messages to individuals and groups, and assess reactions or 'feedback' that indicate how the message has been received.

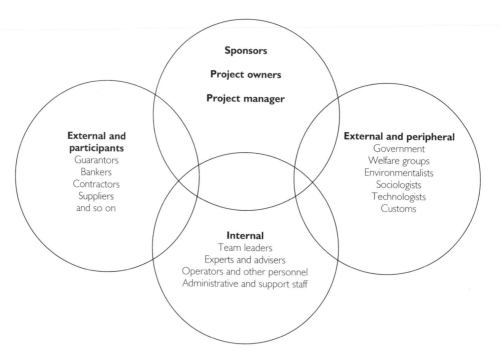

Figure 11.7 Typical stakeholder groups

1. External peripherals may include:

    *   Members of the public in general
    *   Local, state and national governments
    *   Local residents
    *   Environmentalists
    *   Advisory and welfare bodies
    *   Transport and communications companies
    *   Sociologist, technologists, and so on
    *   Industrial or commercial interests in some way related to project outcomes
    *   Private individuals with vested interests related to project outcomes
    *   Trade unions or employer organizations
    *   Ethnic or nationalist groups
    *   Security, defence forces or law enforcement agencies

2. Project peripherals may include:

    *   Guarantors
    *   Diplomatic missions, embassies, UNDP, and so on
    *   Involved government departments
    *   Project bankers or financiers
    *   Contractors and suppliers
    *   Managers of associated projects
    *   Customs, Excise, Inland Revenue, security agencies
    *   Company officials and employees (particularly in the case of in-company projects related to change)

3. Internal stakeholders include:

    *   Team leaders
    *   Managers
    *   Consultants, experts and advisers
    *   Operators and other personnel
    *   Administrative and support staff
    *   Full-time or BOT contractors

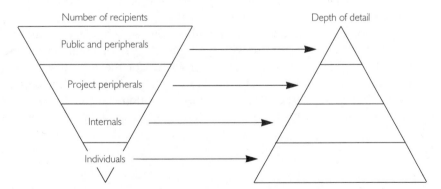

Figure 11.8 Relationship between stakeholder numbers and depth of required information

11.12   UNDERSTANDING THE STAKEHOLDERS

In designing a communications plan, the manager must know who the stakeholders are, their departments, responsibilities and relationships as well as the contribution, support or opposition that they may bring to the project.

Project managers in unfamiliar territory are always aware of differences in language and conditions, but are often oblivious to essential and very important differences of culture. Failure to comprehend the nature of some of the unfamiliar pressures under which local populations and migrant workforces have to live, the diversity between their levels of need and those that we take for granted, or just how the expectations of local residents differ from ours can have a disastrous effect on communication.

It is important to understand the individual and cultural differences that apply to all stakeholder levels, rich and poor, be they sponsors, government officials, contractors, peripheral organizations, external groups or locally engaged project employees (see, for example, Loosemore and Al Muslmani, 1999).

Much of the research into industrial psychology carried out in the 1960s and 70s is now denigrated, taken for granted or has been superseded in western management teaching, but established theories, such as Maslow's Hierarchy of needs and Herzberg's Hygiene-Motivation theories are every bit as appropriate to workers and other stakeholder groups in developing countries as they are in our environment. Assessment and consideration of individual stakeholder needs helps understanding and is an essential basis for effective communication.

11.13   CONFLICT WITH OR BETWEEN STAKEHOLDERS

Not only is effective communication essential for project implementation and control, it is a powerful weapon against conflict. Having established the constituents of stakeholder categories, plans should take into account and seek to obviate potential areas of conflict with and between stakeholders.

But most of the informal communication between external stakeholders will not be known and some of it may not be helpful. External and peripheral stakeholder groups may also hold strong and acutely divergent views, interests and aspirations. Under some circumstances, conflict between stakeholders or groups can be detrimental to the project but with prior knowledge, the communication plan may be able to minimize this and avoid problems for the project itself. Intelligence gathering and circumspect but fruitful face-to-face discussion should begin as early as possible to avoid speculation and misconception.

Timely and regular release of information geared to stakeholder interests should follow.

11.14 COMMUNICATING WITH INTERNAL STAKEHOLDERS

Every aspect of our lives shapes, and is shaped by, communication patterns that have been developed over time. In business, ongoing, routine operations are a maze of complex formal and informal communication patterns, networks and routines. Some are consciously followed or intentional and deliberately engineered. Others reflect haphazard growth that results from experience, contact, emotion, interest or necessity and become deeply ingrained into the fabric of our working lives.

Formal communication patterns can be designed and enforced but, hopefully, a great deal of valuable communication will occur informally between participants. Communication, about which the manager will often be unaware, extends to and between all stakeholders and especially within the project management itself.

The project life cycle commences with few inherited communication systems. It offers a blank page and an exciting opportunity for the manager to establish good communication styles, plan networks, design systems and engineer new standards of effectiveness to see the project through to success. Of course, this will only happen if we take the trouble to set the right tone, design a system that will meet the needs of the project and obviate foreseeable pitfalls.

Whatever the formal project structure, regular informal communication will occur between participants, transactions of which the manager will usually be unaware. Hopefully, communication of the informal kind will be helpful and provide a good basis of cooperation and coordination. The better matched and motivated the team, the more effective that communication will become.

case study

THE NEW HP TURBINE BLADE MACHINING FACILITY (A STAKEHOLDER NEWSLETTER)

Internal stakeholders were well informed of plans, schedules and what to expect during the model Rolls-Royce HP Turbine Blade Machining Project by quarterly newsletters, with background information of topical interest on the project and simple illustrated explanations of technical and administrative processes for those not directly involved with detailed planning and development work. Main topics were described by the responsible development teams, for example:

- The ground breaking ceremony
- What the new facility will look like and how it will be reached (with illustrations)
- Logistics and physical material flow
- Electronic design and data systems
- The technical overview, processes and equipment
- People and the new facility, recruitment, training plans and industrial agreements

▶

In the first issue Mark Hulands, Project Manager, summarized attributes of the facility:

Manufacturing technology

- Simplified manufacturing processes
- Highly flexible CNC machine tools with virtual elimination of setups and changeover delays
- Product verification integrated into the machine tools
- Process understanding and monitoring to ensure product quality

People

- A clean, quiet working environment designed for people and safety, reflecting the precision of parts being produced
- A culture of involvement, continuous improvement and trust
- High levels of appropriate training
- Integration of design and make processes

Integrated information technology and systems

- Use of a turbine key system to share common data with design
- Supply chain management and lean production sysytems
- Statistical process control and quality tracking
- Paperless manufacturing instructions and product records
- Simple, effective computer systems supporting the business environments

Supplier partnerships

- Integration of suppliers into the operation of the facility (from biros to consumables)

Co-location was calculated to enhance simultaneous engineering processes by making the design of the part and the manufacturing method a single continuous process. A model of the building was also displayed for general inspection and information on how new working conditions and processes would affect the working lives of employees was progressively introduced.

Planning and control

From an early stage, stakeholders were informed of the project schedule, milestones and the way in which detailed plans were developed to support them. 'These plans are owned by the relevant team leader for each topic, i.e. technical, building, IT and finance, are updated and reported on a weekly basis. Team leaders provide a monthly brief at a Programme Review Meeting to all interested parties to get others to buy in and help with cross team problems. Alterations are controlled by a change control board which can veto inappropriate changes … ' (A. McLay, Programme Manager).

Problems and adjustments to maintain the objective were also explained. ▶

Major milestones

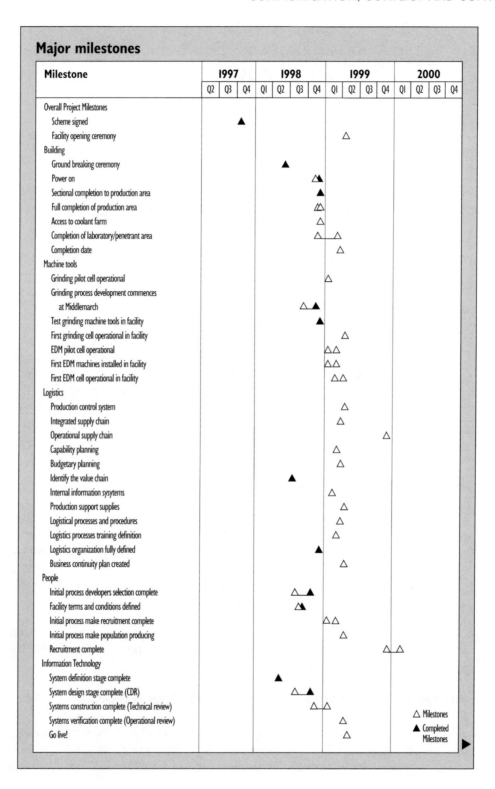

Milestone	1997			1998				1999				2000			
	Q2	Q3	Q4	Q1	Q2	Q3	Q4	Q1	Q2	Q3	Q4	Q1	Q2	Q3	Q4

Overall Project Milestones
- Scheme signed
- Facility opening ceremony

Building
- Ground breaking ceremony
- Power on
- Sectional completion to production area
- Full completion of production area
- Access to coolant farm
- Completion of laboratory/penetrant area
- Completion date

Machine tools
- Grinding pilot cell operational
- Grinding process development commences at Middlemarch
- Test grinding machine tools in facility
- First grinding cell operational in facility
- EDM pilot cell operational
- First EDM machines installed in facility
- First EDM cell operational in facility

Logistics
- Production control system
- Integrated supply chain
- Operational supply chain
- Capability planning
- Budgetary planning
- Identify the value chain
- Internal information sysytems
- Production support supplies
- Logistical processes and procedures
- Logistics processes training definition
- Logistics organization fully defined
- Business continuity plan created

People
- Initial process developers selection complete
- Facility terms and conditions defined
- Initial process make recruitment complete
- Initial process make population producing
- Recruitment complete

Information Technology
- System definition stage complete
- System design stage complete (CDR)
- Systems construction complete (Technical review)
- Systems verification complete (Operational review)
- Go live!

△ Milestones
▲ Completed Milestones

187

Project schedule
for the new HP Turbine Blade Machining Facility

May 1998	–	Main building contractor appointed
June	–	Ground breaking ceremony Contractors start on site
July/August	–	Steelwork arrives from Spalding, Lincs.
August	–	First Makino grinder arrives in NCMT, Coventry
December	–	Roof sealed. Production area handed over. First grinding cell brought into the facility. First EDM cell brought into the facility.
March 1999	–	Completed building handed over to Rolls-Royce.
April	–	First machining cell operational
January 2000	–	Single source on Trent and RB211 family turbine blades

In simple format, the commonsense publication disseminates a wealth of information to a range of stakeholders both allaying misconception and providing a significant aid to communication and project success.

(Information and diagrams courtesy of Rolls-Royce plc)

11.15 COMMUNICATION OF DATA

The communication of data is vital for detailed control and coordination. Integration of activity and resource planning, scheduling and online reporting mechanisms is possible in all but the simplest projects but care should be taken to ensure that everyone responsible for data input is aware of their responsibility and the method and frequency of reporting or direct data input. When online inputting is used, safeguards are essential to avoid inadvertent inputs of incorrect or unauthorized data.

Most software packages provide for automatic integration of information on activities, resources, supplies and payments and other financial information.

11.16 COMMUNICATING WITH PERIPHERAL STAKEHOLDERS

Communication with stakeholder groups will call for a variety of messages, detail, emphasis, timing and, possibly, different channels and combinations of communication media. It is necessary to consider the needs of each group (sometimes each individual), develop a planned communications strategy and update it as the need arises. To avoid a build-up of speculation or rumour, the manager may have to pre-empt difficulties by careful timing and drafting of information to external sources. This need should be carefully considered in the communication plan.

THE CENTRAL ASIA RUNWAY PROJECT

Ashkhatar International Airport is the main point of access to a small, land-locked Central Asian democracy. Formerly part of the USSR, the independent nation is situated in mountainous terrain.

Residents enjoy a simple lifestyle backed by basic welfare and health services. Family income is largely dependent on subsistence agriculture and a lucrative sideline in mink farming which has been developed by the more prosperous inhabitants.

The airport is based on a military airfield and its administrative buildings. The extreme winter climate causes damage to the runway which is constantly in need of repair and is too short to accommodate large passenger and freight aircraft. This limits communication and is detrimental to regional and national development, international travel and tourism.

The government has benefited from programmes of foreign aid in the education and health sectors and this experience has encouraged it to seek financial and technical assistance for airport and runway improvement.

Preliminary proposals envisage lengthening and recarpeting the existing runway, provision of additional taxiways, and runway lighting. It is claimed that these improvements would accommodate modern jets, open the country to tourism, facilitate increased trade and result in a sustainable improvement in prosperity and living standards.

After rejection of the proposal by one aid donor, a new proposal listing a 25 per cent contribution by the government (in the form of materials, local labour and so on), and the provision of engineers and contractors from another donor nation, led to a feasibility study.

The study team consisting of an ICAO specialist in airport design, a civil engineer with runway construction experience and an expert in local conditions were briefed to work within a well-defined framework. A major consideration was the possible effect of runway changes on the local population, any local resistance that might have to be overcome and the suitability of the local labour force for manual and technical work on the project.

▶

189

The team reported favourably, and recommended a realistic budget increase to provide for the construction of an entirely new runway, parallel to the existing one, new taxiways and lighting. Minor repairs would be carried out to the existing runway which would remain in use during construction work. Due to extreme weather conditions, construction would be carried out in two phases during summer weather. The longer runway would also mean moving the transmitter site.

Extensive use of local labour was planned but a problem was foreseen in delivery of some construction materials and cumbersome runway construction machinery. Feasibility of air freighting materials and partly dismantled machines to the site, using the existing runway or making a temporary extension to accommodate large transports was considered.

The team observed that the project might be opposed by a small but potentially influential group of mink farmers because their animals might be adversely affected by increased aircraft noise from the new flightpath. Success of the project relied on the acquiescence of residents whose agreement on relocation, compensation and/or some acceptable form of noise abatement would have to be considered. This would call for a carefully orchestrated discussion and communication plan appropriate to the local conditions and culture.

11.17 THE COMMUNICATION PLAN

A project evolves by stages and there is no universally accepted way to prepare its communication plan. However, a simple communication matrix listing the essentials is a good start. Having roughed out the matrix at the start of planning, additions can be made as the process develops and when all the important items have been included, a bar chart or calendar can be drawn up. In the case of the Long Runway Project, communication with peripheral stakeholders was established in the initial stages of the feasibility study but no proposals were put forward until a final decision had been made as to the choice of airport design methods. A simple communication plan based on stakeholder identification was then drawn up. The first outline matrix is shown in Figure 11.9.

Stakeholder Group	Focus	What does this group need to know?	Media/Method	When?
Public and peripherals	*Individual interests*	*General information*	*Meetings/ circulars*	*At outset and periodically*
Individuals to be displaced or rehoused	Compensation package and assistance	Details of the effect on individuals, dates and proposed arrangements	Meetings Individual interview	After final decision on runway
Project peripherals				
Government and director of civil aviation	Project aid and operational data	Proposals, costs, method and timings	Discussions, project document and progress reports	Prior to implementation, at all milestones and reviews
Contractors, suppliers, labour agency	Project supply	Project needs, method of tendering and payment Conditions of contract	Leaflets, circulars and letter	On decision to proceed; at start of tendering
Air transport operators	Schedule, runway and special conditions	Transport agreement, loading schedules, temporary runway provisions	NOTAMS, fax, e-mail, phone	Prior to delivery of heavy machinery
Project internals				
Sponsor/ programme managers (aid agency)	Programme control info.	Agency/government agreements, project objectives and plan, progress reports and revision proposals, disbursements etc.	Project document and reports, telephone, fax, teleconference, e-mail, etc.	Commencement; weekly progress fax, review dates, special events
Project manager, consultant, team leaders, supply manager	Briefing and full info. update	All background and detail	All	As info. is available
Principal contractors	Contract duties and deadlines	Confirmation of contract, specifications, quality and deadlines	Written, post, fax, e-mail, personal contact	
Project manager, team leaders	Control	Daily update and progress	Daily meeting, online update, telephone/fax	Daily and at will

Figure 11.9 Management communication matrix. Central Asia Runway Project stakeholder matrix – outline considerations

THE CENTRAL ASIA RUNWAY PROJECT – Part II

Investigation into ways, means and costs followed the feasibility report and approval was reached for an adequately funded and well-structured project. Engineering activity was planned, scheduled for approval and monitored by an independent project director who also had responsibility for stakeholder relations. He remained in the country throughout the winter period of construction inactivity and held regular consultations with representatives of government and local residents. The affected mink farmers were resettled before commencement of the second phase and the project was completed on time and within 12 per cent of budget.

The Central Asia Runway Project was more complex than this summary might suggest. However, its success was attributable to a realistic feasibility assessment, careful planning and effective patterns of communication.

(The Central Asia runway project is based on an exchange of experiences and information of airport construction project work in Central Asia.)

11.18 PROJECT CONTROL

Project control is inextricably linked with plans, schedules and reporting procedures.

The project manager is the helmsman who has to chart progress, look ahead, and make allowance for current, crosswind and diversion to navigate a safe and direct course towards project objectives.

Although the bulk of operational control is exercised by way of on-the-spot decisions by experts, team and section leaders, to be able to assess the effect of operational control it is essential the manager be fully informed of changes and their results, so any significant issues must be reported.

Control of projects that involve simultaneous (concurrent) engineering techniques calls for a particularly close team approach with micro-coordination of activities conducted in close cooperation and centred on the mission objective.

Control at manager level is usually occasioned by one or more of the following:

- unexpected difficulty or risk to the achievement of objectives;
- control required by special circumstances, for example cost overrun, budget deficit or delay;
- an activity situation in which further expense or effort would not be justified;
- emergence of some new or unexpected opportunity to enhance project outcome;
- periodic review or planning revision;
- stakeholder change or alteration of strategy affecting objectives and/or plans.

To keep the project on schedule the project manager usually has to make frequent assessments of the programme, manipulating important considerations of time, quality and cost (Figure 11.10). Many control situations that entail a sacrifice of some kind amount to the manipulation of three key variables:

Time: Less time = more cost
Cost: Lower cost = more time or lower quality
Quality: Better quality = higher cost or more time

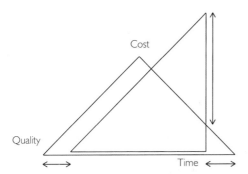

Figure 11.10 Time, cost and quality relationships

For purposes of cost control, limits can be set above or below which actual costs may not exceed budgeted figures (Figure 11.11). When the level moves beyond predetermined limits, the manager is alerted to action, either by cost limitation or a revision of budget estimates. The band also alerts for lower than expected costs so that, after reviewing cumulative expenditure, timely action can be taken to reallocate funds.

11.19 CONTROLLING PROJECT CONTRACTORS

Effective communication and good leadership are the ingredients of day-to-day operational control involving project personnel but control of activity provided by contractors or the work of consultants is often more difficult. Even when tied by contract or agreement, the contractor is likely to have different communication and reporting systems that may not fit project needs. They may have differing priorities and will not, as a rule, come under the project manager's direct control.

In setting up a communication and control system, provision should be made for an information and reporting procedure that will enable the project manager to monitor contractors' progress and coordinate the efforts of all contributors.

Contractual agreements should stipulate minimum reporting requirement for monitoring and provide the project manager with authority to demand timely action in default of a contractor's commitment.

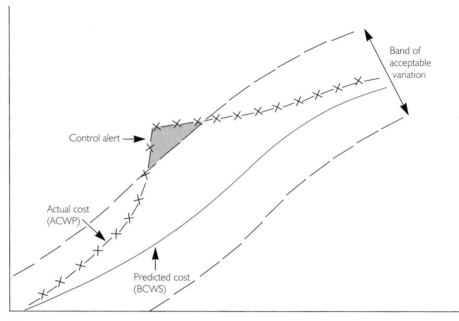

Figure 11.11 Establishing acceptable cost variations

Complex projects (for example, for development and design prior to manufacture or construction) involving several supply and development contractors call for special skill (for example, the Airborne Early Warning System in Chapter 2).

Time scales for research and development are notoriously difficult to predict and when several aspects of development are involved, frequent reappraisal and adjustment may be needed. A control and coordination plan to which all contractors respond with routine information and on attaining agreed milestones or progress stages should be enforced.

REVIEW AND DISCUSSION QUESTIONS

1. Discuss three examples of the effective use of computer generated charts or special graphic material:
    1.1 in day-to-day communication with internal project personnel;
    1.2 as an aid to communication with external or project peripheral stake-holders.
2. Describe instances in which effective communication cam forestall conflict with or between peripheral stakeholders.
3. Consider the scope and objectives of an appropriate CD or videotape production for the Central Asia Runway Project, the stakeholders at whom it might be aimed and ways in which it might best be used.

4. Give six examples of both 'crossed' and 'parallel' transactions between different 'ego-states' and describe how crossed transactions might be brought to a satisfactory conclusion. (Refer to T. Harris's (1967) *I'm OK – You're OK* if necessary.)

5. *Communication planning exercise*

   Some projects have a large number of peripheral stakeholders and call for expertise in communication and lengthy negotiation with diverse stakeholder groups.

   Using the background of the case study *Goodbye Subic Bay* (Chapter 2):

   5.1 Discuss and list the main communication needs of a project leading to the reutilization of a former military base for a combination of light industrial and recreation purposes.

   5.2 Consider and segment probable stakeholders.

   5.3 Discuss and prepare an outline plan for the early stages of a base reuse project.

6. Discuss the basis of day-to-day control and list sources of information and 'feedback' that would be used in the control of a typical project of your experience.

7. Consider the problems of managing a development project or a programme involving a number of different contractors and how reporting and control needs might be met.

8. Explain how a project based on simultaneous engineering concepts can be controlled.

REVIEW, REVISION AND EVALUATION

An historian is a prophet in reverse ... F. VON SCHLEGA

12.1 MANAGEMENT DECISIONS FOR THE FUTURE

Project management is about the future. Situations that have passed, expended time and resources cannot be further managed. One can only manage that which remains.

When communication is good, meetings well conducted and the project goes more or less according to plan, a strong temptation exists to avoid spending time and effort in progress review or evaluation. At the end of a project or a significant project event, we want to press on with new challenges rather than look back on what has passed, so the importance of periodic reviews and final evaluation is often ignored.

So if project management is forward looking and concerned with the future, why should we bother with review and evaluation?

12.2 THE NEED FOR REGULAR REVIEW

Despite what has been said, progress monitoring and evaluation are germane to onward-looking management, so the value of systematic review and project revision should not be underestimated, and the review offers a ready basis for the development of project expertise.

Projects develop, stage by stage in an orderly and logical fashion. The past provides the foundation on which the future is built; past experience influences the way in which we work and the data with which we forecast and measure expectations. It is also a valuable aid for honing individual and collective skills, developing expertise, and establishing standards or 'benchmarks' for continuing improvement.

All comprehensive plans make clear provision for timely reviews of progress and the need for occasional revision, because as we have said, planning and project management is a forward-thinking process. During the project, evaluation confirms results up to the review stage, defines the base on which further progress will be built, and sometimes logical grounds and/or parameters for project revision – major changes or minor adjustments to keep the project on a straight road to its objectives.

12.3 SMALL PROJECT REVIEWS

A review of the simplest in-company project might be limited to a low-key process of regular checks to assess progress and make sure that the remainder of the project can proceed as planned. If difficulty is foreseen, on-the-spot action will be taken to adjust the plan and all concerned will be made aware of the changes. The final review might be in the form of a verbal 'wash-up' or discussion in which the effectiveness of the project is assessed, its cost calculated and, if things went wrong, a post-mortem to determine the cause of difficulty, its consequences and avoidance of similar problems in the future. In this way, costs are justified and lessons learnt from the project experience.

12.4 STRUCTURED REVIEW AND EVALUATION PROGRAMMES

Larger and more complex projects call for a structured programme consisting of all or some of the following reviews:

1. *Initial reviews and inception reports* – important preliminary reviews on establishing a complex or remote project.
2. *Periodic reviews* – in accordance with a programme, at, say, three-monthly intervals. These reviews, akin to a routine medical examination, provide an opportunity to assess the project's overall health and progress, symptoms, problems, and experience gained, and evaluate lessons that have been learnt. Discussion can take place on the best way to proceed, and adjustments or improvements can be made to promote further progress.
3. *'Milestone' progress reviews* – these reviews are conducted on the achievement of agreed goals or project stages.
4. *Special reviews* – required as a result of an owner's request for project revision, a change in project timing, scope or deliverables, or because the project has made better than expected progress or encountered unexpected problems.
5. *Terminal reviews* – comprehensive validation, evaluation and review proceedings held at the completion stage and usually forming the basis of a final report. They confirm project justification; provide details of activity costs and results, and follow-up requirements; summarize accounts, expenditure, and disposal of assets; make acknowledgements; and so on.
6. *Programme and 'cluster' reviews* - multi-project organizations conduct or commission reviews of groups or sector projects.

Most reviews deal with progress in terms of time, cost and quality. Complex techniques have been developed to assist in monitoring the progress of specialized activities. Benchmarking has led to the development of key ratios and performance indicators applicable to many forms of comparable activity. But surveys of review strategies indicate that project appraisal in the private sector has traditionally concentrated on technical and financial viability (Lopes and Flavell, 1998)

An effective review is much more than an audit of cost, an appraisal of progress, or the way in which the project is being conducted. It is a stepping stone to future activity confirming or remapping future direction – as much an indication of what is to be done as a confirmation of what has already been achieved.

Multi-project research or design programmes, for example, need frequent information on progress and detailed updates for continuing management and control purposes, while global organizations need regular news of their individual projects, changes in the political and economic situation, project environment and so on.

Intelligence about new opportunities, discoveries or lessons learnt in pioneering projects included in review reports may be relevant to other situations and such items should be highlighted. This is all part of the process of continuous improvement, constantly checking initial assumptions, establishing stage-by-stage decisions on project continuation and the ongoing quality assessment practised by major international agencies and global enterprises.

> The ability to adjust research (and other programmes) in the light of new knowledge is highly desirable. Regular reviews of research programs and progress should include consultation with all relevant sectors of the industry which is intended to benefit from the research.
>
> (Australian Agency for International Development (AusAID) Agricultural Projects (PNG Cluster Evaluation, 1998)

12.5 EVALUATION

Evaluation methods vary between projects and the type of review. Setting aside complex procedures for special activities, evaluation prior to a periodic review may consist of a financial statement, comparison of planned and actual results, nature and root cause of problems, effectiveness of remedies, and communication and control procedures.

Some projects are sensitive to external changes whether due or unrelated to past project activity, for example political, economic or environmental developments and their impact on the project environment.

In the final (terminal) review, the evaluation of project effectiveness may be quite detailed, including financial statements, audit reports, comparison of results and objectives, cost–benefit assessment, appraisal of the performance of contractors and consultants and, possibly, an assessment of environmental, social, ecological and other project-related outcomes that are not part of its main purpose. There may be some form of 'benchmarking' to establish standards or compare results with:

- other projects by the same organization;
- the operation of similar processes in other fields of work, or elsewhere in the world;

- the work and results of competitors;
- equipment suitability, operating conditions, reliability, performance and value.

12.6 BENCHMARKING AS A MEASURE OF BEST PRACTICE

Benchmarking is the term currently applied to the practice of comparing best practices and results. It is defined as 'the search for industry best practices that lead to superior performance' (Camp, 1989). It can be usefully applied to the evaluation of project performance as a basis of continual improvement in such areas as:

- processes, methods or procedures;
- machinery and equipment;
- manufacturing or production operations;
- quality and value of products or services;
- productivity.

12. 7 INITIAL REVIEW AND INCEPTION REPORTS

The beginning of project implementation is a good time for the manager to conduct a brief initial review. This is the stage in which the project structure and facilities have been established, key personnel joined and project administration set up. At this early stage, unforeseen difficulties, minor errors in initial assumptions or planning mistakes may become apparent, suppliers assessed, changes in project environment noted and if, for any reason, implementation is delayed, early adjustments can easily be made to compensate for changed needs or new opportunities.

The Project Inception Report is usually a brief situation statement confirming (or otherwise) that facilities are adequate and that the project has been successfully established, recommending any minor changes that may be desirable and agreeing the way ahead. It may include administrative details such as information on newly joined personnel, accommodation, transport, equipment, local conditions and other matters.

12.8 PERIODIC REVIEWS

The type of project will determine whether progress reviews should be scheduled on a time-elapsed basis, for example every three or six months, or on achievement of certain 'goals', project stages or 'milestones' (a method favoured by sponsors of major development projects in which large areas of activity are contracted out).

Following the UK AEW project failure, one of the proposals of a UK study team looking into project management for large defence contracts was that progress be measured against milestones rather than work completed or time (Comptroller and Auditor General, 1985).

For many projects, a combination of the two methods may be desirable. The need to monitor progress and avoid liability to a contractor for work that has failed to result in an agreed outcome favours reviews based on the achievement of milestones, but to assist in monitoring the rate of progress, limit the danger of cost escalation caused by delay in scheduled work and monitor the financial situation, periodic reviews may also be required.

12.9   REVIEW COVERAGE

Periodic reviews should not be allowed to become too complex (unless special circumstances demand). They should confirm activities and those results that have been conducted on time, within budget and according to plan, and review the project's financial and resource status.

'Better than planned' results and early completion of activities should be highlighted with reasons contributing to good performance and details of budgetary or scheduling adjustments (surplus funds should not be prematurely deducted from project budgets).

Areas for review would normally include some of the following topics:

- overview of progress and significant events;
- strategy review and progress towards objectives and 'milestones';
- political situation (if applicable);
- environmental impact;
- technical situation;
- human resource and staffing situation (including safety and welfare);
- status of contractor contributions;
- resource situation;
- update on project finances, budgets and justification for funding increases;
- project communications;
- failures, problems and remedial action to overcome constraints;
- overview of future activity and proposals for project revision.

Periodic reviews of complex projects calling for research, development or detailed coordination with other activities and those involving risky or new technologies will usually include technical details of progress and future outlook.

12.10   MILESTONE REVIEWS

Milestone reviews are similar to periodic (time spaced) reviews but for the fact that attention is focused on the achievement of a particular goal, point of progress or the effect of the special event that has made the review necessary.

In complex cases, detailed information may be required for purposes of performance appraisal, analysis, evaluation or integration with other activities.

A financial statement will be prepared and proposals for continuing action, project revision or a revision of contracts (with justification) will be set out, justified and discussed.

12.11 SPECIAL EVENT REVIEWS

Special event reviews are held 'as required' for a variety of reasons, for example, if a major change in strategy and/or planning becomes necessary, after an unexpected setback, failure to maintain scheduled progress, when new opportunity offers the prospect of substantially improved opportunity or outlook, or the project owner seeks an 'owner funded' addition or alteration to objectives or receivables. Owner's requests for project revision often call for in-depth analysis and major planning modification. The consequences of revision proposals should be fully investigated and documented before the review meeting and, if additional cost is involved, supported by a detailed request for extra funds, draft budget amendments and revised cash flow predictions.

12.12 TERMINATION REVIEWS AND EVALUATION

It has already been observed that completion of a project is often accompanied by a temptation to relax, move on to other things and downgrade review priorities. With the passage of time, errors and failures are hopefully forgotten and successes can be magnified in the imagination.

But this attitude is unworthy of the project and those who devoted their time, effort and resources to it. The final evaluation and project terminal report are valuable contributions to both the project itself and the success of future ventures.

The final review would include some of the relevant topics listed for review coverage (paragraph 12.9), not only constituting an immediate post-mortem on project activity when events are still fresh in the participants' minds, but resulting in:

- project justification;
- confirmation of results – verification of objectives achieved, for acceptance by owners and sponsors;
- acceptance of contractor's contributions, completeness of quality and work and authorizing bonus or final payment;
- publicity for the project, its image, outcomes and success;
- a record of project development, progress and achievement;
- a record of the individual and group performance and the achievements of project personnel;

- an audit of expertise, finances and other resources and an evaluation of project cost-effectiveness;
- a record of the disposal of assets;
- a record of historical data for future reference, in research, development, design, construction, and so on, showing methods, lines of research, specifications, tolerances and stress factors;
- a body of learning experience for future reference, training and a basis for continuing improvement in project management;
- a means of recognition for people and agencies whose support helped the project or its personnel;
- a record of advice or instruction on post-project activity, training recommendations, instruction schedules or guidelines for those who will use the project result or operate its equipment;
- a contribution to stakeholder communication and satisfaction;
- a record of the handover and the acceptance of the project by owners and sponsors.

12.13 PROGRAMME AND CLUSTER EVALUATIONS

Many organizations running major programmes or long-term projects conduct or commission a further review some time after project termination. This is particularly necessary for international aid or development projects where lasting benefits or effects may not become apparent for a considerable time, so that sustainability of project purpose, objectives and impact can be realistically assessed. Reviews of this kind cover:

- a study of project scope and mission objectives, and the extent to which they were achieved;
- a review of planning and the conduct of the project;
- a review of problems and impediments encountered during implementation;
- a review of the cause of any failure, unsuccessful or incomplete result, and identification of improvements for future use;
- a review of the cost and long-term effects of the project, and need (if any) for consolidation or follow-up.

12.14 LEARNING FROM LONG-TERM EVALUATIONS

In addition to programme and project justification, lessons resulting from the long-term evaluation of programmes and individual projects may differ from those outlined in the final project report.

Many project organizations such as the OECD, World Bank and AusAID maintain a Lessons and Practices database. Information extracted from a South Pacific Cluster Evaluation report of September 1998 includes:

- Benefits of simplicity in project design and implementation plan for targeting specific need in a technical area:

  The Fiji Meteorological Radar Project was highly relevant to the needs of Fiji. The technical knowledge base of trainees was relevant and had the potential to be upgraded, the equipment supplied was appropriate and the project activities integrated with the day-to-day activities of the Fiji Meteorological service and Civil Aviation Authority of Fiji. These factors contributed to a reduction of project risk, increased sustainability and provided conditions for positive long-term development …

- Suitability of building design for local conditions:

  Options for building designs should be carefully developed and stakeholders fully consulted on optimizing criteria and maximizing cost efficiency … design of buildings in Vila and the Sub-Centre building in Santo were inappropriate in several respects. Selection of materials which minimize maintenance requirements must be one of the design criteria … careful consideration should be given to the capability of the local construction industry to undertake further construction and rehabilitation work after the project.

- Project emphasis:

  Project activities designed to improve marketing of internationally traded commodities such as cocoa should consider where the greatest value-adding can occur in the production chain. It is unrealistic to concentrate on production and not other controlling factors such as transport, storage, grading and shipping …

- Institutional strengthening (IS) and the organizational environment:

  Events in the environment of agencies targeted for IS may influence the quality of outputs and reduce the sustainability of outcomes …

  Or

  Possibly the most important lesson from the evaluation was that IS project designs must retain the flexibility to respond to changes in the external environment (political, cultural and economic) thus increasing the chances of sustainability of outcomes …

  Or

  Training, particularly technical training, needs to be integrated into all IS projects. In addition, the establishment of a centralised training unit may assist the development of training materials …

- Stakeholder participation:

  All stakeholders must be involved in design, implementation and monitoring …

- Performance indicators:

  Performance indicators must be clearly related to project outputs …

(AusAID, reproduced with permission)

REVIEW AND DISCUSSION QUESTIONS

1. Consider an appropriate review programme for a project of your knowledge.
2. List areas that you would consider for a periodic review in a medium-term construction project.
3. Discuss how the conclusions of a late (post terminal) review some time after project completion might differ from those listed in final evaluation and recorded in the project report.

REFERENCES

Chapter 1

Archibald, R.D. (1992) *Managing High Technology Programs and Projects*, 2nd edn. New York: John Wiley & Sons Inc.

Cusumano, M.A. and Nobeoka, K. (1998) *Thinking Beyond Lean: How Multi-Project Management is Transforming Toyota and Other Companies*. New York: Free Press.

Davenport, T.H., DeLong, D.W. and Beers, M.C. (1998) 'Successful knowledge management projects', *Sloan Management Review*, Winter.

Sung Woong Hong (1997) 'Project management in globalizing economies', *Project Management Journal*, December.

Turner, B. (1997) *The Shorter MBA – A Practical Approach to the Key Business Skills* (B. Pearson and G.N. Thomas, eds), Ch. 7. London: Harper Collins Publishers Ltd.

Turner J.R. (1993) *The Handbook of Project Management, Improving the process of achieving strategic objectives*. London: McGraw-Hill International.

Chapter 2

Ashley, M. (1999) 'Searching for a spyplane', *Air Forces Monthly*, April, Key Publications Ltd, UK.

Amalfi, C. (1999) 'Engineering similar to big mine: Clough', *The West Australian*, 26 March.

Andrews, D.C. and Stalick, S.K. (1994) *Business Reengineering, The Survival Guide*, NJ: Prentice Hall.

Hill, The Hon. R., Minister for the Environment and Heritage, and Vale, M., MP, Minister for Agriculture, Fisheries and Forestry (1998) *Australia Gains Action on Antarctic Illegal Fishing*, Joint press release, Canberra 6 November.

Laufer, A. (1997) *Simultaneous Management, Managing Projects in a Dynamic Environment*. New York: American Management Association.

Love, P.E.D, Gunasekaran, A. and Li, H. (1998) 'Concurrent engineering; a strategy for procuring construction projects', *International Journal of Project Management*, 16 (6): 375–383, Elsevier Science Ltd and IPMA.

McManus, T.C and Burke, W. (1997) 'A project outline for military base closures and reuse', *Cost Engineering*, **39** (10), October.

Maylor, H. (1996) *Project Management*. London: Financial Times Management/Pitman.

Morris, P.W.G (1994) *The Management of Projects*. London: Thomas Telford.

Priest, M. (1998) 'Court advisor linked to nuke dump', *Sunday Times* (WA), 4 March.

Rose, R. and Grove, J. (1999) 'Senator backs N-waste plan', *The West Australian*, 26 March.

Sobek, D., Ward, A.C. and Likster, J.K. (1999) 'Toyota's principles of set-based concurrent engineering', *Sloan Management Review*, Winter.

Winner, R.I. (1988) *The Role of Concurrent Engineering in Weapons Systems Acquisition*. Institute for Defense Analysis, December, Report R-338.

Chapter 3

Anderson, D.R., Sweeney, D.J and Williams, T.A. (1991) *An Introduction to Management Science*. Minnesota: West Publishing Company.

Hulands, M. (1998–9) *The New HP Turbine Machining Facility*, issues 1 to 4 Rolls-Royce plc, July 1998 to July 1999.

McLay, A. (1998–9) *The New HP Turbine Machining Facility*, issues 1 to 4 Rolls-Royce plc, July 1998 to July 1999.

Thomas, G (1999) 'Rolls triggers transatlantic air raid panic', *The West Australian*, 3 March.

Shen, L.Y. (1997) 'Project risk management in Hong Kong', *International Journal of Project Management*, **15** (2), 105–7, Elsevier Science Ltd and IPMA.

Webb, A. (1994) *Managing Innovative Projects*. London: Chapman & Hall.

Chapter 4

Al-Khalil, M.I and Al-Ghafly, A (1999) 'Delay in public utility projects in Saudi Arabia', *International Journal of Project Management*, **17** (2), 101–6, Elsevier Science Ltd and IPMA.

Hartman, F., Ashrafi, R. and Jergeas, G. (1998) 'Project management in the live entertainment industry – what is different?', *International Journal of Project Management*, **16** (5), 269–81, Elsevier Science Ltd and IPMA.

Osama Jannadi, M. (1997) 'Reasons for construction business failures in Saudi Arabia', *Project Management Journal*, June.

Chapter 5

Cavinato, J.L. (1984) *Purchasing and Materials Management*. Minnesota: West Publishing Company.

Eden, C., Williams, T. and Ackermann, F. (1998) 'Dismantling the learning curve: the role of disruptions on the planning of development projects', *International Journal of Project Management*, **16** (3), 131–8, Elsevier Science Ltd and IPMA.

Hirshmann, W.B. (1964) 'Profit from the learning curve', *Harvard Business Review*, Jan–Feb.

Jergeas, G.F. and Cooke, V.G (1997) 'Law of tender applied to request for proposal process', *Project Management Journal*, December.

Oxford Dictionary of Law, Oxford University Press, 1997.

Woodward, D.G. (1997) 'Life cycle costing – theory, information acquisition and application', *International Journal of Project Management*, **15** (6), 335–44, Elsevier Science Ltd and IPMA.

Chapter 6

Harrison, F.L. (1981) *Advanced Project Management – A Structural Approach*, 3rd edn. London: Gower.

Hofstede, G. (1980) *Cultural consequences: international differences in work-related values*. Beverly Hills, CA: Sage Publications.

Loosemore, M. and Al Muslmani, H.S. (1999) 'Construction project panagement in the Persian Gulf: inter-cultural communication', *International Journal of Project Management*, **17** (2), 95–100, Elsevier Science Ltd and IPMA.

Morris, P.W.G. (1984) *The Management of Projects*. London: Thomas Telford.

Osama Jannadi, M. (1997) 'Reasons for construction business failures in Saudi Arabia', *Project Management Journal*, June.

Voropajev, V.I (1998) 'Project management development in transitional economies' (Russian case study), *International Journal of Project Management*, **16** (5), 283–93, Elsevier Science Ltd and IPMA.

Chapter 7

Adair, J. (1986) *Effective Team Building*. Aldershot: Gower.

Adair, J. (1988) *Developing Leaders*. Guildford: Talbot Adair Press.

Al-Khalil, M.I. and Al-Ghafly M.A. (1999) 'Delay in public utility projects in Saudi Arabia', *International Journal of Project Management*, **17** (2), 101–6, Elsevier Science Ltd and IPMA.

Belbin, R.M. (1981) *Management Teams – Why they Succeed or Fail*. London: Heineman.

Hersey, P. and Blanchard, K.H. (1977) *Management of Organizational Behaviour: Utilizing Human Resources*. NJ: Prentice-Hall.

Kubr, M. (ed.) (1986) *Management consulting: A guide to the profession*. Geneva: International Labour Office.

Parker, G.M. (1990) *Team Players and Team Work: The New Competitive Business Strategy*. San Francisco: Jossey-Bass.

Chapter 9

Maylor, H. (1996) *Project Management*. London: Financial Times & Pitman Publishing.

PMI (1994) *A Guide to the Project Management Body of Knowledge (PAMBOC)*. Upper Darby, PA: Project Management Institute.

Saldanha, C. and Whittle, J. (1998) *Using the Logical Framework for Sector Analysis and Project Design*. Manila: Asian Development Bank.

USAID (1980) *Design and Evaluation of Aid-Assisted Projects*. Training and Development Division, Office of Personnel Management, US Agency for International Development, Washington DC.

Chapter 10

Baki, M.A. (1998) 'CPM Scheduling and Its Use in Today's Construction Industry', *Project Management Journal*, March.

Fox, T.L. and Spence, J.W. (1998) 'Tools of the trade; A survey of project management tools', *Project Management Journal*, September.

Hegazy, T.M. and El-Zamzamy, H. (1998) 'Project management software that meets the challenge', *Cost engineering*, **40** (5), 5 May.

Chapter 11

Adair, J. (1988) *Developing Leaders The Ten Key Principles*. UK: Talbot Adair Press.

Berne, E. (1968) *Games People Play*. London: Penguin Books.

Galpin, T.J. (1996) *The Human Side of Change: A Practical Guide to Organization Redesign*. San Fransisco: Jossey-Bass Inc.

Hallowell, E.M. (1999) 'The human moment at work', *Harvard Business Review*, January–February.

Harris T.A. (1967) *I'm OK – You're OK – A Practical Guide to Transactional Analysis*. New York: Harper & Row.

Hulands, M. (1998–9) *The New HP Turbine Machining Facility*, Issues 1–4, Rolls-Royce plc, July 1998 to July 1999.

Loosemore, L. and Al Muslmani, H.S. (1999) 'Construction project management in the Persian Gulf; inter-cultural communication', *International Journal of Project Management*, **17** (2), 95–100, Elsevier Science Ltd and IPMA.

McLay, A. (1999) *The New HP Turbine Machining Facility*, Issues 1 to 4, Rolls-Royce plc, July 1998 to July 1999.

Chapter 12

AusAID (1998) *South Pacific Cluster Evaluation No. 8.* Canberra: Australian Agency for International Development, September.

Camp, R.C. (1989) *Benchmarking: The Search for Industry Best Practices That Lead to Superior Performance.* Milwaukee, WI: ASQC Quality Press.

Comptroller and Auditor General, National Audit Office (1985) *Ministry of Defence: control and management of the development of major equipment.* London: HMSO.

Lopes, M.D.S and Flavell, R. (1998) 'Project appraisal – a framework to assess the non-financial aspects of projects during the project life cycle', *International Journal of Project Management,* **16** (4), 223–233, Elsvier Science Ltd and IPMA.

BIBLIOGRAPHY

Note: In addition to items listed in chapter references, this bibligraphy includes some useful related items.

Adair, J. (1986) *Effective Teambuilding*. UK: Gower.
Adair, J. (1988) *Developing leaders: the ten key principles*. Guildford: Talbot Adair Press
Adair, J. (1989) *Great Leaders*. UK: Adair Press.
Al-Khalil, M.I and Al-Ghafly, A. (1999) 'Delay in public utility projects in Saudi Arabia', *International Journal of Project Management*, **17** (2), 101–6, Elsevier Science Ltd and IPMA.
Amalfi, C. (1999) 'Engineering similar to big mine; Clough', *The West Australian*. 26 March.
Anderson, D.R., Sweeny, D.J. and Williams, T.A. (1991) *An Introduction to Management Science*. Minnesota: West Publishing Company.
Andrews, D.C and Stalick, S.K. (1994) *Business Reengineering, the Survival Guide*. NJ: Prentice Hall.
Archibald, R.D. (1992) *Managing High Technology Programs and Projects*, 2nd edn. NY: J. Wiley.
Asian Development Bank (1998) *Logical framework*. Manila: Asian Development Bank.
Ashley, M. (1994) 'Searching for a spyplane', *Air Forces Monthly*, April, Key Publications Ltd, UK: Prentice Hall.
AusAID (1998) *South Pacific Cluster Evaluation No. 8*. Canberra: Australian Agency for International Development, September.
Baki, M.A. (1998) 'CPM Scheduling and its use in today's construction industry', *Project Management Journal*, March.
Belbin, R. Meredith (1981) *Management Teams – Why they Succeed or Fail*. London: Heinemann.
Berne, E. (1968) *Games People Play*. London: Penguin Books.
Bion, W. (1961) *Experiences in Groups*, London: Tavistock.
Blake, R.T. and Mouton, J.S. (1964) *The Managerial Grid*. Houston: Gulf Publishing.
Body, D. and Buchanan, D. (1992) *Take the Lead*. Prentice Hall.
Burnett, N.R. and Youker, R. (1980) *Analyzing the Project Environment* CN848. Economic Development Institute (World Bank), Washington, July.
Burns, J.M. and McGregor, (1978) *Leadership*. NY: Harper & Row.
Camp, R.C. (1989) *Benchmarking: The Search for Industry Best Practices That Lead to Superior Performance*. Milwaukee, WI: ASQC Quality Press.
Cavinato, J.L. (1984) *Purchasing and Materials Management*. Minnesota: West Publishing Company.
Chapman and Ward (1987) *Project Risk Management*. NY: Wiley.
Clark, N. (1994) *Teambuilding: a practical guide for trainers*. London and NY: McGraw-Hill.
Comptroller and Auditor General, National Audit Office (1985) *Ministry of Defence; Control and management of the development of major equipment*. London: HMSO.
Cusumano, M.A. and Nobeoka, K. (1998) *Thinking Beyond Lean – How Multi-Project Management is Transforming Toyota and other Companies*. New York: Free Press.
Davenport, T.H., DeLong, D.W., Beers, M.C. (1998) 'Successful knowledge management projects', *Sloan Management Review*, Winter.

Eden, C., Williams, T. and Ackermann, F. (1998) 'Dismantling the learning curve; the role of disruptions on the planning of development projects', *International Journal of Project Management*, **16** (3), 131–8, Elsevier Science Ltd and IPMA.

Englebert, R.D. (1990) *Winning at Technological Innovation.* NY: McGraw Hill, Inc.

Fisher, K. (1993) *Leading Self-Directed Workgroups.* McGraw-Hill.

Flippo, E.B. (1984) *Personnel Management* (6th edn). McGraw-Hill, SA.

Fox, T.L and Spence, J.W. (1998) 'Tools of the trade: A survey of project management tools', *Project Management Journal*, September.

Galpin, T.J. (1996) *The Human Side of Change. A Practical Guide to Organizational Redesign.* San Francisco: Jossey-Bass Inc.

Garg, D., Kaul, O.N. and Deshmukh, S.G. (1998) 'JIT implementation, a case study', *Production and Inventory Management Journal*, Third Quarter.

George, C.S. and Cole K. (19) *Supervision in Action.* Australia: Prentice Hall.

Gilbreth, R.D. (1986) *Winning in Project Management.* John Wiley & Sons Inc.

Greer, M. (1996) *The Project Manager's Partner.* Amherst, MA: HRD Press.

Hallowell, E.M. (1999) 'The human moment at work', *Harvard Business Review*, January–February.

Handy, C. (1990) *Inside Organizations.* London: BBC Books.

Harris, T.A. (1967) *I'm OK – You're OK – A Practical Guide to Transactional Analysis.* NY: Harper & Row.

Harrison, F.L. (1992) *Advanced Project Management – A Systems Approach,* 3rd edn. Aldershot: Gower.

Hartman, F., Ashrafi, R. and Jergeas, G. (1998) 'Project management in the live entertainment industry – what is different?', *International Journal of Project Management*, **16** (5), 269–81, Elsevier Science Ltd and IPMA.

Hegazy, T.M. and El-Zamzamy, H. (1998) 'Project management software meets the challenge', *Cost Engineering*, **40** (5), 5 May.

Hersey, P. and Blanchard, K.H. (1977) *Management of Organizational Behavior; Utilizing Human Resources.* NJ: Prentice-Hall

Hicks, R.F. and Bone, D. (1991) *Self Managing Teams.* London: Kogan Page.

Hill, the Hon. R., Minister for the Environment and Heritage, and Vale, M., MP, Minister for Agriculture, Fisheries and Forestry (1998) *Australia gains Action on Antarctic Fishing,* Joint press release, Canberra, 6 November.

Hirshmann, W.B. (1964) 'Profit from the learning curve', *Harvard Business Review*, Jan–Feb.

Hofstede, G. (1980) *Cultural consequences; International differences in work-related values.* Beverly Hills, CA: Sage Publications.

Hortensius, R. and Barthel, M. (1997) *ISO 14001 and Beyond, Environmental Management Systems in the Real World.* UK: Greenleaf Publishing

Kubr, M. (ed.) (1986) *Management consulting – A guide to the profession,* Geneva: International Labour Office.

Laufer, A. (1997) *Simultaneous Management. Managing Projects in a Dynamic Environment.* American Management Association.

Lich, H.G. (1997) *Transport Systems – A Management Approach.* Melbourne: RMIT Press.

Lockyer, K.G. and Gordon, J. (1996) *Project Management and Project Network Techniques.* London: Pitman.

Loosemore, M. and Al Muslmani, H.S. (1999) 'Construction project management in the Persian Gulf: inter-cultural communication', *International Journal of Project Management*, **17** (2), 95–100, Elsevier Science Ltd and IPMA.

Lopes, M.D.S. and Flavell, R. (1998) 'Project appraisal – a framework to assess the non-financial aspects of projects during the project life-cycle', *International Journal of Project Management*, **16** (4), 223–233, Elsevier Science Ltd and IPMA.

Love, P.E.D., Gunasekararan, A. and Li, H. (1998) 'Concurrent Engineering: a strategy for procuring construction projects', *International Journal of Project Management*, **16** (6), 375–383, Elsevier Science Ltd and IPMA.

Mant, A. (1997) *Intelligent Leadership.* Australia: Allen & Unwin.

Margerison, C. and McCann, D. (1990) *Team Management.* Mercury.

McGregor, D. (1960) *The Human Side of Enterprise*. NY: McGraw-Hill.

McManus, T.C and Burke, W. (1997) 'A project management outline for military base closures and reuse', *Cost Engineering*, **39** (10), October.

Maylor, H. (1996) *Project Management*. London: Financial Times & Pitman Publishing.

Morris, P.W.G. (1994) *The Management of Projects*. London: Thomas Telford.

Osama Jannadi, M. (1997) 'Reasons for construction business failures in Saudi Arabia', *Project Management Journal*, June.

Oxford Dictionary of Law, Oxford University Press, 1997.

Parker, G.M. (1990) *Team Players and Team Work; The New Competitive Business Strategy*. San Francisco: Jossey-Bass.

Pearson, B. and Thomas, G.N. (eds) (1994) *The Shorter MBA – A Practical Approach to the Key Business Skills*. London: Harper Collins.

Peters, T. and Waterman, R. (1982) *In Search of Excellence*. NY: Harper Collins Publishers.

Priest, M. (1998) 'Court Advisor linked to nuke dump', *Sunday Telegraph* (WA), 4 March.

Project Management Institute (1994), *A Guide to the Project Management Body of Knowledge (PAMBOK)*. Upper Darby, PA: PMI.

Project Management Institute (1996); *Global Status of the Project Management Profession*. Upper Darby, PA: PMI.

Rose, R. and Grove, J. (1999) 'Senator backs N-waste plan', *The West Australian*, 26 March.

Saldanha, C. and Whittle, J. (1998) *Using the Logical Framework for Sector Analysis and Project Design*. Manila: Asian Development Bank.

Shen, L.Y. (1997) 'Project risk management in Hong Kong', *International Journal of Project Management*, **15** (2), 105–7, Elsevier Science Ltd and IPMA.

Sobek, D., Ward, A.C. and Liker, J.K. (1999) 'Toyota's principles of set-based concurrent engineering', *Sloan Management Review*, Winter.

Spinner, A.P. (1983) *Elements of Project Management (An Engineering Approach)*. McGraw-Hill.

Stone, R. (1988) *The Management of Engineering Projects*. London: Macmillan Education.

Sung Woong Hong (1997) 'Project management in globalizing economies', *Project Management Journal*, December.

Thomas, G. (1999) 'Rolls triggers transatlantic air raid panic', *The West Australian*, 3 March.

Toney, F. and Powers, R. (1997) *Best Practices of Project Management Groups in Large Functional Organizations*. Upper Darby, PA: Project Management Institute.

Turner, B. (1997) *The Shorter MBA – A Practical Approach to the Key Business Skills*. LondonL Harper Collins.

Turner, J.R. (1993) *The Handbook of Project Management, Improving the process of achieving strategic objectives*. London: McGraw-Hill International.

USAID (1980) *Design and Evaluation of Aid-Assisted Projects*. Training and Development Division, Office of Personnel Management, US Agency for International Development, Washington DC.

Voropajev, V.I (1998) 'Project management development in transitional economies' (Russian case study), *International Journal of Project Management*, **16** (5), 283–93, Elsevier Science Ltd and IPMA.

Webb, A. (1994) *Managing Innovative Projects*. London: Chapman & Hall.

Winner, R.I. (1988) *The Role of Concurrent Engineering in Weapons Systems Acquisition*. Institute for Defense Analysis, December, Report R-338.

Woodcock, M. and Francis, D. (1981) *Organization Development Through Team Building*. Aldershot: Gower.

Woodward, D.G. (1997) 'Life cycle costing – theory, information acquisition and application', *International Journal of project Management*, **15** (6), 335–44, Elsevier Science Ltd and IPMA.

INDEX